PRAISE FOR *LEAFS 365*

Leafs 365 is a fantastic read for any Toronto Maple Leafs fan, whether new, old, or so old that they can remember what the Stanley Cup looks like.

— SEAN MCINDOE, senior NHL writer, the Athletic, and author of *The Down Goes Brown History of the NHL*

Amazing stories and very well told. A must for Leafs fans who want the behind-the-scenes story.

— GORD MILLER, NHL, and international commentator, TSN

Like a Leafs version of This Day in History. A must-read!

— GORD STELLICK, former Leafs GM and NHL hockey media personality

The best part of hockey is the stories you tell for decades after, so Mike's given you 365 *more* to tell your friends. This is a can't miss book.

— ADAM WYLDE, co-host of *The Steve Dangle Podcast* and CEO, SDPN

Leafs 365 is a must-have Maple Leafs diary for dyed in the wool Toronto hockey fans who follow their team 24/7.

— CHRIS CUTHBERT, commentator for Sportsnet and *Hockey Night in Canada*

Mike Commito's *Leafs 365* is an absolute treasure trove for Toronto Maple Leafs fanatics. His exceptional grasp of the team shines through on every page, making this book a remarkable tribute to the Leafs' rich history.

— JESSE BLAKE, co-host of *The Steve Dangle Podcast* and CEO, SDPN

Insightful, fascinating, and a further education for even the world's most informed Leafs fans.

— JUSTIN BOURNE, NHL analyst for Sportsnet and author of *Down and Back*

Mike's love of "his" Maple Leafs and his scrupulous attention to detail make *Leafs 365* a breezy day-by-day stroll through the franchise, rich with facts, figures, anecdotes, and trivia.

— DAVE STUBBS, NHL.com columnist and historian

The self-confessed Leafs fan serves hockey's most passionate (and most tortured) audience with a forgotten nugget or compelling anecdote for each calendar day.

— LUKE FOX, senior writer, Sporstnet

Flipping through each day of *Leafs 365* will make any hockey fan feel a bit wistful. A must-have for a Leafs fan or a masochist.

— DAVID ALTER, Leafs reporter, *Sports Illustrated* and the *Hockey News*

A must-have for Leafs fans. One story every day of the year to remind us why we still love this horrible, beautiful, cursed team.

— STEFAN BABCOCK, vocalist and guitarist for PUP

One of hockey's most passionate historians, Mike Commito's *Leafs 365* is a must-read for any Leafs fan interested in the team's rich past.

— JD BUNKIS, host of *Leafs Talk* on Sportsnet and the *JD Bunkis Podcast* on Sportsnet 590 The FAN

Unlike paying for a ticket to game one of the first round at home for the Toronto Maple Leafs in 2023, this book is well worth the price of admission.

— MARISSA ROBERTO, host of TSN's Digital SportsCentre

Whether you're a die-hard fan or a hockey historian, Commito captures the highs, the lows, and the iconic times of everything Toronto Maple Leafs.

— OMAR WHITE, NHL content creator,
Yahoo Sports and the Athletic

Mike takes us back in time through the ups and downs of the storied franchise. Reading this book brought back so many fond memories and is must-have for any Maple Leafs fan.

— MATT MARCHESE, sports radio host/producer

What happens in the present becomes history. To relive those moments that were once present time, Mike delivers an in-depth recollection that brings them to life.

— CRAIG BUTTON, TSN analyst and scout

If you're a sports fan, this book is for you. If you're a hockey fan, this book is really for you. If you're a Maple Leafs fan, this book is mandatory!

— BRYAN HAYES, co-host of TSN's *OverDrive*

LEAFS 365

The Hockey 365 Series

Leafs 365
Hockey 365, The Second Period
Hockey 365

MIKE COMMITO

LEAFS 365

DAILY STORIES FROM THE ICE

DUNDURN
PRESS

Publisher: Kwame Scott Fraser | Acquiring editor: Kathryn Lane | Editor: Patricia MacDonald

Library and Archives Canada Cataloguing in Publication

Title: Leafs 365 : daily stories from the ice / Mike Commito.
Other titles: Leafs three hundred and sixty-five
Names: Commito, Mike, author.
Description: Series statement: Hockey 365 ; 3
Identifiers: Canadiana (print) 20230466931 | Canadiana (ebook) 20230466958 | ISBN 9781459751378 (hardcover) | ISBN 9781459751385 (PDF) | ISBN 9781459751392 (EPUB)
Subjects: LCSH: Toronto Maple Leafs (Hockey team)—Anecdotes. | LCSH: Toronto Maple Leafs (Hockey team)—Miscellanea. | LCSH: National Hockey League—Anecdotes. | LCSH: National Hockey League—Miscellanea. | LCSH: Hockey players—Ontario—Toronto—Anecdotes. | LCSH: Hockey players—Ontario—Toronto—Miscellanea. | LCSH: Hockey—Ontario—Toronto—Anecdotes. | LCSH: Hockey—Ontario—Toronto—Miscellanea. | LCGFT: Anecdotes. | LCGFT: Trivia and miscellanea.
Classification: LCC GV848.T6 C66 2023 | DDC 796.962/6409713541—dc23

We acknowledge the support of the Canada Council for the Arts and the Ontario Arts Council for our publishing program. We also acknowledge the financial support of the Government of Ontario, through the Ontario Book Publishing Tax Credit and Ontario Creates, and the Government of Canada.

Care has been taken to trace the ownership of copyright material used in this book. The author and the publisher welcome any information enabling them to rectify any references or credits in subsequent editions.

The publisher is not responsible for websites or their content unless they are owned by the publisher.

Printed and bound in Canada.

Dundurn Press
1382 Queen Street East
Toronto, Ontario, Canada M4L 1C9
dundurn.com, @dundurnpress 𝕏 f ⊚

For my mom, Patti,
who is the reason I became a Leafs fan

AUTHOR'S NOTE

The history of the Toronto Maple Leafs doesn't start with the Leafs.

When Toronto entered the NHL in 1917, the team was operated by the Toronto Arena Company and known simply as the Toronto Arenas, but often called the Blueshirts as well. A couple of years later, under a change in ownership, the Arenas were renamed the St. Patricks. For the next eight years, the St. Pats sported green uniforms, a nod to their Irish label.

In the midde of the 1926–27 season, Conn Smythe purchased the St. Patricks and rechristened them as the Maple Leafs. The following season they switched up their colour scheme and have been blue and white ever since.

There are stories in this book about the Arenas, St. Patricks, and Leafs, oh my, but they are all the same franchise. I've also referred to the team as the blue and white, but only in the Leafs era, though they did wear blue as the Arenas. And, of course, you may also know them as the Buds because, well, buds turn into Leafs. One of my favourite Twitter follows, Platinum Seat Ghosts, popularized the expression "the Buds are all day," so hopefully they appreciate that now, the Buds are all book.

Notice I did not call them the Laughs because that is simply not funny — and you should dissociate yourself from anyone in your orbit who uses that term with a straight face.

Finally, I poured my heart into researching this book. And while I have double- and triple-checked my work, mistakes happen — but any errors are mine and mine alone. One thing I did want to note is that our understanding of history is always changing. Take, for an example, a story I included about Larry Murphy. On March 27, 1996, he scored his 1,000th career point, becoming the fourth defenceman to accomplish the feat. All the newspaper coverage the next day focused on that milestone, and if you watch the clip on YouTube, you will see his teammates mob him in celebration after he notches the landmark point.

But if you were to go to the NHL's website and look up Murphy's stats, it appears he actually hit the 1,000-point mark two days earlier. As researchers have reviewed game sheets over the years, particularly when the league underwent a major digitization project in the lead-up to its centenary in 2017, our prior knowledge has been challenged by new information. While this means Murphy technically hit his milestone on March 25, it doesn't change the fact that for him and his teammates, he made history two nights later on the road in Vancouver. The numbers may have changed, but you cannot substitute the emotion. So, with that in mind, I kept my Larry Murphy story the way it was, because that particular moment in time was when he wrote his name into the record books.

PRE-GAME SKATE

've been a Leafs fan for as long as I can remember. And if you're reading this, chances are you're a Leafs fan, too. As far as I can tell, I didn't pick the Leafs. My mom is actually an even bigger Leafs fan than me, and I suppose she's the reason I started cheering for the team. I'm not sure how someone who hails from Sault Ste. Marie, Ontario, a place that boasts the likes of players such as Phil Esposito, ended up cheering for Toronto instead of the Boston Bruins, but I am certainly glad she did.

The Leafs have been with me throughout my life. Some of my earliest memories of trying to stay up late was when Toronto was playing on *Hockey Night in Canada*. My parents would let me stay up, especially if the Leafs were in the play-offs, but I realize now, as a parent myself, they agreed to it because they knew I'd fall asleep partway through the game. And sure enough, no matter how hard I tried to stay up, I would always wake up later in my bed. I'd learn the score from my mom the next morning and tell myself that next time I would catch the entire thing, although I never would.

As I got older, the Leafs were part of some important milestones in my world. When my mother's authentic Doug Gilmour jersey was stolen from my locker because I forgot to lock it up, I remember how disappointed she was with me. I eventually understood it was not because it was expensive, but because it was a parting gift from some of her friends and colleagues before we moved to a new city. While I eventually replaced the jersey many years later, I learned the importance of protecting something valuable, especially if it doesn't belong to you — a lesson that has always stuck with me.

A couple of weeks after my first daughter, Zoe, was born, the Leafs started the 2016–17 campaign. I remember how excited I was to put her into her teeny tiny Maple Leafs pajamas for the season opener. That night Auston Matthews made his NHL debut. And although Zoe slept soundly through all four of his goals, I will always be able to tell her we experienced that together. It was an important moment in Leafs history, but as a new father, it was a special memory I will always cherish.

Even some of my career benchmarks have Leafs footnotes. After earning a big promotion in 2018, I wanted to treat myself to something to mark the occasion. We happened to be in Toronto at the time, and I could think of nothing better than to buy a Matthews jersey. While I had collected a number of replica, and even counterfeit, jerseys over the years, mostly for my regular shinny ice times, I had always shied away from buying an authentic one because of the price tag. But since my hard work at the office had paid off, I rewarded myself.

It remains my most prized Leafs item, and I only wear it for important games.

As you can tell, the Leafs have been with me for some important parts of my life, and they have probably been there for you as well. Since the Leafs are often such an important backdrop in our lives, day after day and year after year, it only made sense that I would put together a book so you could experience a different piece of Leafs history for every day of the year. When I wrote the first *Hockey 365* in 2017, it had never crossed my mind that it would lead to this. Although both volumes of *Hockey 365* include plenty of Leafs stories, I had never considered there would be a full book there. But of course there would be. The franchise has been around for more than a century, and there are more than enough tales to fill these pages.

From the team's first Stanley Cup in the NHL to some of the more recent struggles to avenge the ghosts of the past, *Leafs 365* includes stories from across eras. While there are recurring characters such as Doug Gilmour, Börje Salming, and Darryl Sittler, there are also stories featuring players you may have forgotten about but are still an important part of the team's fabric. Many of these tales will, hopefully, make you smile, but some of them will undoubtedly frustrate you as you relive some of the moments that have pushed your fandom to the limits. There have been plenty of times when the Leafs have probably made you want to tear your hair out, and there's more than a few of those stories in this book, but it's those episodes that really make the good ones worth celebrating.

Some people say the Leafs are cursed, but anything that's able to give you this many memories worth revisiting year after year is obviously a blessing. And while you may disagree with my optimism, we certainly have one thing in common: You're reading this because no matter what has happened in the past or how the season unfolds, you're a Leafs fan until the bitter end.

JANUARY 1

LEAFS PLAY OUTDOOR GAME
AT THE BIG HOUSE, 2014

t was the largest crowd to ever watch a hockey game. On January 1, 2014, the Maple Leafs took on the Detroit Red Wings as part of the NHL's annual Winter Classic. Played at Michigan Stadium, fittingly known as "the Big House," in Ann Arbor, Michigan, the game saw 105,491 fans brave frigid temperatures to take in the spectacle. The record crowd surpassed the previous mark of 104,173 spectators when Michigan University and Michigan State competed in the same stadium in 2010 in what was billed as "the Big Chill."

Following a scoreless first period, the Leafs and Red Wings each scored goals in the final two frames to head to overtime knotted 2–2, but neither team could break the deadlock. Heading into the shootout, Maple Leafs goaltender Jonathan Bernier, who sported a toque over his helmet for the contest, had made 41 saves, a record for the most in an outdoor regular-season game. With snow falling during the shootout, Tyler Bozak played hero, scoring the clinching goal for Toronto.

JANUARY 2

LEAFS ACQUIRE DOUG GILMOUR, 1992

Doug Gilmour remembers learning he was being traded while sitting in his hotel room on the road, when he apparently heard Calgary Flames GM Doug Risebrough talking about it in the next room. It didn't come as a surprise. Gilmour had been disgruntled and wanted his contract renegotiated. Following arbitration in November 1991, which left neither side satisfied, the writing was on the wall.

On January 2, 1992, two days after scoring a goal and assisting on the overtime winner in Calgary's win over the Montreal Canadiens, Gilmour, along with Rick Wamsley, Jamie Macoun, Ric Nattress, and Kent Manderville, was traded to the Leafs for Gary Leeman, Michel Petit, Alexander Godynyuk, Craig Berube, and Jeff Reese. At the time, the 10-player deal was the biggest in NHL history. A day later, Gilmour made his debut for the Buds, scoring a goal and picking up an assist in a 6–4 loss in Detroit. Gilmour, who will be a recurring character throughout this book, would become one of the greatest players in Leafs history.

JANUARY 3

GUY LAFLEUR SCORES 545TH GOAL AGAINST THE MAPLE LEAFS, 1990

There are three guarantees in life. Death, taxes, and players reaching milestones against the Maple Leafs. It's true. When something significant happens in the NHL, there's a good chance it happened against Toronto. Sure, it was to be expected in a six-team league, but even after the circuit has more than quintupled in size, it seems as though the Leafs just can't shake being on the wrong side of history.

Case in point: On January 3, 1990, Guy Lafleur, who was playing his first season with the Quebec Nordiques after the New York Rangers lured him out of retirement the year before, scored his 545th career goal against Toronto to move him past Maurice Richard and into eighth place on the NHL's all-time goal-scoring list. Lafleur would score one more goal against the Maple Leafs the following season before hanging his skates up for good in 1991. While this may seem like a footnote in Maple Leafs history, it is part of the team's fabric, and there will be other moments like this throughout the book.

JANUARY 4

BÖRJE SALMING PLAYS
1,000TH GAME, 1988

t was a momentous occasion worthy of celebration. On January 4, 1988, Maple Leafs defenceman Börje Salming became the first European-born and -trained player to appear in 1,000 career NHL games. Salming signed with Toronto in 1973 as part of an early wave of European players to join the league. A hard-nosed blueliner from Sweden, Salming was tough as nails and quickly dispelled the notion of the "chicken Swede" stereotype. But despite being just the fifth player in Maple Leafs history to reach the 1,000-game mark, Salming's salute would have to wait.

At the time team owner Harold Ballard was out of the country and insisted that his player not be honoured until he returned. It wasn't until nearly two months later, when the Maple Leafs hosted the St. Louis Blues on February 27, that the durable defenceman was officially recognized by the club. During the belated tribute at Maple Leaf Gardens, Salming was presented with a sparkling blue Chevy S-10 Blazer. Emblazoned on the doors were the Maple Leafs logo, Salming's No. 21, and the number 1,000 to signify his accomplishment.

JANUARY 5

TREVOR MOORE SCORES
FIRST NHL GOAL, 2019

Trevor Moore brought the Leafs crowd to its feet. During a game against the Vancouver Canucks on January 5, 2019, the Toronto rookie carried the puck out of the defensive zone and effortlessly made his way around Vancouver defenceman Derrick Pouliot to put a shot past goaltender Jacob Markstrom and score his first NHL goal. Moore, who went undrafted playing collegiate hockey for the University of Denver, signed with the Leafs organization in the summer of 2016. He spent the next two seasons playing for the Toronto Marlies of the American Hockey League, where he won a Calder Cup championship in 2018.

After starting the 2018–19 campaign with the Marlies, Moore was called up to the big club in December 2018, playing in 25 games down the stretch. He made the Leafs roster to start the following season, but on February 5, 2020, the native of Thousand Oaks, California, was traded, along with a third-round draft pick and a conditional selection, to his hometown Los Angeles Kings for goaltender Jack Campbell and Kyle Clifford.

JANUARY 6

LEAFS END 30-GAME ROAD WINLESS STREAK, 1983

The Maple Leafs had not exactly been road warriors. After defeating the Chicago Black Hawks at Chicago Stadium on January 31, 1982, they failed to record a victory in their next 30 games away from home, recording six ties and 24 losses in that span. It would take almost a full calendar year before they picked up another victory on the road. Finally, on January 6, 1983, taking on the Washington Capitals in Maryland, Toronto snapped the skid.

With the game tied 1–1 in the second period, Rick Vaive scored on the power play to give the Maple Leafs the lead. Jim Korn added another in the final frame to secure a 3–1 victory. Breaking their road ineffectiveness against the Capitals was rather fitting. In Washington's inaugural season in 1974–75, the team managed just one victory on the road. When the Caps finally won in an opposing rink, they celebrated by hoisting a garbage can and calling it "the Stanley Can" — after so much road futility, it felt like they had won a championship.

JANUARY 7

LEAFS CLAIM LARRY REGAN FROM BRUINS, 1959

Larry Regan finally got his shot at the NHL. After spending a decade playing the semi-professional circuit, Regan made his debut for the Boston Bruins in the 1956–57 season. The 27-year-old winger finished the campaign with 14 goals and 33 points in 69 games to earn the Calder Trophy as the league's top rookie that year. At the time, Regan was the oldest player to win the award, a distinction he would hold until 31-year-old Sergei Makarov won it in 1989, which led to a rule change.

Following his first year with the Bruins, Regan spent another full season in Boston before he was claimed by the Maple Leafs on January 7, 1959. He would play two full seasons in Toronto before finishing his hockey career abroad in Europe, later returning to the NHL as a scout for the Los Angeles Kings. Not long into the 1968–69 season, Regan, who was the Kings' GM at the time, was fined $1,000 by NHL president Clarence Campbell after he slugged referee Bruce Hood following a game against the California Seals.

JANUARY 8

HOWIE MEEKER SCORES
FIVE GOALS, 1947

O n January 8, 1947, Maple Leafs rookie Howie Meeker scored five goals in a game. Or did he? In the newspaper coverage following the game, it was noted that two of the goals were originally credited to Wally Stanowski, but after a conference between the officials and the players, they were attributed to Meeker. More than six decades later, Stanowski suggested there was more to that story.

In an interview with the *National Post*'s Joe O'Connor in 2015, Stanowski says when he returned to the bench after scoring a goal, Toronto coach Hap Day told him they were going to give the goal to Meeker. Following another supposed goal by Stanowski, Day issued the same directive. According to Stanowski, the team was trying to build up Meeker's case to win the Calder Trophy as the league's top rookie. After the five-goal game, Meeker added 11 more goals down the stretch to finish with 27 and win the Calder. While there may be some truth to Stanowski's claim, we will never know for sure.

JANUARY 9

LEAFS TRADE FÉLIX POTVIN TO
ISLANDERS FOR BRYAN BERARD, 1999

After the Maple Leafs signed goaltender Curtis Joseph to a four-year deal during free agency in 1998, the Félix Potvin era in Toronto was over. It wasn't a matter of whether Potvin would be moved elsewhere, it was when. A few months into the season, Potvin had appeared in only a handful of games and was eager to end the saga. After several deals fell through, he was finally sent to the New York Islanders on January 9, 1999, along with a sixth-round pick, in exchange for defenceman Bryan Berard and a sixth-round pick.

In Toronto, Berard, an offensively gifted blueliner, picked up 19 points in 38 games down the stretch. The following season, after recording 30 points through the first 64 games, Berard sustained what many believed would be a career-ending injury to his right eye in a game against the Ottawa Senators. Although he never played for Toronto again, Berard did return to the NHL after taking a year off and won the Bill Masterton Memorial Trophy, awarded annually to the player who best exemplifies the qualities of perseverance, sportsmanship, and dedication to hockey in 2004.

MIKE NYKOLUK BECOMES HEAD COACH, 1981

nstead of broadcasting Maple Leafs games from the radio booth, Mike Nykoluk would be calling them from behind the team's bench. On January 10, 1981, Nykoluk was named head coach, replacing Joe Crozier, who was fired two days earlier following a 13-22-5 start to the season, one of the worst openings in franchise history. Back in his playing days, Nykoluk suited up for 32 games for Toronto in the 1956–57 season.

After hanging up his skates, Nykoluk got into coaching, becoming one of the first full-time assistant coaches in NHL history when he worked with Fred Shero and the Philadelphia Flyers in the early 1970s. Following a stint with the New York Rangers as an assistant coach, he worked as a radio broadcaster for the Maple Leafs until he got the call to join the bench. Under Nykoluk's direction, Toronto went 15-15-10 to close out the campaign and qualify for the playoffs. In the opening round, however, the Leafs were swept by the New York Islanders, who went on to win their second straight Stanley Cup.

JANUARY 11

LEAFS STOMP AMERICANS 9–0, 1941

For the second straight game in Toronto, the penalty box was quiet. After defeating the New York Rangers 3–2 in overtime a couple of nights earlier at Maple Leaf Gardens, with neither team incurring an infraction, the Maple Leafs provided a penalty-free encore on January 11, 1941, when they trounced the New York Americans 9–0. After Toronto jumped out to a 2–0 lead early into the first period, the club added four goals in the middle frame and three more in the final to record their largest margin of victory in nearly two decades, back when the team was still known as the St. Patricks.

Following the back-to-back games in Toronto without penalties, the Maple Leafs didn't play at home again for a week. When they returned to action at the Gardens, hosting the Boston Bruins, they were shut out 1–0 and the penalty-free streak was halted. At the team's next home game against the Montreal Canadiens, 12 penalties were called, but neither the Leafs nor their opponents were able to capitalize on their respective power plays.

JANUARY 12

LEAFS TRADE TOM KURVERS TO VANCOUVER, 1991

The Leafs had originally acquired defenceman Tom Kurvers from the New Jersey Devils for a 1991 first-round draft pick on October 16, 1989. While Kurvers was an offensively gifted blueliner who put up 66 points for the Devils in 1988–89, the move carried significant risk. The first-round pick Toronto gave up was for the year Eric Lindros would be eligible for the draft.

The plan was that the Maple Leafs wouldn't be in contention for the Lindros sweepstakes, but early into the 1990–91 campaign, with the team sputtering, it seemed like a distinct possibility that the club could finish in last place to earn the rights to draft the dynamic power forward. With the season seemingly lost, the Leafs traded Kurvers, who had just three assists through 19 games, to the Vancouver Canucks for Brian Bradley on January 12, 1991. The Leafs didn't bottom out in the standings, but they forfeited the third overall pick to the Devils, which they used to take Scott Niedermayer, who would go on to have a Hall of Fame career.

JANUARY 13

TOM FITZGERALD AND GARY ROBERTS PLAY 1,000TH GAME, 2004

Whenever an NHL player reaches the 1,000-game milestone, his teammates usually chip in to get him a gift to mark the occasion. Sometimes it's a Rolex, but other times it could be a Sea-Doo, which is what Doug Bodger received from his Los Angeles Kings teammates in 1999 when he pulled it off. But on January 13, 2004, Maple Leafs players had to reach into their wallets twice.

On that day both Tom Fitzgerald and Gary Roberts suited up for their 1,000th career game, marking the first time in NHL history that two teammates accomplished the feat on the same night. The pair were honoured before the game by the league and showered with gifts from their teammates and even their opponents, the Flames. Calgary captain Jarome Iginla presented Roberts, who played 10 seasons with the Flames, with a print of Western Canada. But the best gift for both Leafs players was that they picked up the victory as part of their special evening. Toronto defeated Calgary 4–1, with Fitzgerald recording the final goal.

HAP DAY SCORES FIRST MAPLE LEAFS HAT TRICK, 1928

After Conn Smythe bought the Toronto St. Patricks in February 1927 and rechristened the team as the Maple Leafs, no player had been able to score a hat trick with a maple leaf on their chest. The following season, on January 14, 1928, team captain Clarence "Hap" Day finally put on a three-goal performance in a 6–1 victory over the New York Rangers.

Day, a native of Owen Sound, Ontario, originally made his NHL debut with the St. Patricks as a winger in the 1924–25 season but was moved to the blue line the next year. Following Smythe's purchase of the team, Day became the first Maple Leafs captain. Five years after his first career hat trick, Day played a critical role in helping the club earn its first Stanley Cup in the Maple Leafs era, scoring three goals and six points in seven games that post-season. Day would pick up one more hat trick, his last in the NHL, on November 19, 1929, when he lit the lamp four times in a game against the Pittsburgh Pirates.

JANUARY 15

BRIT SELBY SCORES ONLY NHL HAT TRICK, 1966

B rit Selby needed just 47 seconds to complete his first NHL hat trick. On January 15, 1966, in a game against the Boston Bruins, after the Toronto winger scored in the first period, he notched two goals in quick succession in the middle frame to accomplish the feat. Selby, a rookie, would finish the season with 14 goals and 27 points in 61 games to win the Calder Memorial Trophy, becoming the ninth Maple Leaf to earn the award since it was first handed out in 1937.

Although Selby went on to play eight more seasons in the NHL, this proved to be his only three-goal performance. After hanging up his skates in 1975, following three seasons in the World Hockey Association, Selby went into teaching. He started at Parkview Secondary School in Toronto before spending the rest of his time at North Toronto Collegiate Institute, where he, fittingly, coached the school's hockey team. Following more than three decades teaching, he retired in 2010. Seven years after Selby left the classroom, Auston Matthews won the Calder, becoming the first Leafs player to earn the award since the player-turned-teacher.

PETER ZEZEL ACQUIRED
BY THE LEAFS, 1991

I t was a homecoming for Peter Zezel. On January 16, 1991, the centre, who was born and raised in Scarborough, Ontario, a neighbouring Toronto community where he still made his home in the off-season, was traded from the Washington Capitals, along with Bob Rouse, to the Maple Leafs in exchange for Al Iafrate. Prior to being selected 41st overall by the Philadelphia Flyers in the 1983 entry draft, Zezel had played junior for his hometown team, the Toronto Marlboros of the Ontario Hockey League.

Zezel made the NHL the following year and quickly established himself as a strong two-way player with plenty of offensive upside. In his rookie season with the Flyers, Zezel scored 15 goals and 60 points in 65 games but was overshadowed by another newcomer that year by the name of Mario Lemieux. After being acquired by Toronto, Zezel made his debut for the blue and white the next night at Maple Leaf Gardens, scoring a goal and picking up two assists in a 6–5 overtime loss to the Pittsburgh Penguins.

STEVE THOMAS SCORES
ANOTHER OT GOAL, 2000

Fighting off a pair of defencemen in overtime, Maple
Leafs winger Steve Thomas looked more like a running
back than a hockey player. That's at least how his goaltender, Curtis Joseph, saw it. Following the game, in which
Thomas scored the game-winning goal with just five seconds
remaining in the extra frame to give Toronto a 5–4 victory
over the Vancouver Canucks, Joseph told reporters that he
"looked like Marshall Faulk breaking tackles." While Faulk
set records on the gridiron during his time in the NFL with
the Indianapolis Colts and St. Louis Rams, Thomas was no
slouch himself on the ice.

That night, January 17, 2000, Thomas's sudden-death
goal was his 11th career overtime winner, which surpassed
Mario Lemieux for the most in NHL history since the league
reintroduced regular-season overtime in 1983. Thomas eventually scored two more to pass Nels Stewart for the all-time
record, but he has long since been surpassed by other players
such as Alex Ovechkin, who at the time of this writing leads
with 25 tallies.

RICK VAIVE SCORES SEVENTH CAREER HATTY, 1984

Heading into the 1983–84 season, Rick Vaive had three career hat tricks to his name. Although the right winger was already a back-to-back 50-goal scorer for the Maple Leafs, he wasn't exactly known for scoring in bunches. But by the halfway point of the 1983–84 campaign, he had already more than doubled his career total for three-goal performances.

On January 18, 1984, Vaive recorded his seventh career hat trick, his fourth of the season, in a 9–4 victory over the Minnesota North Stars. His effort also helped the Maple Leafs break out of a seven-game winless skid. The performance brought the winger's season total up to 38, and with plenty of games remaining on the schedule, he was poised to hit the 50-goal mark for the third year in a row. Sure enough, on March 14, in a game against the North Stars no less, Vaive scored a pair of goals to reach the milestone. He would add two more tallies down the stretch to finish with 52 goals and 93 points, a career high.

JANUARY 19

CHARLIE CONACHER SCORES FIVE, 1932

efore players like Bernie "Boom Boom" Geoffrion and Bobby Hull became synonymous with the slapshot, Charlie Conacher boasted one of the most fearsome shots in the NHL. Known as "the Big Bomber," Conacher had a thundering shot that made goaltenders quiver in the 1930s. After scoring 31 goals in his second season with the Maple Leafs in 1930–31, he christened Maple Leaf Gardens with his cannonading shot, becoming the first Leaf to score a goal in the new Toronto arena on November 12, 1931.

As the season wore on, Conacher continued to fill the back of the net. On January 19, 1932, he became the first player in a Maple Leafs sweater to score five goals in a game in an 11–3 victory over the New York Americans. Although that type of production wasn't unexpected for Conacher, he had some help. New York's regular goaltender, Roy Worters, left the game early in the second period with a knee injury and was replaced by defenceman Allan Shields, who allowed seven goals in relief.

JANUARY 20

LEAFS TRADE DARRYL SITTLER, 1982

After a long and bitter falling out, the saga was finally over. On January 20, 1982, Darryl Sittler, the long-time Maple Leafs captain, agreed to waive his no-trade clause and was sent to the Philadelphia Flyers for the rights to Rich Costello, a second-round pick, and future considerations. The trouble began a few years earlier when Toronto owner Harold Ballard brought back Punch Imlach as general manager. It wasn't long before Imlach and Sittler didn't see eye to eye.

With Imlach unable to move the captain because of his no-trade-clause protection, he instead targeted his close friend and linemate, Lanny McDonald, sending him to the Colorado Rockies. In response, Sittler grabbed the trainer's shears, excised the *C* from his jersey, and said he could no longer serve as captain. Although the situation was thought to have improved over the 1981 off-season when Ballard attempted to make amends with his skipper, things deteriorated again not long into the 1981–82 campaign. Sittler played three seasons in Philadelphia and another in Detroit before hanging up his skates in 1985.

JANUARY 21

COLONEL CHRIS HADFIELD
DROPS THE PUCK, 2013

t was a puck drop that was out of this world. From 400 kilometres above the Earth in the International Space Station, Colonel Chris Hadfield kicked off the Maple Leafs' first home game in the lockout-shortened season on January 21, 2013. Beamed into the Air Canada Centre onto the Jumbotron, Hadfield tells the fans he is proud to be the first member of Leafs Nation in space.

After Hadfield drops the puck in zero gravity, the video feed switches to footage of a winking Félix Potvin — on the roof of the arena — catching the puck as it falls from the sky before tossing it down an open hatch to a waiting Darcy Tucker. After a quick elevator ride, Tucker gives the puck to Darryl Sittler. The video continues to feature Sittler as he runs through the ACC, then stops when he appears live behind the Maple Leafs' bench, puck in hand. He gives it to Johnny Bower and the two proceed to centre ice, along with Potvin and Tucker, for the ceremonial faceoff.

JANUARY 22

AUSTON MATTHEWS SIGNALS
GOOD GOAL, 2018

Auston Matthews wanted to make sure there was no doubt. On January 22, 2018, after putting his 21st goal of the season past Colorado Avalanche goaltender, and former Maple Leaf, Jonathan Bernier to give Toronto a 2–1 lead, Matthews emphatically signalled it was a good goal by pointing his arm at the net to mimic referee Gord Dwyer. Less than two minutes earlier, Matthews thought he had scored the go-ahead goal, but it was not meant to be.

Following a scramble in the Colorado crease that led to Matthews tapping in a loose puck past Bernier, Avalanche coach Jared Bednar challenged it for goaltender interference. When the officials eventually overturned the goal, Matthews subtly rolled his eyes from the bench while the Toronto faithful broke into a raucous "ref, you suck" chant. But instead of dwelling on it, the Maple Leafs phenom went out and got it back. Skating down the ice with William Nylander, he scored off his linemate's rebound and responded with an outburst of emotion rarely displayed thus far in his young career.

JANUARY 23

KIRK MULLER TRADED TO LEAFS, 1996

After finishing out the 1994–95 season with the New York Islanders, Kirk Muller told general manager Don Maloney in the off-season that he wanted to be traded. Maloney, who had acquired Muller, along with Mathieu Schneider and Craig Darby, a few months earlier from the Montreal Canadiens for Pierre Turgeon and Vladimir Malakhov, asked the veteran winger to be patient. He told him to come to training camp and said he would look to trade him.

But by November 1995, Maloney had still not made a deal. Muller's performance slid — he had just four goals and seven points in 15 games — and he was becoming a distraction, so the team told him to go home and wait to be traded. The saga was finally resolved on January 23, 1996, when, as part of a three-way deal with the Islanders and the Ottawa Senators, the Maple Leafs acquired Muller. The next day, in his first game in more than two months, Muller made his debut for Toronto, scoring a goal, his first since October 28, 1995.

LEAFS TRADE PAUL FENTON AND
JOHN KORDIC TO THE CAPITALS, 1991

M aple Leafs centre Eddie Olczyk was in the delivery room with his wife, Diana, preparing for the birth of their second child, Tommy, when he received an urgent phone call from the team. He quickly reassured them he'd be ready for the game that night against his hometown Chicago Blackhawks, but he really couldn't talk just then. But before he could hang up, he was informed he had been traded to the Winnipeg Jets.

Olczyk was stunned, but he had more important things to worry about. It turned out that Toronto sent him, along with Mark Osborne, to Winnipeg in exchange for Dave Ellett and Paul Fenton. The latter, a former 30-goal scorer, was not with the Maple Leafs for very long. A couple of months later, on January 24, 1991, Fenton and John Kordic were sent to the Washington Capitals for future considerations. While Fenton's time with the Maple Leafs was fleeting, his stint with the Capitals was even shorter. That same day he was flipped to the Calgary Flames for Ken Sabourin.

JANUARY 25

THE BIG M SETS SEASON GOAL-SCORING RECORD, 1961

Frank Mahovlich was known as "the Big M." It may not have been the most imaginative nickname; he was one of the biggest players of his day and his surname started with an *M*. A better sobriquet for Mahovlich might have been the one King Clancy bestowed on him. The former Maple Leafs coach called him "Moses," because he believed that, like the biblical character, Mahovlich would lead the team out of the wilderness.

After winning the Calder Trophy in 1958, it seemed like Mahovlich might do just that. On January 25, 1961, in a game against the Montreal Canadiens, Mahovlich scored his 39th goal of the season, surpassing Tod Sloan and Gaye Stewart to establish a new franchise record for most goals in a season. Although the Big M missed out on the 50-goal mark that campaign, the next year he would indeed lead the Maple Leafs to the promised land, scoring six goals in the playoffs to help the club win its first Stanley Cup in more than a decade.

CORB DENNENY SCORES SIX, 1921

With the St. Patricks outside of the playoff picture, the stands were all but empty at the Arena Gardens on Mutual Street in Toronto on January 26, 1921, when the team hosted the Hamilton Tigers. There may not have been much at stake for the home team, but Corb Denneny put on a show for the fans in attendance. After getting the St. Patricks on the board just before the halfway mark of the first period, he added another one five minutes later. In the middle frame he provided the closing tally to make it 5–3 heading into the second intermission.

But Denneny saved his best for the final frame. In a span of just over six minutes, he scored three straight goals to finish the game with six, establishing a franchise record that still stands to this day. With Denneny making headlines, it seemed as though his older brother, Cy, who played for Ottawa, wasn't going to let his younger sibling have all the glory. Less than two months later, Cy also scored six goals against Hamilton.

JANUARY 27

LARRY MURPHY SCORES HIS 250TH CAREER GOAL, 1997

Following a scoreless first period, Adam Foote got the Colorado Avalanche on the board just before the midway mark of the second period in a game against Toronto on January 27, 1997. Less than a minute later, Maple Leafs blueliner Larry Murphy tied it up to record his 250th career goal, becoming just the seventh defenceman in NHL history to reach the milestone. The typical jeers that Murphy received from the home crowd at the Gardens were replaced by a chorus of cheers, but it was fleeting.

After going into the second intermission tied 2–2, Colorado scored three unanswered goals to take the game 5–2 and drop the Leafs to last place in the standings. While it should have been a celebratory night for Murphy, there wasn't much of a silver lining for the defenceman, who had been the whipping boy for an abysmal campaign that still had 32 games remaining. Fortunately for Murphy, he wasn't around much longer. On March 18, 1997, he was traded to Detroit for future considerations and would go on to win back-to-back championships with the Red Wings.

FRANK McCOOL RECORDS BACK-TO-BACK SHUTOUTS, 1945

Every time Frank McCool retired to the dressing room between periods, the Maple Leafs goaltender would sip on milk to calm his stomach ulcers. McCool had actually been discharged from the Canadian army during the Second World War because of his condition. Following his discharge, the netminder spent the 1943–44 season recuperating at his home in Calgary and writing for the *Calgary Albertan* while he received treatment. Although he was well enough to join the Maple Leafs the next year, his ulcers plagued him for the rest of his life.

But on January 28, 1945, McCool posted his second straight shutout in a 7–0 victory over the New York Rangers at Madison Square Garden. The night before, he stopped everything the Rangers threw his way in Toronto. McCool would finish the season with five shutouts and win the Calder as the league's top rookie. In the playoffs he elevated his game further, recording four shutouts, including three straight in the Stanley Cup Final, a franchise record, as Toronto defeated Detroit to win its fifth championship.

JANUARY 29

OLIVER EKMAN-LARSSON SCORES FROM OWN BLUE LINE, 2015

S ometimes the milestones that happen against the Leafs are the ones you least expect, but if you have been a fan of the team long enough, they are exactly the type of incidents you presume could only happen to the Toronto Maple Leafs. Take this one for example. On January 29, 2015, the Leafs were hosting the Arizona Coyotes and were leading 1–0 heading into the third period.

When the final frame began, the Coyotes were still killing off an interference penalty. Five seconds after Arizona won the faceoff, defenceman Oliver Ekman-Larsson flipped the puck into the Maple Leafs' end from just above his own blue line. The puck took a funny bounce, fooled goaltender Jonathan Bernier, and went into the back of the net, tying a Coyotes franchise record for the fastest goal of any kind to start a period. Toronto ended up allowing two more goals and lost 3–1, the club's eighth straight defeat. Despite the gaffe, Bernier still managed to stop a commendable 42 shots that game.

CURTIS JOSEPH RECORDS 36TH CAREER SHUTOUT, 2002

The Atlanta Thrashers had the fewest wins in the NHL. Heading into a game against the Maple Leafs on January 30, 2002, the Thrashers were sitting at just 13 victories. And while it appeared to be a lopsided matchup on paper, two of Atlanta's wins that season were against the Leafs. The Thrashers defeated Toronto in overtime after the holiday break and a couple of weeks later on the road.

So when the two teams squared off at Philips Arena at the end of the month, the Leafs were due. Just fifteen seconds after the opening faceoff, Jonas Höglund scored his 11th of the season to make it 1–0. The Maple Leafs added three more goals before the midway mark of the game to chase goaltender Milan Hnilička from his crease. Pasi Nurminen, who was making his NHL debut, stopped 25 shots in relief but allowed three more goals in a 6–0 loss. When the final buzzer sounded, Maple Leafs netminder Curtis Joseph had stopped all 17 shots he faced to record his 36th career shutout.

JANUARY 31

PAT QUINN RECORDS 600TH CAREER WIN, 2004

After an embarrassing 7–1 loss at home to Ottawa, in which Senators captain Daniel Alfredsson mocked Toronto captain Mats Sundin by pretending he was about to throw his broken stick into the stands, a move that earned Sundin a one-game suspension earlier in the month, the Maple Leafs redeemed themselves two weeks later. On January 31, 2004, Toronto hosted the Senators again. Although Alfredsson opened the scoring late in the first period, the Maple Leafs took over, scoring five unanswered goals to win 5–1.

Sundin scored the game-winning goal just after the half-way mark of the middle frame. But the victory had more significance than simply avenging a humiliating loss a couple of weeks earlier — it was also head coach Pat Quinn's 600th career victory. Quinn became just the fourth bench boss in NHL history to reach the milestone, joining Dick Irvin, Al Arbour, and Scotty Bowman. Quinn and the Leafs ultimately got the last laugh against the Senators a few months later when they picked up their fourth series victory against their provincial rivals.

FEBRUARY 1

HAP DAY REPLACES CONN SMYTHE, 1955

After three decades with Conn Smythe at the helm, the Maple Leafs had a new general manager. On February 1, 1955, Smythe appointed his protege, Clarence "Hap" Day, his long-time assistant GM, to the role. In becoming general manager, Day made history as the first person to serve as captain, coach, and GM of the Maple Leafs. After Smythe purchased the St. Patricks in 1927 and renamed the club the Maple Leafs, Day became its first captain and, five years later, led the team to its first Stanley Cup in the blue-and-white era.

Following his playing career, Day moved behind the bench and guided the Maple Leafs to five championships. His time as GM, however, would not be as glorious. While Day controlled the day-to-day hockey operations, Smythe still wielded significant power as team owner. Before the Leafs were even eliminated from the 1957 playoffs, Smythe stated on a broadcast that it was unclear whether Day would return the following year. After the post-season, an embarrassed Day resigned from his GM duties.

FEBRUARY 2

IAN TURNBULL SCORES FIVE, 1977

an Turnbull was making up for lost time. After failing to find the back of the net in December and much of January, the Leafs defenceman broke out of his goal-scoring slump in a big way on February 2, 1977. That night, in a 9–1 victory against the Detroit Red Wings, the 23-year-old rearguard notched five goals, establishing a new NHL record for the most goals in a game by a defenceman. The last time a blue-liner had scored even four goals in a game was nearly five decades earlier when fellow Leaf Hap Day and Pittsburgh's John McKinnon each found the back of the net four times in a high-scoring affair.

Following the game Turnbull was beaming when he greeted reporters. "When they go in, you smile. When they don't, you try again," he said. When Turnbull went 21 games without scoring a goal, he had fired 84 shots on net with nothing to show for it. That night against Detroit, he needed only five shots to score five goals. Sometimes you just need a little puck luck.

FEBRUARY 3

BILLY TAYLOR RECORDS HAT TRICK, 1946

Even Billy Taylor wouldn't have bet he'd pick up his first hat trick in a game against the New York Rangers on February 3, 1946. But actually, he might have. A couple of years later, after a stopover in Detroit, where he recorded a league-record seven assists in a game, Taylor was playing for the Bruins. During his time in Boston, Taylor and his teammate Don Gallinger started gambling on hockey games, including some against their own team.

The pair got away with it until their activities were uncovered in a police surveillance operation against Detroit gangster James Tamer. They had been placing bets with him and were caught on a wiretap. With the notorious Black Sox Scandal, in which eight players of the Chicago White Sox were accused of throwing the 1919 World Series, making big headlines three decades earlier, NHL president Clarence Campbell came down hard on the duo. Gallinger was suspended indefinitely and Taylor, who was then with the Rangers, was banned for life. While Campbell rescinded the punishments in 1970, the two never played hockey again.

FEBRUARY 4

BRAD MARSH TRADED TO DETROIT, 1991

When the NHL started moving toward publicly disclosing player salaries in the early 1990s, Maple Leafs defenceman Brad Marsh had some colourful words. "Now instead of calling some guy a bleeping jerk, we'll call him an overpaid bleeping jerk," he said. Marsh was never one to mince words. Not long after Toronto traded him to Detroit on February 4, 1991, in exchange for an eighth-round draft pick, the veteran blueliner took a shot at some of his former teammates, saying they didn't take as much pride in wearing the Maple Leaf as he did.

"I think hockey, in general, needs Toronto to be a strong franchise," Marsh added. "Considering what it used to be and what it is now, it is unfortunate." Despite his comments, which were tough to argue with, the Leafs reacquired him in June 1992 for cash. Marsh, however, didn't sport the blue and white again. Just over a month later, he was sent to Ottawa, where he played his final NHL season, for future considerations.

FEBRUARY 5

AUSTON MATTHEWS SIGNS FIVE-YEAR EXTENSION, 2019

After scoring four goals in his NHL debut and breaking franchise benchmarks for most goals and points in a season by a rookie, it was pretty obvious that Auston Matthews was going to earn a significant raise following the expiration of his entry-level contract. The only question was how long the term would be. Many Leafs fans, myself included, wanted to see Matthews sign an eight-year extension, which he was eligible for, but like many of his predecessors, including Tampa Bay's Steven Stamkos and New York's John Tavares, who ended up joining the Leafs in 2018 as a free agent, Matthews opted for a shorter contract that would make him an unrestricted free agent while he was still in his prime.

On February 5, 2019, the Leafs announced they had signed Matthews to a five-year, $58.17 million contract extension. Since inking the deal, Matthews has won the Rocket Richard Trophy twice, along with the Hart Trophy and the Ted Lindsay Award. He's certainly lived up to the deal, but will he still be a Maple Leaf beyond 2024?

FEBRUARY 6

CHARLIE CONACHER WASTES NO TIME AGAINST BOSTON, 1932

Charlie Conacher was in a hurry to get the Leafs on the board. On February 6, 1932, just seven seconds after the puck was dropped in a contest against the Boston Bruins, Conacher scored, demolishing the team record for the fastest goal from the beginning of a game. Reg Noble originally set the mark when he bulged the twine 30 seconds into a matchup against the Canadiens in 1918. After Conacher made short work of Noble's milestone, the Leafs added five straight goals, including another from the quick-scoring centre, to trounce the Bruins 6–0.

While Conacher's accomplishment was a couple seconds off the league benchmark set by the Montreal Maroons' Merlyn Phillips in 1926, he stood alone in the Leafs record books for nearly nine decades. On January 3, 2019, seven seconds into a duel against the Minnesota Wild, Mitch Marner backhanded the puck into the back of the net to match Conacher's franchise record for the fastest goal to start a game. More recently, William Nylander came close, opening the scoring against Chicago in nine seconds on February 15, 2023.

FEBRUARY 7

DARRYL SITTLER SCORES 10 POINTS, 1976

D arryl Sittler always stuck to his pre-game routine. He would go to morning skate and then return home for a meal and a nap before heading back to Maple Leaf Gardens from his home in Mississauga. But on February 7, 1976, he had to change his routine slightly. His wife usually prepared his meal, but on that day Wendy was out and about running errands, so Sittler was on his own.

On his way back from the rink, he picked up some chicken from Swiss Chalet and ate it in his car. Although it wasn't what he would typically do before a game, it worked. That night against the Boston Bruins, Sittler put up a performance for the ages. The Maple Leafs captain scored six goals and 10 points to establish a new NHL record, which has yet to be matched, for the most points in a single game. If anyone from Swiss Chalet is reading this, here's an idea on the house: the 10-point chicken dinner every February 7.

FEBRUARY 8

DARRYL SITTLER HONOURED, 2003

t was a bittersweet moment for Darryl Sittler and his family. On February 8, 2003, the Maple Leafs raised their former captain's No. 27 to the top of the Air Canada Centre. Although Sittler was joined by his children, Ryan, Meaghan, and Ashley, there was a notable absence on the ice. Wendy, his wife of three decades, passed away the previous year following a courageous battle against cancer. Sittler was supposed to have been honoured early into the 2001–02 campaign, on the same day as Frank Mahovlich, his predecessor who wore the same number with the blue and white, but Wendy was in the final stages of her illness and his ceremony was ultimately postponed.

Although Wendy was not there, Sittler tearfully acknowledged to the crowd that she was certainly there in spirit. As he tenderly embraced his children, he watched his banner join the other Toronto greats high above the rafters. Following the ceremony, after which there was probably not a dry eye in the house, the Maple Leafs defeated the Montreal Canadiens 3–1.

FEBRUARY 9

LEAFS ACQUIRE JOFFREY LUPUL, 2011

Joffrey Lupul believed he still had a lot of hockey ahead of him. Although the 27-year-old winger had reached the 20-goal mark three times in his NHL career, he missed most of the 2009–10 season with back problems. When he returned to the Anaheim Ducks lineup the next year, he got off to a slow start, scoring five goals and 13 points in 26 games. But then, on February 9, 2011, he was traded to the Maple Leafs, along with Jake Gardiner and a fourth-round draft pick, for defenceman François Beauchemin.

Playing on a line with Tyler Bozak and Clarke MacArthur, Lupul recorded nine goals and 18 points down the stretch. In his first full campaign with the Buds, he proved he still had plenty of game left, scoring 25 goals and 67 points, a career high. Following his offensively explosive season, the Leafs inked Lupul to a five-year, $26.25 million contract extension. Although Lupul reached the 20-goal plateau one more time in Toronto, injuries did get the better of him, and by 2016 he was placed on long-term injured reserve.

FEBRUARY 10

LEAFS ACQUIRE RED KELLY
FROM DETROIT, 1960

When the Detroit Red Wings traded Red Kelly to the New York Rangers — along with Billy McNeill for Bill Gadsby and Eddie Shack — the defenceman, who had won four championships for the Motor City, threatened to retire. Despite NHL president Clarence Campbell suggesting he sleep on it before making a decision, Kelly was adamant that he would hang up his skates rather than report to New York.

Although he did not want to go to Broadway, he did say he would go to Toronto if a deal with the Maple Leafs could be arranged. A few days later, on February 10, 1960, after the initial trade to the Rangers was cancelled, Kelly was dealt to the Buds for Marc Reaume. Although Kelly patrolled the blue line for the Red Wings, he was shifted up front in Toronto. Centring a line with rising star Frank Mahovlich, Kelly quickly established himself as one of the game's top pivots. He would go on to add four more Stanley Cup rings to his collection during his tenure with the Leafs.

FEBRUARY 11

DAVE ANDREYCHUK SCORES 350, 1993

t didn't take Dave Andreychuk long to reach an important milestone with his new team. Just over a week after being acquired by the Maple Leafs from the Buffalo Sabres, as part of a trade that included Grant Fuhr, Daren Puppa, and a pair of draft picks, Andreychuk, a power-play specialist, recorded his 350th career goal in a game against the Vancouver Canucks on February 11, 1993.

Before he was traded to Toronto, Andreychuk had already racked up 29 goals in 52 games for the Sabres and would pick up 25 more tallies with the Leafs to finish the season with 54, a career high. Of those goals that season, 32 were recorded on the man advantage. When Andreychuk parked his big frame in front of the opposing team's net, few could move him, and he was a master at banging in rebounds and loose pucks from the blue paint, particularly on the power play. The next year, his first full season with the Leafs, Andreychuk potted 53 goals and 99 points.

BALDY COTTON TRADED TO THE LEAFS, 1929

After the final buzzer sounded to close a game between the Pittsburgh Pirates and the Montreal Canadiens on February 12, 1929, Pittsburgh winger Harold "Baldy" Cotton was informed he had been traded to the Maple Leafs in exchange for fellow winger Gerry Lowrey. Two nights later, Cotton made his debut for the blue and white when the club hosted the New York Rangers. He scored his first goal for the Maple Leafs a couple of days later in a 3–0 victory against the Montreal Maroons.

The next year, in his first full season in Toronto, Cotton recorded 21 goals and 38 points, a career high, and was second in team scoring behind Ace Bailey. Cotton played five more seasons for the Maple Leafs and was part of the team's Stanley Cup victory in 1932. In 1935, Toronto traded him to the New York Americans, where he played for two more seasons before hanging up his skates. Following his playing career, Cotton served as a scout for the Boston Bruins and Minnesota North Stars.

FEBRUARY 13

PEA SOUP MAKES GILMOUR HAPPY, 1993

t must have been something he ate. On February 13, 1993, in a game against the Minnesota North Stars, Doug Gilmour assisted on all six of Toronto's goals in a 6–1 rout. His six helpers matched a franchise record originally set by defenceman Babe Pratt in a matchup against the Bruins on January 8, 1944. You have already read that a pit stop at Swiss Chalet may have played a part in Darryl Sittler's 10-point performance nearly two decades earlier, but it turns out Gilmour's achievement might also have been fuelled by an unusual pre-game meal.

Years later on TSN 1050's radio show *Overdrive*, Gilmour told the hosts that when he came home from the rink after the morning skate he had a tuna sandwich and pea soup. "That night I had six assists, so you guys figure that one out," he said. It's personally not something I would have chosen to eat before a game, or for any meal for that matter, but I can't knock it because clearly it worked out well.

WILF PAIEMENT SCORES 200TH CAREER GOAL, 1981

Wilf Paiement was the last player not named Wayne Gretzky to wear No. 99 in the NHL. Originally drafted second overall by the Kansas City Scouts in 1974, Paiement started his professional career wearing No. 9. When he was traded from Colorado to the Maple Leafs on December 29, 1979, as part of a contentious deal that sent Lanny McDonald to the Rockies, he donned No. 14 down the stretch. But for his first full campaign in Toronto, Paiement wore No. 99.

Meanwhile, Gretzky, who had just won his first Hart Trophy, was also sporting the number. While Gretzky was starting to rewrite the record books in Edmonton, Paiement notched a milestone of his own that year in Toronto. On February 14, 1981, he scored his 200th career goal in a 6–3 victory against the New York Rangers. Paiement wore No. 99 until he was traded to Quebec in 1982. Gretzky, of course, went on to make the number iconic and was the last player to wear it until it was retired league-wide in 2000.

FEBRUARY 15

LEAFS BLOW 5–1 LEAD TO OTTAWA, 2021

While the world was still navigating through the Covid-19 pandemic, the NHL put all the Canadian teams into a single division, known as the Scotia NHL North Division, for an abbreviated 2020–21 season. The Canadian clubs would only play each other and square off at least nine times each. When Toronto played Ottawa for just the third time, on February 15, 2021, I was already sick of the Senators.

With nine seconds remaining in the second period, Ottawa's Nick Paul scored a short-handed goal. No matter, the Leafs still had a 5–2 lead heading into the final frame. But early in the third, Artem Zub potted his first of the season to close the gap. After Connor Brown, a former Leaf, scored just over five minutes later, Evgenii Dadonov found the back of the net with two minutes to go to force overtime. Early into sudden death, Dadonov scored again to give the Senators the victory, marking the first time in franchise history that Ottawa overcame a deficit of at least four goals to win.

FEBRUARY 16

JOHN TAVARES NEARLY
GETS HIT BY PUCK, 2019

John Tavares was too focused on the game to notice. On February 16, 2019, on the road against the Arizona Coyotes, an errant puck crashed into the Maple Leafs' bench. While all of his teammates and coaches blocked their faces and attempted to avoid its path, Tavares just sat there stoically as chaos erupted around him. When the team held practice a couple of days later, he and his teammates addressed the incident with the media.

Tavares, who said he'd received a flurry of concerned texts from friends and family, chalked it up to being too deep in thought about the game. Auston Matthews told reporters it didn't seem to faze Tavares. "Our whole bench, even coaches, flinched, but he was just in deep thought thinking about I don't know what, but thank god it didn't hit him," he said. A few nights after his near miss, Tavares scored his first goal in a handful of games. He would finish his first season with the Maple Leafs with 47 goals and 88 points, both career benchmarks.

FEBRUARY 17

FIRST MAPLE LEAFS GAME, 1927

As Toronto's NHL team skated out onto the ice to take on the New York Americans on February 17, 1927, they were sporting a new look. Rechristened as the Maple Leafs just a few days earlier after a new ownership group, led by Conn Smythe, purchased the St. Patricks, the club played its first game under its new banner. They wore white sweaters with a green maple leaf and *Toronto* emblazoned across the chest.

Although the Americans opened the scoring four minutes into the first period, the newly minted Maple Leafs took over the rest of the way. After recording four unanswered goals, including two from rookie Ace Bailey, they defeated their opponents 4–1 to record the first victory in the Leafs era. While the team continued to sport green sweaters for the rest of the season, the following year they adopted the white-and-blue uniforms that have become forever synonymous with the franchise, a nod to the colours Smythe wore when he played hockey for the Varsity Blues at the University of Toronto.

FEBRUARY 18

KIRK MULLER SCORES 300TH CAREER GOAL, 1996

N ot long into a matinee game against Detroit on February 18, 1996, Toronto pugilist Tie Domi two-handed Red Wings star Sergei Fedorov over the head. Domi maintained he was trying to hit his opponent's stick, but after his own twig struck Detroit's net, the truculent winger's blade came down on top of Fedorov's helmet. The smooth-skating Russian was able to shake it off and stay in the game, picking up an assist on the power-play goal that resulted from the incident, and another helper later in the frame.

Domi, on the other hand, earned a tripping minor, a high-sticking major, and a 10-minute game misconduct. Lost in Domi's antics was the fact that just over the halfway mark of the first period, Kirk Muller, who was playing in his 13th game with the Maple Leafs since being acquired from the New York Islanders, scored his 300th career goal to tie the game 1–1. The two teams exchanged another pair of goals before captain Steve Yzerman scored the eventual game-winner in the second period.

FEBRUARY 19

DARRYL SITTLER RECORDS FIRST CAREER HAT TRICK, 1972

n a game in which Buffalo's Rick Martin scored his 39th goal of the season, establishing a new modern NHL rookie record, Darryl Sittler stole the show. On February 19, 1972, in a 4–1 victory against the Sabres, the 22-year-old continued to break out of a goal-scoring slump by recording his first career hat trick. Sittler found the back of the net a few nights earlier in Pittsburgh but had been mired in an eight-game goalless drought before that matchup.

After Martin scored just before the halfway mark of the middle frame to tie the game 1–1 for the Sabres, it was all Sittler. He scored his first of the night with just over five minutes to go before the second intermission. In the third period, he scored two more goals within a span of 10 seconds to complete the milestone and firmly put the game out of reach for Buffalo. Sittler would go on to record 17 more regular-season hat tricks over the course of his career with the Maple Leafs.

FEBRUARY 20

LEAFS PLAY FIRST GAME AT THE ACC, 1999

The Leafs went out like a lamb at Maple Leaf Gardens but came in like a lion at the Air Canada Centre. On February 13, 1999, the team played its final game at the Gardens, a 6–2 loss to the Blackhawks. More than six decades earlier, the Maple Leafs played their first game in their arena against Chicago and also came up short in a 2–1 defeat.

This time around, however, the Leafs would start their tenure in their new building in the win column. Exactly one week after the loss at the Gardens, the club hosted the Montreal Canadiens at the ACC. Toronto's Todd Warriner scored the first goal in the new barn, putting the puck past goalie Jeff Hackett early in the opening frame. When regulation ended the game was tied 2–2, but with just over a minute remaining in overtime, Steve Thomas scored to seal the victory. While the Buds won a championship at the end of their first season at Maple Leaf Gardens, the team is still waiting for its Stanley Cup at the ACC, now Scotiabank Arena.

FEBRUARY 21

MATS SUNDIN RETURNS, 2009

You couldn't have scripted a better homecoming. On February 21, 2009, Mats Sundin returned to Toronto as a member of the Vancouver Canucks. During his 13 seasons with the blue and white, Sundin scored 420 goals and 987 points in 981 games and dutifully served as captain for most of those years. Although some Leafs fans were still perturbed that he did not waive his no-movement clause the previous year, he was one of the best players the franchise had known.

In his first game back, Sundin choked back tears during a video tribute that brought everyone in the building to their feet. After regulation ended in a deadlock and overtime solved nothing, it went to a shootout. Through five shooters each team had a goal, and then it was Sundin's turn. With the game on his stick, he put the puck past goalie Vesa Toskala to give the Canucks a 3–2 victory. Sundin had scored 79 game-winning goals with the Maple Leafs, so it was only fitting he decided the game in Toronto once again.

FEBRUARY 22

ZAMBONI DRIVER BEATS
THE LEAFS, 2020

t's the type of story that could only happen to the Leafs. On February 22, 2020, they were defeated by a Zamboni driver. While David Ayres did more than drive the ice resurfacer at the Mattamy Athletic Centre in Toronto, he will forever be remembered as the Zamboni driver who beat the Leafs. When Toronto hosted Carolina that night, Ayres, who was serving as the emergency backup goaltender, was in the building should he be called upon.

After former Leafs goaltender James Reimer, who started for the Hurricanes, left the game six minutes in, Ayres became Petr Mrazek's backup. But when Mrazek was bowled over halfway through the second period, Ayres was suddenly the last Carolina goaltender standing. Making his NHL debut at the age of 42, he allowed goals on the first two shots he faced. But the team rallied around Ayres and he stopped the next, and final, eight shots he faced to backstop the Hurricanes to a 6–3 victory, becoming the first emergency backup goaltender in NHL history to win a game.

FEBRUARY 23

ROCKY SAGANIUK SCORES ONLY CAREER HAT TRICK, 1980

Playing in his first full season with the Maple Leafs after winning the Les Cunningham Award as most valuable player in the American Hockey League the year before with the New Brunswick Hawks, Rocky Saganiuk had one of his best nights on the road in Winnipeg. After opening the scoring in a game against the Jets on February 23, 1980, he tallied two more to record his first, and only, career hat trick in a 9–3 victory. Saganiuk would play three more campaigns in Toronto before he was traded to Pittsburgh in 1983, where he wrapped up his NHL career.

Following the better part of a decade in the British Hockey League as a player and coach, he founded a youth hockey program in Chicago. Known as Rocky Hockey, it gave Saganiuk the chance to mentor his grandson, Colby, who was raised in the Windy City. More than four decades after Saganiuk scored his lone hat trick for the Leafs, Colby was invited to Toronto's development camp before the start of the 2021–22 season.

FEBRUARY 24

LEAFS BEAT BRUINS TO MATCH HOME WIN STREAK, 2018

Hosting the Boston Bruins on February 24, 2018, the Maple Leafs had some history on the line. A victory would give the team its ninth straight win at the ACC to match a franchise record for most consecutive home wins. The benchmark was originally set by the St. Patricks in 1924–25 and was matched two times since then. But there was more than history at stake. It was the last regular-season meeting between the two clubs and a potential preview for the playoffs.

Although Auston Matthews was out of the lineup with a shoulder injury, William Nylander, who took his spot on the top line, set up two goals, including the game-winner with less than two minutes remaining in regulation. Following a four-game road trip, the Leafs picked up their 10th straight home victory to establish a new franchise record. They would stretch that number to 13 before losing to Buffalo on March 26, 2018. And although the outcome against Boston seemed promising for the post-season, the Leafs would come up short in seven games.

FEBRUARY 25

LEAFS FIRE 61 SHOTS ON DETROIT, 1976

J im Rutherford did the best he could. Although the
Detroit goaltender allowed the first goal just 15 seconds
into a game against the Maple Leafs on February 25,
1976, he didn't exactly get much help from his blue line. Just
over the halfway mark of the first period, the Leafs put three
more goals past him in only 52 seconds. When the opening
session came to a close, Toronto had already fired 30 shots on
net, a franchise record for most shots in a single frame, and
was up 4–0.

And the shots just kept coming. The Leafs scored two
more goals in the second period, including Lanny McDonald's
30th of the season to make his line with Errol Thompson and
Darryl Sittler just the second unit in the league in which each
player reached the 30-goal mark. Toronto added two more
goals in the final stanza to take an 8–0 victory. When the
dust settled, the Leafs had taken 61 shots on net, another club
record, which more than doubled Detroit's output that game.

MITCH MARNER SCORES SIX POINTS, 2022

I t was certainly one for the books for Mitch Marner. On February 26, 2022, in a road game against the Detroit Red Wings, the wizardly winger scored four goals, his first NHL hat trick, and six points, a career high. After assisting on rookie Michael Bunting's first-period goal to make it 2–0 for Toronto, Marner took over in the middle frame. He notched his first goal of the night 33 seconds in and completed a natural hat trick just before the halfway mark. And with less than two minutes to go until the second intermission, he picked up another helper on an Auston Matthews goal that made it 7–2.

But Detroit nearly ruined the storyline. They scored four unanswered goals to open the final period to pull within one. After Ilya Mikheyev made it 8–6 for Toronto, the Red Wings scored again to make it a one-goal game. Luckily for the Leafs, the team potted two more, with Marner notching the 10th and final goal to close out a wild victory on the road.

FEBRUARY 27

FRANK MAHOVLICH PICKS UP FOUR POINTS AGAINST CHICAGO, 1963

Heading into a game against the Chicago Black Hawks on February 27, 1963, the Maple Leafs were nine points behind their first-place opponents. But Toronto's strapping, skilled winger Frank Mahovlich kept the club's shot at the league title alive with an impressive performance. The Big M opened the scoring early in the first period with his 31st goal of the campaign, tying him with Gordie Howe for the league lead.

After the teams exchanged a pair of goals to close out that frame and another apiece in the middle session, Toronto went into the third period leading 3–2. Mahovlich set up three goals in the final stanza to power the Leafs to a 6–3 victory. Prior to the game, the Big M was eighth in the NHL in points, but his four-point effort shot him into third place. Although he would cede the goal-scoring and points titles to Howe, the Leafs rattled off six more victories down the stretch to pass the Hawks and win the Prince of Wales Trophy as the top regular-season team.

LEAFS ACQUIRE CONNOR CARRICK, 2016

Connor Carrick led the 2016 American Hockey League playoffs in scoring and he didn't even play in the final series. Carrick, a blueliner for the Toronto Marlies, recorded 18 points in 15 games before the Marlies were eliminated in the Eastern Conference Final by the Hershey Bears, the AHL affiliate of the Washington Capitals. It was a team Carrick knew quite well.

Drafted 137th overall by the Capitals in 2012, Carrick had established himself as one of the top defencemen in Hershey before he was sent to the Maple Leafs, along with Brooks Laich and a second-round draft pick for Daniel Winnik and a fifth-round pick on February 28, 2016. Carrick played 16 games down the stretch for the Maple Leafs before joining the Marlies for the post-season. The following year he played his first full NHL campaign, suiting up for 67 games for the blue and white. Carrick played one more season for Toronto before he was traded to the Dallas Stars in exchange for a conditional seventh-round draft pick in 2019.

FEBRUARY 29

LEAFS ACQUIRE NICK KYPREOS, 1996

eafs captain Doug Gilmour made sure to give Nick Kypreos a warm welcome to his new team. After Kypreos, a Toronto native, was traded from the New York Rangers to the Leafs on February 29, 1996, along with Wayne Presley, for Bill Berg and Sergio Momesso, he travelled to Dallas where the team was scheduled to play in a few days. In his book *Undrafted*, Kypreos recounts how during his first morning skate, he noticed that captain Doug Gilmour was hunched over beside him on the bench tying his skates.

But when Kypreos went over the boards for a drill, he learned that Gilmour, a well-known prankster, had only been pretending to tie his skates. Instead, he was untying one of his new teammate's, and Kypreos nearly fell out of his skate once he hit the ice. He learned pretty quickly that you need to keep your head on a swivel when Gilmour was around. Later that day, Kypreos made his debut for the blue and white, fighting Bill Huard in a 5–1 loss to the Stars.

MARCH 1

NORTH STARS SNAP 20-GAME WINLESS STREAK, 1970

The Minnesota North Stars were due for a victory. The team's last triumph was on January 14, 1970, and since then they had racked up a 20-game winless streak, which included nine consecutive losses. So when the North Stars hosted the Maple Leafs on March 1, 1970, they had something to prove. Even head coach Charlie Burns, who had started the season as a player but had been appointed full-time bench boss in January, suited up for his first game in a few months.

Although Burns did not get on the scoresheet, he motivated his team to an 8–0 win, its first in 45 days. "This showed everybody we're not going to take this lying down," Burns told reporters after the game. When the Leafs had a rematch against the North Stars at home less than a week later, the result was somehow much the same. Although Toronto managed to get three goals past veteran goaltender Gump Worsley, Minnesota once again racked up eight tallies, chasing Bruce Gamble from the net.

MARCH 2

SWEENEY SCHRINER SCORES FINAL CAREER HAT TRICK, 1946

Sweeney Schriner was set to retire. But before he hung up his skates, the veteran winger had some unfinished business. With eight games left on the schedule, Schriner was just four goals back from reaching the 200-goal mark. Originally born in Saratov, Russia, in 1911, when Schriner made his debut for the New York Americans in 1934, he was believed to be the first Russian-born player to play in the NHL. He finished his rookie campaign with 18 goals and 40 points to win the Calder Trophy. After five years with the Americans, Schriner was traded to the Maple Leafs in 1939.

Following five more seasons in Toronto, which included two championships, Schriner was ready to ride off into the sunset at the end of 1945–46, but not without hitting one last milestone. In a game against Chicago on March 2, 1946, he scored three goals, his final NHL hat trick, to move within one of 200. Just over a week later, he reached the benchmark. He played his last game on March 17, adding one more goal for good measure.

MARCH 3

DOUG GILMOUR GETS 100, 1993

Doug Gilmour was giving back with every assist he dished out. During the 1992–93 season, Gilmour partnered with the Children's Wish Foundation, now known as Make-A-Wish Canada, which fulfills the wishes of children suffering from critical illness, on the Give with Gilmour campaign. For every assist the playmaker earned, he would personally donate $93, a nod to his jersey number, to the special cause.

On March 3, 1993, in a game against the Minnesota North Stars, he added to his pledge with a helper on Dave Andreychuk's second-period goal. The assist also gave Gilmour 100 points on the season, making him just the second player in Leafs history to reach the century mark in a campaign. Darryl Sittler did it twice during his tenure and last accomplished the feat in the 1977–78 season, when he racked up 117 points. Gilmour would add 19 more helpers down the stretch to finish the season with 95 assists, a franchise record that continues to stand the test of time, and donate $8,835 to Children's Wish.

MARCH 4

RON ELLIS SCORES 300TH CAREER GOAL, 1978

When Ron Ellis abruptly announced his retirement in October 1975 at the age of 30, he still had four years remaining on his contract that he was leaving on the table. While some speculated Ellis was walking away because Darryl Sittler was awarded the captaincy when Dave Keon joined the World Hockey Association, Ellis maintained he was simply unhappy with the hockey player's lifestyle.

But after a couple of years, he was ready to put his skates back on. After playing for the Canadian national team at the 1977 Ice Hockey World Championships, Ellis was lured out of retirement a few months later and returned to the Leafs. Now the team's elder statesman, Ellis was also the last remaining player from the 1967 championship. Sitting at 24 goals back from the 300-goal mark, he was zeroing in on the milestone down the stretch. On March 4, 1978, before the home crowd at Maple Leaf Gardens, Ellis scored his 300th career goal, becoming just the second player in franchise history to accomplish the feat.

MARCH 5

LEAFS ACQUIRE OWEN NOLAN, 2003

Landing Owen Nolan was a big deal for the Leafs. The San Jose power forward was the most sought-after player leading up to the 2003 NHL trade deadline and was drawing interest from teams around the league, including Philadelphia and Montreal. But on March 5, 2003, the Leafs acquired the Sharks captain for Alyn McCauley, Brad Boyes, and a first-round draft pick in 2003.

It had been quite some time since the Leafs landed a big-name acquisition, but GM and head coach Pat Quinn felt the team was in a strong position to start moving assets to shore up for a playoff run. A few days after the deal, Nolan made his debut for Toronto, scoring two goals in a 3–3 tie against the Vancouver Canucks. He racked up seven goals and 12 points in 14 games down the stretch for the Buds but could not find the back of the net in the playoffs. The next year, his first and only full campaign with the Leafs, Nolan scored 19 goals and 48 points.

MARCH 6

ST. PATRICKS TROUNCE BULLDOGS, 1920

The Quebec Bulldogs travelled to Toronto without their goaltender, Frank Brophy. But with the St. Patricks out of contention, they loaned one of their netminders, Howard Lockhart, to the Bulldogs for a game on March 6, 1920. Although the two teams went into the first intermission tied 1–1, Lockhart had his work cut out for him in the middle frame. After his usual teammate Mickey Roach scored his first of the night three minutes into the session to make it 2–1, the St. Patricks scored eight unanswered goals, four of which belonged to Roach, to take a 10–1 lead.

In the third period, Roach added another to his tally as Toronto cruised to an 11–2 victory. Although it was the most goals Lockhart had ever allowed in a game, the newspaper coverage was charitable. According to reports, he had been hung out to dry by his defencemen. It wouldn't be the last time Lockhart was pelted by Toronto. The next season, as a member of the Hamilton Tigers, he gave up 10 goals in a 10–3 loss.

MARCH 7

DEFENCEMAN-TURNED-FORWARD JIM KORN BAGS HAT TRICK, 1984

As a defenceman, Jim Korn wasn't exactly known for his scoring touch. Through the first 48 games of the 1983–84 season, the Maple Leafs blueliner had just one goal. But with the team struggling down the stretch, head coach Mike Nykoluk had an idea. He told his assistant, Dan Maloney, to move Korn up to forward. Nykoluk later said Maloney didn't put him exactly where he wanted him, but it still worked out.

In his first game playing on a line with Dale McCourt and Peter Ihnačák, Korn scored two goals in a 4–4 tie on the road against the Vancouver Canucks. A few nights later, he scored another goal when the Leafs hosted the New York Rangers. Just over a week after being moved up front, on March 7, 1984, Korn bagged his first, and what would prove to be his only, career hat trick in an 8–4 victory against the New Jersey Devils. Korn's three-goal performance gave him seven goals in five games as a forward. The next year, however, he was moved back to defence.

MARCH 8

BUD POILE SCORES THREE IN LANDSLIDE, 1947

Eight different Maple Leafs scored goals in a 12–4 rout of the Chicago Black Hawks on March 8, 1947, but only Bud Poile managed to bag a hat trick. The right winger, who was not known for scoring in bunches, completed his second and final three-goal performance just over halfway through the third period. He would finish the regular season with 19 goals and 36 points, both career benchmarks. In the playoffs Poile contributed meaningful goals for the Leafs. He found the back of the net twice in the Stanley Cup Final against the Montreal Canadiens as the team earned its sixth championship.

Just four games into the following season, Poile was traded to Chicago, along with Gus Bodnar, Ernie Dickens, Bob Goldham, and Gaye Stewart for Max Bentley and Cy Thomas. Poile played two seasons in the Windy City before rounding out his NHL career with stops in Detroit, New York, and Boston. After hanging up his skates, he served as the inaugural general manager for both the Philadelphia Flyers and Vancouver Canucks.

MARCH 9

RON FRANCIS TRADED TO THE LEAFS, 2004

Not long after Ron Francis left a Carolina Hurricanes practice, he got a call from general manager Jim Rutherford on March 9, 2004, to let him know a deal was done. He was heading to the Maple Leafs in exchange for a 2005 fourth-round draft pick. A few weeks earlier, Francis actually brushed off the idea of a trade. Although the Hurricanes were out of the playoff picture for the second straight year, Francis insisted on finishing out the season in Carolina. But as the trade deadline approached, he had a change of heart.

Looking to get one last Cup before hanging up his skates, he waived his no-trade clause to accept the trade to Toronto, telling reporters it was "just something I felt I had to do." But unfortunately for Francis, who won back-to-back titles with Pittsburgh in the early 90s, he would not add another championship to his collection. Although the Leafs knocked off Ottawa in the first round, they were eliminated in the conference semifinals by Philadelphia. Following the 2004–05 lockout, Francis announced his retirement.

DAN MALONEY RECORDS SIX POINTS, 1979

Dan Maloney had a fractured cheekbone and his nose was still broken, for reportedly the fifth time in his career, from when he took a stick to the face from Detroit's Terry Harper a few weeks earlier, but the tough left winger had every reason to smile. He had just finished a game against the Los Angeles Kings in which he scored a goal and picked up five assists in a 9–4 victory on March 10, 1979. "It usually takes me a month to get that many points," Maloney told reporters after the matchup.

Originally drafted 14th overall by the Chicago Black Hawks in 1970, Maloney was traded to the Kings after just a couple of seasons in the Windy City. Following two full campaigns on the West Coast, he was part of the trade that brought Marcel Dionne to Los Angeles from Detroit. Maloney eventually made his way to the Leafs as part of another deal in 1978. After four years with the blue and white, Maloney retired but returned to Toronto as a coach for two seasons.

MARCH 11

APPLE CHEEKS LUMLEY RECORDS 13TH SHUTOUT, 1954

As far as hockey nicknames go, Harry Lumley's was pretty wholesome. He was known as "Apple Cheeks" because of his reddish complexion. But don't let the sobriquet fool you — he was one of the best goalies of his generation. Born and raised in Owen Sound, Ontario, Lumley broke into the NHL in 1943 with the Detroit Red Wings. Although he did not become a regular until 1945, he played a handful of games for the Wings, including one in which he was loaned to the New York Rangers for a period in a game against Detroit on December 23, 1943.

After six seasons in the Motor City, which included a Stanley Cup in 1950, Lumley played two seasons in Chicago. Following two abysmal campaigns with the cellar-dwelling Black Hawks, the goaltender was traded to Toronto, where he found his game again. On March 11, 1954, he picked up his 13th shutout of the year, extending his own franchise record, a mark that still stands. At season's end Lumley was awarded the Vezina as the league's top netminder.

MARCH 12

DARRYL SITTLER HITS 100, 1978

t was just another day at the office for Darryl Sittler. On March 12, 1978, in a matchup against the Pittsburgh Penguins, the 27-year-old Maple Leafs captain potted two goals and three assists to record his second five-point game of the season. His efforts also pushed him over the 100-point mark for the second time in his career. A couple of years earlier, he became the first player in franchise history to join the century club. Sittler would finish the 1977–78 campaign with 117 points, a career high, and a franchise record that would stand for 15 years.

It's hard to believe that just a few years later, the Maple Leafs' cantankerous owner Harold Ballard began publicly feuding with the star player, and his relationship with the club deteriorated. Ballard once said that Sittler should not expect to be given a sucker every time he went on the ice. In response, Sittler's teammates, who evidently disagreed with Ballard, reportedly taped a bunch of lollipops to his locker in the club's dressing room.

MARCH 13

GILMOUR'S LAST GAME, 2003

t was supposed to be a triumphant homecoming. A few days after the Maple Leafs reacquired Doug Gilmour from the Canadiens in exchange for a sixth-round draft pick, the former captain was making his much-anticipated return on March 13, 2003. Although he was no longer the player he once was when he led Toronto to back-to-back conference final appearances in the mid-90s, he was still Doug freaking Gilmour. But in his first shift back in a Leafs uniform, he collided with Calgary Flames winger Dave Lowry.

Gilmour was slow getting up and although he remained on the bench for a few minutes, he eventually retired to the dressing room and did not return to the game. A couple of days later, the team announced Gilmour would be out for four to six weeks with a left knee injury. While that ruled him out for the rest of the regular season, there was still hope he could return for the playoffs. Unfortunately, that March 13 game proved to be Gilmour's final NHL appearance. He announced his retirement on September 8, 2003.

MARCH 14

BOB PULFORD SCORES 100TH CAREER GOAL, 1962

arly in the third period in a game against the Montreal Canadiens on March 14, 1962, Bob Pulford put the puck past goalie Jacques Plante to record his 100th career goal. Pulford made his debut for the blue and white in 1956 following five seasons of junior with the Toronto Marlies of the Ontario Hockey Association. In his first six campaigns with the Leafs, the winger reached the 20-goal mark twice.

While Pulford had no problem finding the back of the net, he was also known as one of the best forecheckers in the league. Gordie Howe once famously said that Pulford was "one of his private headaches" because he was so skilled on both sides of the puck. Pulford's style of play was well suited for the post-season, but in the 1962 playoffs, it proved to be his goal scoring that made the difference. He scored the series winner against New York in the semifinals and then scored a hat trick against Chicago in the Stanley Cup Final as the Leafs clinched their first title since 1951.

MARCH 15

ALEXANDER MOGILNY RECORDS
1,000TH CAREER POINT, 2004

Just a month after Anaheim's Sergei Fedorov became the first Russian-born player to record 1,000 NHL points, Alexander Mogilny matched the feat. Fedorov might have been the first, but Mogilny reached the milestone in more dramatic fashion. On March 15, 2004, in a game against the Buffalo Sabres, the Leafs were down 5–2 heading into the final frame.

Mogilny had earned an assist on Mats Sundin's second goal in the first period to move within one point of the vaunted benchmark, but after Buffalo scored three unanswered goals in the middle session, it seemed as though Mogilny might have to wait for another night to etch his name into the record books. Toronto, however, scored two goals in the third to pull within one, and with just 38 seconds remaining in regulation, Mogilny assisted on the tying goal to force overtime. The helper gave him 1,000 points, but he wasn't done just yet. Mogilny picked up his third assist of the night on Tomáš Kaberle's game-winner to cap off his historic night with a comeback victory.

MARCH 16

BERNIE GEOFFRION SCORES 50, 1961

With time winding down in the third period in a game against the Maple Leafs on March 16, 1961, Montreal's Bernie Geoffrion found the back of the net to reach the 50-goal mark for the first time in his career. He became just the second player in NHL history to reach the milestone, joining former teammate Maurice Richard, who originally accomplished the feat in 1945. As the faithful at the Montreal Forum gave Geoffrion a standing ovation, the Leafs could only hope that, with two games still remaining on the schedule, their own Frank Mahovlich, who had been stuck at 47 goals for a handful of contests, might somehow find a way to join him.

Although Mahovlich scored two nights later at home in Boston, that was as far as he would get. Earlier in the season it seemed likely that Mahovlich would have punched his ticket before Geoffrion, but after potting his 40th on January 26, 1961, the Big M managed just eight more goals in 22 games down the stretch.

MARCH 17

KING CLANCY NIGHT, 1934

rish eyes were certainly smiling on the Leafs on St. Patrick's Day in 1934. That night, the team held King Clancy Night to recognize the club's favourite Irishman before hosting the New York Rangers. Before the game began, a parade of floats, including a giant shamrock, made their way across the ice at Maple Leaf Gardens. The final piece in the procession was a sleigh that was pulled by captain Hap Day. On the sleigh was a figure in a flowing robe, beard, and crown. It was, of course, Clancy.

After the crowd erupted into raucous applause, Clancy removed his costume to reveal he was wearing a green Maple Leafs sweater. Instead of his usual No. 7 on the back, he was sporting a shamrock. He wore the special jersey for the first period but returned to the blue and white for the rest of the game following complaints from Rangers coach Lester Patrick. Although Clancy didn't get on the scoresheet, the Leafs still had the luck of the Irish, defeating New York 3–2.

MARCH 18

VESA TOSKALA GOAL GAFFE, 2008

I f you mention Vesa Toskala to a Leafs fan, or any hockey fan for that matter, this story is probably what immediately comes to mind. On March 18, 2008, late in the first period in a road game against the New York Islanders, the Leafs were on a power play. With the puck deep in the Islanders' zone, New York blueliner Rob Davison, who started his NHL career in San Jose with Toskala, cleared it the length of the ice. Somehow, the 195-foot shot took a funny bounce and then skipped over Toskala's outstretched glove.

While everyone remembers that gaffe, what usually gets lost is that Toskala was perfect for the rest of the game. Other than Davison's fluke goal, he stopped 27 of the 28 shots he faced that night. The Maple Leafs also rebounded from the demoralizing blunder, scoring three unanswered markers in the third period to win 3–1. Following the game, Toskala was able to find the humour in it. "At least my good friend Robbie scored that goal," he told reporters with a smile.

MARCH 19

THE CROW GETS BACK BEHIND NHL BENCH, 1980

Joe Crozier started the week in his usual spot: behind the bench of the American Hockey League's New Brunswick Hawks, but he was soon back in the big leagues. After making his NHL coaching debut for the Buffalo Sabres in 1971–72, Crozier was named Coach of the Year by the *Hockey News* in 1973. Following another season in Buffalo, he jumped to the World Hockey Association for a few seasons. In 1979, after taking some time away from coaching, Crozier was named bench boss of the Hawks, Toronto's AHL affiliate.

But after Leafs head coach Floyd Smith got into a car accident in March, there were some personnel changes while he recuperated. Although GM Punch Imlach initially named himself as Smith's replacement, he elevated assistant coach Dick Duff for a pair of games, and then hired Crozier to run practice and help out behind the bench. On March 19, 1980, Crozier, who was known as "Joe the Crow," found himself on a big-league perch for the first time in six years when the Leafs trounced Winnipeg, his hometown team, 9–1. He was named head coach in the off-season but was dismissed 40 games into the 1980–81 campaign.

MARCH 20

AL SECORD SCORES NUMBER 50 AGAINST TORONTO, 1983

Just over five minutes into the second period in a game against the Maple Leafs on March 20, 1983, Chicago winger Al Secord scored his 50th of the season to give the Black Hawks a 5–0 victory. Secord, a native of Sudbury, Ontario, became just the second player in Chicago franchise history to achieve the milestone, joining Bobby Hull, who did it five times in the Windy City. Secord finished the season with 54 goals, the most by a Black Hawks player in more than a decade.

Following two injury-plagued campaigns, Secord found the back of the net 40 times in the 1985–86 season, but after one more year in Chicago, he was traded to Toronto, along with Eddie Olczyk, for Rick Vaive, Steve Thomas, and Bob McGill on September 3, 1987. Vaive, of course, was the first Maple Leafs player to reach the 50-goal mark. Secord spent the better part of two seasons with the blue and white before making his way back to Chicago to close out his NHL career. After hanging up his skates, he became a commercial airline pilot.

MIKE GARTNER TRADED TO MAPLE LEAFS, 1994

ooking back, it was a tough day for Mike Gartner. On March 21, 1994, just hours before the NHL trade deadline closed, the New York Ranger was sent to the Maple Leafs for Glenn Anderson, the rights to Scott Malone, and a fourth-round draft pick. Gartner, who was the NHL's fifth-highest all-time goal scorer at the time, was still searching for his Stanley Cup after 15 seasons, while Anderson already had five under his belt from his years with the Edmonton Oilers.

Although the Leafs were playoff bound, Gartner left a serious contender that would finish atop the standings with 112 points to win the Presidents' Trophy. Had the Maple Leafs defeated the Vancouver Canucks in the conference final, Gartner would have squared off against his former team for the right to Lord Stanley's mug, but it was not meant to be. The Rangers went on to defeat the Canucks to hoist the Cup for the first time in more than five decades, with Anderson adding yet another championship ring to his collection and Gartner left literally empty-handed.

RICK VAIVE BEATS THE BIG M'S RECORD, 1982

Rick Vaive was one of the few bright spots in an otherwise hopeless season. With just a handful of games remaining on the schedule, the Maple Leafs had long been eliminated from playoff contention, but Vaive still gave Toronto fans something to cheer about. On March 22, 1982, the 22-year-old captain (who wore No. 22) scored four goals, his second career hat trick, in an 8–5 victory against the Chicago Black Hawks.

The win didn't mean much in the standings, but Vaive's fourth of the game, an empty-netter, gave him 49 on the season to surpass Frank Mahovlich's record for the most goals in a season by a Maple Leaf. When Vaive spoke to reporters after the game he said, "It's always great when you score goals and win, but it doesn't make up for the season." While the team could only look ahead to next year, Vaive managed to end things on a high note. Two days later he scored his 50th goal, becoming the first player in franchise history to reach the milestone.

MARCH 23

DAVE ANDREYCHUK SCORES 50, 1993

On a night in which Teemu Selänne scored two goals and picked up an assist to establish a new NHL rookie points record, Toronto's Dave Andreychuk stole the headline because, much like this book, it's always about the Leafs. Although all eyes were on the hotshot newcomer from Finland, Andreychuk was on quite the heater himself. Since being acquired from the Buffalo Sabres nearly two months earlier, the burly winger had scored 20 goals in 19 games with Toronto.

Andreychuk had already racked up 29 goals with the Sabres, so when the Leafs landed in Winnipeg for a game on March 23, 1993, there was a distinct possibility he would collect his 50th. But he could not get anything past Jets goaltender Bob Essensa. Early into the final frame, Andreychuk had already fired a dozen shots on net, and the netminder had turned them all away. Finally, on his 13th shot of the game, he beat Essensa with a high wrister to reach the 50-goal mark for the first time in his career.

MARCH 24

DAVE ANDREYCHUK SCORES 50 ... AGAIN, 1994

The second time Andreychuk reached the benchmark was the next year with the Leafs. Although it was a significant accomplishment to record 50 goals in a season in which he split time with two teams, this one was obviously more special because he potted every goal in a Maple Leafs sweater. When Toronto hosted San Jose on March 24, 1994, Andreychuk was sitting at 49 goals. A second before the halfway mark of the first period, he rifled a shot past Sharks goaltender Artūrs Irbe to pick up his 50th of the season, becoming just the third player in franchise history to accomplish the feat.

While the home crowd celebrated Andreychuk's achievement, it proved to be the only goal they cheered for that night. The Sharks defeated the Leafs 2–1 to record their first-ever victory at Maple Leaf Gardens. Andreychuk would pick up three more goals down the stretch to finish the campaign with 53. It would take nearly three decades before another Leafs player joined Andreychuk, Rick Vaive, and Gary Leeman in the 50-goal club.

MARCH 25

SYL APPS SCORES HAT TRICK IN RETURN, 1941

Syl Apps had been out for a month with a knee injury, but it certainly didn't show when he hit the ice against the Boston Bruins on March 25, 1941. With the Bruins leading 2–1 early in the second period, the Toronto captain sparked a comeback. After Apps scored the tying goal, Bucko McDonald — I really just wanted to include his name in the book — found the back of the net on the power play to give Toronto the lead.

Before the period came to a close, Apps scored another to give the Leafs a 4–2 advantage heading into the second intermission. While Apps scored the first in a series of three unanswered tallies, Nick Metz set up the trio of goals, becoming just the second player in NHL history to get three assists in one period of a playoff game. After Toronto added to its lead in the final stanza, Apps completed the hat trick with just over three minutes remaining, with Metz adding a final goal to give the Leafs a 7–2 victory.

MARCH 26

LEAFS SCORE FOUR IN A FLURRY, 2002

Tampa Bay's goalie must have felt like he had been struck by lightning. In the third period in a game against the Maple Leafs on March 26, 2002, Bolts netminder Dieter Kochan, who had come in to relieve Nikolai Khabibulin with less than 15 minutes remaining on the clock, allowed three goals in a span of 42 seconds. After Toronto's Robert Reichel made it 4–2 just over five minutes into the final frame to chase Khabibulin from the net, Kochan, who had been called up from the American Hockey League a week earlier, entered the crease for his second NHL appearance that season.

Just 43 seconds later, Mats Sundin scored his 36th goal of the season. A mere 16 seconds after that, Tie Domi found the back of the net. And then, as if it couldn't get any worse, 26 seconds later, the feisty winger scored again. When the dust settled, the Leafs had scored four goals in 85 seconds, breaking a franchise record that had stood for more than eight decades.

MARCH 27

LARRY MURPHY HITS 1,000 POINTS, 1996

t was really a shame for Larry Murphy that the Leafs were on the road against the Vancouver Canucks on March 27, 1996. The defenceman, who was often maligned for his play on the blue line, was frequently subjected to boos on home ice, but that evening he gave the fans every reason to root for him. Just before the halfway mark of the first period, with the Leafs on the power play, Mats Sundin dished the puck to Murphy, who scored a nifty backhand goal to record his 1,000th career point.

When the goal light went off, he was mobbed by his teammates, who poured off the bench to celebrate the achievement. Murphy became just the fourth defenceman in NHL history to reach the milestone, joining Denis Potvin, Paul Coffey, and Ray Bourque. Although there were more than a few Leafs fans in attendance that night at General Motors Place, it was unfortunate that Murphy was unable to accomplish the feat at Maple Leaf Gardens to a chorus of cheers instead of the usual jeers.

MARCH 28

LEAFS SIGN GARRETT GAMBLE, 2015

Hockey is just a game, but sometimes it's so much more. There is no greater example of that than a paper transaction the Maple Leafs inked as the season came to a close. On March 28, 2015, working with the Children's Wish Foundation, the club signed Garrett Gamble to a one-day contract. Gamble, an 11-year-old boy from Duck Lake, Saskatchewan, was born with a rare genetic condition called Morquio syndrome.

When Gamble arrived in Toronto, he was asked what number he wanted. He said No. 42, which, of course, belonged to Tyler Bozak, so coach Peter Horachek joked that he would get the centre to switch numbers. It just so happened that after Gamble dropped the puck for a ceremonial faceoff, he watched Bozak score his first career hat trick in a 4–3 overtime victory against Ottawa. It was a dream come true for Gamble, but it meant just as much to the team. They had lost 25 of their last 30 games, but Gamble's presence helped put things in perspective and show what's truly important in life.

MARCH 29

WATCH THE LAWSUIT, TIE, 2001

Harry Neale warned him. "Watch the lawsuit, Tie," the colour commentator said as scrappy Leafs forward Tie Domi suddenly found himself nose to nose with a fan in the penalty box at First Union Center in Philadelphia on March 29, 2001. It all started when Domi, sitting in the sin bin, decided to give it back to the Flyers faithful by spraying his water bottle up into the crowd. A few rows up, Chris Falcone, a concrete worker, took exception.

Falcone leaped onto the glass surrounding the penalty box to grab the water bottle. When the glass suddenly gave way, he found himself in a confined space with one of the NHL's toughest players. "It was like watching someone fall into the lion's den at the zoo," said Leafs goalie Curtis Joseph. Although Domi landed a few quick shots before the officials intervened, it could have been a lot worse for Falcone. The Philly fan did indeed end up filing a lawsuit against Domi, but the bruising winger was able to settle the matter out of court.

MARCH 30

ARENAS WIN FIRST NHL-ERA STANLEY CUP, 1918

For much of the game, it seemed like the first Stanley Cup in the NHL era would be decided in overtime. On March 30, 1918, the Toronto Arenas were taking on the Vancouver Millionaires, champions of the Pacific Coast Hockey Association, in the fifth and final game for the rights to hockey's ultimate prize. After two periods of play, the game was scoreless.

But 30 seconds into the final frame, Toronto's Alf Skinner, who was arrested earlier in the season for a violent on-ice episode in a game against Montreal, broke the deadlock. And just when it seemed as though Skinner's tally might hold up, nine minutes later, Frederick "Cyclone" Taylor got Vancouver on the board. But the Arenas would not be denied. Just one minute after the Millionaires knotted it up, Corb Denneny gave Toronto a 2–1 lead. There would be no more scoring after that, and the Arenas would become the first NHL team to lay claim to Lord Stanley's mug. The next time Toronto won a title it was as the St. Patricks.

MARCH 31

AUSTON MATTHEWS HITS 50, 2022

For a goal scorer like Auston Matthews, it may not have been how he envisioned reaching the 50-goal mark, but he took it just the same. On March 31, 2022, with Winnipeg goalie Eric Comrie on the bench for the extra attacker, Toronto's superstar centre fired the puck into the empty net to notch his 50th goal of the season, becoming the first Leaf in nearly three decades to accomplish the feat.

Matthews likely would have added his name to the 50-goal club a couple of years earlier, joining Rick Vaive, Gary Leeman, and Dave Andreychuk, had the world not been ground to a halt by the Covid-19 pandemic, but he was in it now and that's all that mattered. The reason Matthews probably never imagined scoring a milestone goal like that on an empty net was because he'd scored so few of them during his career. Prior to that game against the Jets, Matthews had 248 regular-season goals to his name, but just a handful of those happened with no goalie between the pipes.

APRIL 1

LANNY MCDONALD SCORES 200TH GOAL, 1979

L anny McDonald had himself quite the weekend. After scoring his fifth career hat trick in a 6–2 victory against the Minnesota North Stars on Saturday, March 31, 1979, he followed it up with another milestone performance the very next night. Early in the opening period, after Paul Gardner made it 1–0 for the Leafs, McDonald scored his 200th career goal to extend Toronto's lead, becoming the 10th player in franchise history to reach the benchmark.

Before the session came to a close, he would also pick up an assist on Börje Salming's goal to make it 4–1 for the blue and white. Just over the halfway mark of the middle frame, McDonald beat goaltender Don Edwards again to record his 40th goal of the campaign. It was his third consecutive 40-goal season, making him the first Leafs player to accomplish the feat. McDonald would add another tally with less than two minutes remaining in the game to complete the hat trick, his last with the Leafs, and seal a 6–3 victory for Toronto.

APRIL 2

PAT QUINN KNOCKS OUT BOBBY ORR, 1969

Pat Quinn was public enemy number one in Boston. On April 2, 1969, in the first game of Toronto's playoff series against the Bruins, Quinn knocked out superstar defenceman Bobby Orr late in the second period with the Maple Leafs trailing 6–0. As Orr lay prone on the ice, the Maple Leafs blueliner received a five-minute major penalty for elbowing. But as Quinn was sitting in the penalty box, the Boston Garden faithful tried to take matters into their own hands.

The fans threw everything they could at him, and there were even reports that Quinn's teammates had to use their sticks to try to keep angry fans away from getting too close to their bench. When the middle frame ended, police officers had to escort Quinn to the dressing room for his own protection. Orr spent the night in hospital, but he returned to action the following day, picking up an assist in another blowout victory. Although Bruins fans never forgave Quinn, Orr later said it was a clean hit and the two became friends.

APRIL 3

LEAFS THWART OTTAWA'S
DIVISION TITLE, 2004

I f the Senators could beat the Maple Leafs in their final game of the season, they would clinch the Northeast Division title and secure home ice for the first round of the playoffs. But the Senators had defeated the Leafs only once in the regular season, and if any team was going to thwart Ottawa's plans, it would be their provincial rival. And sure enough, that's exactly what happened when they squared off on April 3, 2004.

After Ron Francis made it 1–0 in the first period, the Leafs scored four more unanswered goals in the middle frame to put the game away. While Tie Domi added the final goal in the final session to seal a 6–0 victory, goaltender Ed Belfour stopped all 28 shots he faced to head into the post-season with back-to-back shutouts. Instead of earning a fourth division title and facing a lower-seeded team in the first round, the Senators finished third in the Northeast and would take on the Leafs in the fourth Battle of Ontario playoff series.

APRIL 4

AUSTON MATTHEWS TIES FRANCHISE RECORD FOR MOST GOALS IN A SEASON, 2022

At least one hat landed on the ice at Amalie Arena in Tampa Bay on April 4, 2022. Although the Leafs were on the road against the Lightning, that didn't stop visiting fans from commemorating another Auston Matthews milestone. After scoring two goals in the second period, the superstar centre was just one goal back from matching Rick Vaive's three-decade franchise record for the most goals in a single season.

Just over seven minutes into the final frame, Matthews beat goalie Andrei Vasilevskiy through a crowd in the slot to complete the hat trick and bag his 54th goal of the campaign, becoming the first player to match Vaive's milestone. While some Tampa fans bolted for the exits — Matthews's goal made it 5–2 for Toronto — the broadcast zeroed in on one of the hats that made it to the ice. A few days later in Dallas, Matthews scored a power-play goal late in the second period to set a new Maple Leafs record; he also scored the overtime game-winner for good measure.

APRIL 5

LEAFS ADVANCE TO CUP FINAL, 1947

The Leafs had a berth to the Stanley Cup Final on the line. On April 5, 1947, Toronto hosted Detroit for the fifth game of their semifinal matchup. The Leafs had a commanding 3–1 series lead and were looking to punch their ticket before their faithful fans at Maple Leaf Gardens. Just over the halfway mark of the first period, Toronto's Nick Metz put the puck past goalie Johnny Mowers to put the Leafs up 1–0.

Although the Leafs added to their lead before the frame came to a close, the Red Wings got on the board a couple of minutes before intermission to cut the deficit to one. But in the middle session, Metz assisted on his younger brother Don's goal and picked up another helper on a Gaye Stewart tally that gave Toronto a 4–1 lead heading into the final stanza. The elder Metz added another goal to round out a four-point performance and seal a 6–1 victory that sent the Leafs to the Final to take on the defending champions, the Montreal Canadiens.

APRIL 6

LEAFS FIRE PUNCH IMLACH, 1969

L eafs president Stafford Smythe didn't waste any time. Not long after Toronto was swept out of the playoffs by the Boston Bruins on April 6, 1969, Smythe marched over to the office of general manager and head coach Punch Imlach to inform him that his services were no longer needed. Although Imlach had guided the club to four Stanley Cups since taking over in 1958, the Punch era was over. Upon learning the news that Imlach had been fired, veterans Tim Horton and Johnny Bower both immediately announced their retirements to reporters in the dressing room.

Although Horton still had a year on his contract, he told reporters, "This is it for me," while Bower tearfully confirmed he had played his last game with the Leafs. While both play-ers had strong allegiances to Imlach, particularly Bower, who felt he owed much of his success in Toronto to his bench boss, they would return. After talking with captain George Armstrong over the summer, both Horton and Bower were back with the blue and white that fall.

APRIL 7

YANIC PERREAULT SCORES
FOUR GOALS, 1999

anic Perreault was humble in his assessment of his performance. "It was one of those nights," he told reporters following Toronto's 4–2 win over the Ottawa Senators on April 7, 1999. But Perreault's modesty understated his performance on the ice that evening. He scored all four of the Leafs' goals. Acquired from the Los Angeles Kings just a couple of weeks earlier for Jason Podollan and a third-round draft pick, Perreault had made an immediate impact with his new club.

Before leaving the West Coast, he had 10 goals and 27 points in 64 games, but through his first eight games with the Buds, he had already collected seven goals and 12 points. Although Perreault chalked it up as just one of those nights, the significance of what he accomplished wasn't lost on him. "I'll remember this a long time," he said. It was also an extraordinary night for Perreault's coach, Pat Quinn. The victory against Ottawa gave Quinn his 400th career win, making him the 13th coach in NHL history to reach the milestone.

APRIL 8

LEAFS REACH 100-POINT MARK, 2000

With one game left in the schedule, the Maple Leafs had something to shoot for. A victory against the Tampa Bay Lightning would give the club its 45th win of the season and propel them to the 100-point mark for the first time in franchise history. Just over halfway through the first period on April 8, 2000, Nik Antropov opened the scoring to give Toronto a 1–0 lead. Although the Bolts tied it up 30 seconds before intermission, the Leafs put the game out of reach in the middle frame.

Following a short-handed goal by Mats Sundin just over five minutes into the session, the Buds added two more unanswered goals to take a 4–1 lead. The Lightning added another in the third, but it was too little, too late. While the victory put the Leafs into the century club for points, it was also a milestone performance for goaltender Curtis Joseph. Joseph, who made 33 saves that night, recorded his 36th win of the season, breaking his own club record from a year earlier.

APRIL 9

FIRST LEAFS CUP, 1932

A t the end of their first season at Maple Leaf Gardens, Toronto was on top of the hockey world. On April 9, 1932, the Leafs defeated the New York Rangers 6–4 to complete the sweep in a best-of-five series to win their first Stanley Cup in blue and white. It was the club's first championship in a decade, from back when they were still the green St. Patricks, and was the first in what would be a string of title-clinching victories on home ice at the Gardens in the coming years.

Although the Rangers had home ice advantage to start the final, they played only one game in New York. Following an opening 6–4 loss at Madison Square Garden, the second game was actually played in Boston because of a scheduling conflict. In what would prove to be an ongoing logistical challenge for the Rangers, the circus was in town, so the game was moved to Boston Garden. The Blueshirts wound up losing that contest 6–2 and then allowed another six goals in the finale in Toronto.

APRIL 10

SID SMITH SCORES HAT TRICK, 1949

After scoring 112 points with the Pittsburgh Hornets, Toronto's American Hockey League affiliate, Sid Smith was called up for the playoffs. The 23-year-old Toronto native had played some games for the Maple Leafs over the past few seasons but hadn't been able to find a regular spot in the lineup. When he returned to the club for the 1949 playoffs, he made the most of his opportunity.

After scoring two goals and picking up an assist in his first game at the tail end of Toronto's semifinal series against the Boston Bruins, Smith continued to play a critical role when the Leafs took on the Detroit Red Wings in the Stanley Cup Final. Although he didn't get on the scoresheet in the first game at the Olympia, he silenced the Motor City crowd in the second matchup on April 10, 1949. After opening the scoring in the first period, Smith scored two more goals to record his first NHL hat trick and guide Toronto to a 3–1 victory and a 2–0 series lead.

HOWIE MEEKER BECOMES HEAD COACH, 1956

Howie Meeker picked up an extra gig heading into the 1951–52 campaign. Over the off-season the Maple Leafs winger won a byelection to become the member of Parliament for the Waterloo South riding for the Progressive Conservative party. In winning the seat, Meeker, who would be turning 28 in a few months, was the youngest MP in Canada. He continued to play in the NHL while representing his constituents in Ottawa, but he decided not to contest the seat in the country's general election in 1953.

Following his brief political career and his retirement from hockey a couple of years later due to an ailing back, Meeker got into coaching. After serving as the bench boss for the Pittsburgh Hornets, Toronto's American Hockey League affiliate, for a pair of seasons, he was named head coach of the Maple Leafs on April 11, 1956. Similar to his political appointment four years earlier, Meeker became the youngest active coach in the NHL. But after just one season behind the bench in Toronto, he joined the team's front office as general manager.

APRIL 12

EDDIE OLCZYK COMPLETES HAT TRICK IN OT, 1988

The Leafs were looking to put an embarrassing loss behind them. Following an 8–0 drubbing by the Detroit Red Wings on home ice in the first round of the playoffs, fans hurled jerseys, hats, and pretty much everything else they could get their hands on. Centre Eddie Olczyk later said the team was hurt by a display that, for him, seemed so out of place for Toronto. So when the Leafs looked to lick their wounds at Joe Louis Arena on April 12, 1988, Olczyk led the charge.

Less than four minutes into the game, he notched a short-handed goal to open the scoring. He scored another halfway through the second period. And when his team needed him the most, in overtime, he came up big again. Just 34 seconds into sudden death, Olczyk completed the hat trick, his first in the NHL, to stave off elimination and give the Leafs a chance to redeem themselves at home. Although Toronto was knocked out two days later at home, they managed to get on the board this time, scoring three goals in a 5–3 defeat.

APRIL 13

MITCH MARNER SCORES FIRST PLAYOFF GOAL, 2017

Less than two minutes into the game on April 13, 2017, Mitch Marner scored his first career playoff goal to give the Maple Leafs a 1–0 lead over the Presidents' Trophy winners, the Washington Capitals. Sure, there was a lot of time left on the clock, but you could forgive Leafs fans for being excited. The team wasn't even supposed to be in the post-season. But after clinching a berth in the penultimate game of the regular season, Toronto was playoff-bound for the first time since 2013 and just the second time since 2004.

Having the team's dynamic cadre of rookies, namely Auston Matthews, Mitch Marner, and William Nylander, getting unexpected post-season experience was a nice bonus in a year that already included Matthews' racking up 40 goals and eventually taking home the Calder Trophy. After Marner's goal, defenceman Jake Gardiner scored to extend the lead, but the Capitals potted two unanswered goals of their own to force overtime. Just over five minutes into sudden death, Tom Wilson put the puck past Frederik Andersen to give Washington a 1–0 series lead.

LEAFS WIN SECOND STRAIGHT STANLEY CUP, 1948

After dropping the first three games in the Stanley Cup Final against the Maple Leafs, Detroit was on the ropes. After failing to score a goal in their first home game of the series at the Olympia on April 11, 1948, they were fighting for their lives a few days later. With the Motor City squad sputtering, the Buds put their foot on the gas. Less than three minutes into the game, Ted "Teeder" Kennedy scored on the power play to give the blue and white a 1–0 advantage.

Toronto's special teams continued firing on all cylinders when, just over two minutes later, Garth Boesch recorded a short-handed goal to extend the lead. Just over the halfway mark of the first period, Harry Watson found the back of the net again for the Leafs to put the game out of reach. Although the Red Wings got on the board early in the middle session, Toronto added four more goals to win 7–2, completing the sweep and clinching their second consecutive Stanley Cup.

APRIL 15

TIE DOMI SETS SINGLE-SEASON
PIM RECORD, 1998

Nobody racked up more penalty minutes in a season than Tie Domi. But after surpassing Tiger Williams for that record in a game against the Chicago Blackhawks on April 15, 1998, Toronto's noted pugilist didn't want to talk about it. It was the way it happened that made Domi shy away from discussing the milestone with reporters. Less than five minutes into the game, he got into a fight with Blackhawks defenceman Cam Russell.

During the tilt Domi pulled Russell's jersey up over his head and connected with a flurry of punches that eventually sent the Chicago blueliner to the ice, knocking him unconscious. Russell was taken to hospital for a concussion, and Domi earned minor, major, and misconduct penalties to push him past Williams's single-season mark of 351 penalty minutes. Although Domi felt bad for what happened to Russell, he dropped the gloves with heavyweight Bob Probert later that game. Domi finished the season with 365 PIM, a Leafs record that will likely stand the test of time.

APRIL 16

ED BELFOUR MAKES 72 SAVES AGAINST THE FLYERS, 2003

You had to feel for Ed Belfour. The Maple Leafs goaltender had stood on his head through regulation and nearly three full periods of overtime on April 16, 2003, trying to steal the game for his team, but the puck just didn't go their way. After allowing goals from the Philadelphia Flyers early into each of the first and second periods, Belfour was flawless through the rest of regulation. He continued to stop everything that came his way in the overtime sessions.

But finally, with just over six minutes remaining in the third sudden-death period, Philadelphia's Mark Recchi scored his second of the night to give the Flyers a 3–2 victory and even the series at two games apiece. When it was all said and done, Belfour had made 72 saves, a franchise record that surpassed the mark of 62 set by Johnny Bower more than four decades earlier. While Belfour couldn't have done more that game, the same could not be said for his teammates. They mustered just 38 shots against their opponents through nearly six periods.

APRIL 17

HAROLD BALLARD IS BURIED, 1990

When Jeff Marek reported for his first day of work at Park Lawn Cemetery, he remembers his foreman telling him to be prepared for a crazy day because it was "Ballard burial day." On April 17, 1990, the cantankerous long-time owner of the Maple Leafs, Harold Ballard, was interred at the Toronto graveyard. Before Ballard arrived at his final resting place, the family held a very private service at a church in the Forest Hill neighbourhood.

But the family actually said the ceremony would be at the Turner & Porter funeral home across town to avoid drawing a crowd of reporters and onlookers. Even Ballard's long-time partner, Yolanda, was not given the correct location. Although Marek didn't have a hand in the actual burial that day, it was a memorable first shift in an occupation that still calls to him. He's done well for himself as a host on Sportsnet and the *32 Thoughts* podcast, but Marek says, "The minute this media thing is over for me, I'm going to work at a cemetery."

LEAFS COMPLETE INCREDIBLE
COMEBACK TO WIN THE CUP, 1942

"We did it the hard way," said Leafs bench boss Clarence "Hap" Day. It was difficult to argue with the coach's words. After Toronto lost the first three games of the Stanley Cup Final to the Red Wings, the team battled back to win the next three and force a seventh and decisive game on April 18, 1942. Despite having the support of the home crowd, the Leafs surrendered the opening goal to Detroit's Syd Howe early in the second frame.

For nearly the rest of the game, Toronto couldn't solve goaltender Johnny Mowers and it seemed as though their luck may have finally run out. But just before the halfway mark of the third period, Sweeney Schriner, who was born in Russia but immigrated to Canada as an infant, got the Leafs on the board to tie the game. Toronto would add two more, including another from Schriner, to clinch the Stanley Cup with a 3–1 victory, becoming the first team in NHL history to win a best-of-seven series after losing the first three games.

APRIL 19

LEAFS WIN FOURTH STANLEY CUP, 1947

For Conn Smythe, there were three reasons why his team won the Stanley Cup. The Maple Leafs owner said it came down to coaching, the team's veteran players, and the rookies who wanted to win. Those key ingredients were certainly a factor when Toronto closed out its series against the defending champion Montreal Canadiens on April 19, 1947, to win the fourth title in the blue-and-white era.

Just 25 seconds into the game, the Leafs fell behind 1–0. But coach Hap Day, who had already won two championships with the club, kept his troops calm. From that point on, veteran goaltender Turk Broda, who backstopped the Leafs to a title in 1942, stopped everything else that came his way. And up front, it was the rookies who put the puck in the net. Vic Lynn, playing in his first full NHL season, tied the game up; 21-year-old Ted Kennedy scored the game-winning tally; and rookie Howie Meeker, who would take home the Calder Trophy the next month, assisted on both goals.

LEAFS DEFEAT SENS IN PLAYOFFS ... AGAIN, 2004

After the Senators defeated the Leafs in double overtime to force a decisive seventh game in their opening-round playoff series, Ottawa owner Eugene Melnyk had a prediction. "We're going to kill 'em," he said. It was a bold forecast. Since entering the league in 1992, the Senators had never won a Game 7 in three attempts and, more importantly, had been defeated by Toronto each of the three times they had squared off in the post-season so far.

And by the end of the first period in the pivotal match-up on April 20, 2004, Melnyk would eat his words. The Leafs scored three unanswered goals, including two by Joe Nieuwendyk, and chased goaltender Patrick Lalime from his net. Although the Senators scored just 22 seconds into the second period, that was the only time they would light the lamp that evening. So instead of killing the Leafs, the Sens bowed out of the playoffs in the first round for the third time in the last five years, all at the hands of their provincial rivals.

APRIL 21

BILL BARILKO'S FINAL GOAL, 1951

The last goal Bill Barilko scored won the Leafs the Cup. If you're like me and countless other Canadians, the Tragically Hip's song "Fifty-Mission Cap" is probably playing in your head. But I didn't steal this from a hockey card — it actually happened on April 21, 1951. Less than three minutes into overtime in the fifth game of Toronto's Stanley Cup Final series against the Montreal Canadiens, Bill Barilko fired the puck past goaltender Gerry McNeil to give the Maple Leafs their fourth title in five years.

But while the team celebrated another championship that summer, tragedy struck. While Barilko was returning from a fishing trip with his dentist, Henry Hudson, their single-engine plane disappeared. If you're a Hip fan, you already know the Leafs didn't win another Stanley Cup until 1962, when the defenceman's body was finally recovered. That year, the Leafs defeated the Black Hawks to win their first championship since that memorable goal. A few months later, the wreckage of the plane was found not far from Barilko's hometown of Timmins, Ontario.

PYRAMID POWERS SITTLER TO FIVE-GOAL PERFORMANCE, 1976

R ed Kelly believed in the power of pyramids. He felt the shapes had supernatural powers that could be tapped into. So for the 1976 Stanley Cup Playoffs, he brought pyramid power to the Leafs. Under Kelly's direction, Toronto qualified for the post-season in each of his first two seasons but failed to advance beyond the quarterfinals, so it was time to try something new. Midway through the team's quarter-final series against the Philadelphia Flyers, he placed small pyramids under the Leafs' bench.

After the Leafs won the game, Kelly brought his club in on his secret. Prior to the next contest in Toronto on April 22, 1976, he hung a large pyramid from the ceiling in the dressing room and encouraged his players to harness its power. Darryl Sittler placed his sticks below and stood beneath it before hitting the ice. He ended up scoring five goals that night, tying the NHL record, as the Leafs forced a decisive Game 7. Kelly's pyramid power, however, was fleeting. Toronto was eliminated a few nights later.

APRIL 23

LEAFS FORCE GAME 7 IN CUP FINAL, 1964

With the Leafs facing elimination in the Stanley Cup Final on April 23, 1964, defenceman Bobby Baun put it all on the line after blocking a blistering shot from Gordie Howe with his right ankle. Although Baun was in pain, he played a few more shifts. But after taking a defensive zone faceoff against Howe, Baun recalled hearing a snapping sound and he collapsed. He desperately tried to get up, but when he tried and failed, he was stretchered off the ice.

With the game set to go to sudden death, Baun wasn't going to miss another shift. He got the team's physician, Dr. Jim Murray, to freeze and tape his ankle as tightly as he could. When overtime started, Baun was on the bench. Less than two minutes into the extra frame, he fired the puck past goaltender Terry Sawchuk to force a decisive seventh game. Although Baun had likely fractured his right fibula, the tough blueliner refused to get an X-ray ahead of the pivotal matchup. There was still work to be done.

APRIL 24

LEAFS FLIP "IT WAS 4–1" SCRIPT, 2023

For nearly a decade, the Leafs were the yardstick for playoff futility. Following a catastrophic third-period meltdown against the Bruins in Game 7 in 2013, in which the Buds squandered a three-goal lead only to lose in overtime, it seemed as though every post-season comeback or collapse was measured against that performance. And until the team could find playoff success, that narrative followed them around.

That is until April 24, 2023. With just over 10 minutes remaining in the fourth game of the opening-round series against the Lightning, Toronto was down 4–1. Many Leafs fans, who figured it was over, turned off the game and went to bed. But Auston Matthews scored two straight goals to ignite a response to force overtime. Less than five minutes into the extra session, Alexander Kerfoot tipped in the game-winning goal to cap off an incredible comeback that would usually only happen against the Leafs. Although the team may have vanquished that cursed narrative, there was still more work to be done to ensure it would stay buried.

APRIL 25

LEAFS WIN THIRD STRAIGHT STANLEY CUP, 1964

For Gordie Howe, Bobby Baun's overtime goal that forced a seventh game was a back-breaker. "The fluke goal by Bob Baun Thursday night in overtime is what killed us. It gave the Leafs the momentum they needed for this game and seemed to take a lot out of us," he told reporters following Toronto's Stanley Cup victory on April 25, 1964.

Although the Red Wings had plenty of chances in the third period, after a pair of goals by Dave Keon and Red Kelly in an 87-second span early into that frame, they were all but out of the game. Captain George Armstrong added another goal with less than five minutes remaining to make it 4–0. The Red Wings failed to get on the board and Toronto won its third straight Stanley Cup. While Baun was able to celebrate that night with his teammates, he missed the parade a couple of days later. Leaving Maple Leaf Gardens, he slipped and aggravated his fractured right ankle and had to sit out the procession.

AUSTON MATTHEWS SCORES 60, 2022

t wasn't a question of if Auston Matthews could be a 60-goal scorer but when. During the 2020–21 season, which was shortened because of the Covid-19 pandemic, the superstar centre scored at a fiery clip in the all-Canadian Scotia NHL North Division. Although Matthews missed four games with injuries, he still managed to record 41 goals in 52 games, which put him on track for 65 goals in an 82-game regular season.

The next year, as the 2021–22 season came to a close, Matthews was sitting at 58 goals with two games remaining on the schedule. He probably would have reached 60 earlier in the campaign had he not missed nine games to injury and suspension, but hey, that's hockey, and if anybody could still pull it off it was Matthews. And sure enough, on April 26, 2022, Matthews scored two goals in a game against the Red Wings to reach the milestone, becoming the first player in Maple Leafs history to accomplish the feat and just the third NHL player this century to reach the mark.

APRIL 27

THE FOLIGNO LEAP, 1993

M ike Foligno was jumping for joy. Just over two minutes into overtime against the Red Wings, on April 27, 1993, he fired a shot from between the faceoff circles to beat goaltender Tim Cheveldae and give the Maple Leafs a 5–4 victory. Once the puck found the back of the net, Foligno did his signature celebration, known as "the Foligno leap," in which he jumped jubilantly into the air, driving his knees up toward his chest and raising his arms high above his head.

As his teammates mobbed him, head coach Pat Burns was all smiles behind the bench. Foligno's goal had capped off an incredible comeback that night, with the Maple Leafs recovering from a 4–1 deficit to take the game and a 3–2 series lead. That was probably the most memorable Foligno leap, but you could make the case for another one. Fourteen years later, when his son Nick scored his first NHL goal for the Ottawa Senators, Nick mimicked his old man's patented move to celebrate the milestone goal. Like father, like son.

APRIL 28

GORD STELLICK NAMED MAPLE LEAFS GM, 1988

L ittle did Gord Stellick know that, after joining the Maple Leafs as a press box attendant as a 17-year-old, just over a decade later, he would be given the reins to the club. On April 28, 1988, Stellick was named general manager. The appointment, which came just a month before he turned 31 years old, made him the youngest GM in NHL history.

Stellick's first order of business was the draft, which was just over a month away. That year, the Leafs had the sixth overall pick, and Stellick wasn't shy about saying he was willing to trade. But the right deal never came along and the Leafs ended up taking Scott Pearson, who would suit up for 62 games to start his career in Toronto, and one more almost a decade later. The newly minted GM missed out on the opportunity to take Martin Gélinas, Jeremy Roenick, Rod Brind'Amour, or Teemu Selänne, who were all taken immediately after Pearson. The draft, however, wasn't a complete wash. Stellick nabbed the pugnacious Tie Domi in the second round and goaltender Peter Ing in the third.

APRIL 29

LEAFS ADVANCE TO SECOND ROUND, 2023

Finally! Finally, after 19 long years, the Maple Leafs won a playoff series. The last time they were in the second round, I was finishing my first year of university, and on April 29, 2023, when they defeated the Lightning 2–1 in overtime, I was a father of two. While my daughters slept upstairs, I clapped as quietly as I could, letting out nearly two decades' worth of frustration and revelling in the moment.

It wasn't a highlight reel goal by any means, but it was perfect just the same. It is fitting that captain John Tavares was the one who scored it. While there are some revisionist historians out there who think the team shouldn't have signed him in 2018, he proved he was, once again, worth every penny. And, as a matter of fact, he was the first captain in franchise history to score a series-clinching goal in overtime. Although it marked just the fourth win in a long climb to 16, it was hard not to get caught up in the excitement, and you could be forgiven for believing this could really be the year.

APRIL 30

LEAFS WIN DRAFT LOTTERY, 2016

Leafs Nation held its collective breath. Toronto had the best odds, a 20 percent chance, of winning the NHL's draft lottery in 2016. After coming up just one number short of earning the pick that would have netted them superstar Connor McDavid the year before, despite having the fourth-best odds, Leafs fans hoped that this time around, the ping pong balls would fall in their favour.

Luckily, on April 30, 2016, the Leafs cashed in on their last-place finish and retained their position in the draft order to land the coveted first overall selection. That year, the consensus number one pick was Auston Matthews, a dynamic goal scorer who grew up in Arizona and spent the past season playing professionally in Switzerland. Matthews had nearly been eligible for the 2015 NHL Entry Draft, and many believed that had he been available, he would have challenged Jack Eichel for second overall behind McDavid. But fortunately for Leafs fans, Matthews's birthday fell just two days after the draft age cut-off that year, and the rest is history.

MAY 1

LEAFS WIN GAME 7, 1993

For the first time in more than four decades, Detroit and Toronto needed overtime to decide the final game of a best-of-seven series. On May 1, 1993, after Doug Gilmour tied it up with less than three minutes remaining in regulation, the two clubs went to sudden death in a decisive seventh game. The last time it happened, the Red Wings ended up scoring the lone goal to take their semifinal against the Leafs.

Early in the extra frame, Gilmour passed the puck to a streaking Bob Rouse, who one-timed a shot at the net. Standing in front of the crease, Nikolai Borschevsky, who had returned to the lineup that night after missing five games with a fractured orbital bone in his right eye, tipped the puck past a sprawling Tim Cheveldae to win the game. As the team poured onto the ice, Borschevsky's overtime heroics weren't the most enduring memory. Rather, it was equipment manager Brian Papineau jubilantly spraying water from the bench as if he were popping a bottle of champagne.

MAY 2

LEAFS WIN CUP, 1967

Jim Pappin is often best remembered for scoring the game-winning goal that clinched the Stanley Cup for the Leafs on May 2, 1967, but did he actually score it? Late in the second period of Toronto's sixth game against the Canadiens, it looked as though Pappin tickled the twine to make it 2–0. But during the game, public address announcer Paul Morris said the goal actually belonged to Pappin's linemate Pete Stemkowski.

The story goes that Pappin, who was in line for a nice bonus if he won the playoff goal-scoring race, negotiated a deal with Stemkowski to lobby for the goal to go to him. As part of the pact, Pappin was reportedly going to build a pool in his backyard with the bonus money and give Stemkowski unfettered access to it in the summer. Heading into the game, Pappin was sitting at six goals, tying him with Montreal's Jean Béliveau. With "le Gros Bill" held off the scoresheet that night, Pappin took the goal-scoring title and Stemkowski got as many swims in as he wanted.

GILMOUR ENDS DOUBLE OT WITH WRAPAROUND, 1993

Curtis Joseph thought Doug Gilmour was going left, but when the Blues netminder moved to that side of the cage, it was already too late. Gilmour had spun around and gone back toward the opposite side. Joseph sprawled across the crease, but by the time he made it back to his far post, Gilmour had tucked the puck into the net with a wraparound. As the Leafs mobbed Gilmour in celebration, Joseph just lay in the blue paint.

The Buds had just taken the first game in the Norris Division final series, on May 3, 1993, in double overtime. Off the ice, Gilmour's move inspired a generation of Leafs fans. Whenever I played road hockey, the wraparound was always my go-to move. Although I rarely pulled it off with the same skillful execution as Gilmour, there was nothing better than fooling the goalie from behind the net under the soft glow of the streetlights. In moments like that, I wasn't Mike, I was Killer, winning the game for my teammates before our parents hollered for us to come in for the night.

MAY 4

LEAFS BEAT OTTAWA IN TRIPLE OT, 2002

For Gary Roberts, it was the biggest goal he had ever scored as a member of the blue and white. On May 4, 2002, just over four minutes into the third overtime period against Ottawa, Roberts snagged the loose puck after the Leafs won a faceoff deep in the Senators' zone and wired it past goalie Patrick Lalime to give Toronto a 3–2 victory and even their semifinal series at one game apiece.

Early in the game, however, it hadn't seemed like overtime was looming. The Leafs scored two quick goals in a span of three minutes and 34 seconds in the first period to take a 2–0 lead, but the Senators clawed their way back, scoring the tying goal less than three minutes into the final frame to eventually force overtime. When it was all said and done, it was the longest game the Leafs had played in nearly six decades. It was also the fourth consecutive playoff game, dating back to three straight post-season matchups in 2000, in which Toronto triumphed over Ottawa in overtime.

MAY 5

BLUES TOP LEAFS IN DOUBLE OT, 1993

The Leafs were all over the Blues. By the time Brett Hull recorded St. Louis's third shot of the night on May 5, 1993, Toronto had already fired 15 shots on goaltender Curtis Joseph. But despite the Leafs' lopsided advantage in shots, it was actually St. Louis that got on the board first. Just over eight minutes into the opening frame, Hull beat Félix Potvin for his sixth of the post-season. The Leafs kept pressing, and less than five minutes later, Doug Gilmour got one by Joseph to tie the game.

When the two teams adjourned for intermission, the Leafs had already registered 23 shots on net, the third most in a playoff period in franchise history. When the matchup resumed, Toronto continued its onslaught. They outshot St. Louis 15–4 in the third period, and when regulation was completed with the score knotted at one goal apiece, they had outshot the Blues 48–26. But St. Louis managed to break through in sudden death. They added 13 more shots on Potvin until Jeff Brown broke the deadlock three minutes into the second overtime.

MAY 6

LEAFS ACQUIRE TURK BRODA, 1936

The story goes that Maple Leafs owner and general manager Conn Smythe was interested in goaltender Earl Robertson from the Windsor Bulldogs of the International Hockey League. But when Smythe went to check out one of Robertson's games, the netminder let in eight goals, so the Toronto executive turned his attention to the goalie between the pipes at the other end of the ice: Walter Broda of the Detroit Olympics.

When Smythe needed to replace veteran netminder George Hainsworth during the 1936 off-season, he thought of Broda. On May 6, 1936, the Leafs acquired the goaltender, who had recently backstopped the Olympics to a league championship, for $8,000, a record sum for a minor-league player. It might have been an unprecedented amount, but it paid off for the Leafs. Broda, who was affectionately known as "Turk," would tend the twine for the Leafs for more than a decade, earning the Vezina Trophy twice as the league's top goaltender, receiving First Team All-Star honours on two occasions, and winning the Stanley Cup five times.

MAY 7

PENS TAKE GAME 1, 1999

t was a slow night in the creases. On May 7, 1999, neither goaltender was very busy in the first game of Toronto's semifinal series against Pittsburgh. At one end of the rink, the Maple Leafs' Curtis Joseph faced just 18 shots, while the Penguins' Tom Barrasso turned aside all 20 shots that came his way. While Barrasso got the better of his counterpart, Joseph was nearly flawless in a 2–0 defeat. After allowing a goal from Dan Kesa, a career minor-leaguer who scored on his first shot of the post-season, halfway through the first period, Joseph clamped down the rest of the way.

It remained a one-goal game until the final 37 seconds when winger German Titov added an empty-net goal to seal the Penguins' victory. Toronto's anemic performance was a holdover from their opening-round series against Philadelphia. Despite leading the league in goals, the Maple Leafs became the first team in NHL history to win a best-of-seven series without scoring at least three goals in any game.

MAY 8

LEAFS MUSTER JUST SIX SHOTS, 2000

T he Leafs certainly didn't play with the desperation of a team facing elimination. On May 8, 2000, in Game 6 of the Eastern Conference semifinal against the Devils, after surrendering the first goal just 18 seconds into the contest, they played nearly half the first period before finally getting a shot on goal. The Leafs managed just two more shots before intermission, tying a franchise record for the fewest shots in a period. After New Jersey made it 2–0 early in the second period, Toronto still couldn't break through the Devils' suffocating defence and were limited to just two shots that frame, a new benchmark in futility.

The Leafs, however, broke their own record again in the third period, when they mustered just one shot. After New Jersey centre John Madden scored with six seconds remaining in the game, the final buzzer sounded to mercifully end Toronto's ineffectiveness. The officials didn't need to do much math to determine that the Leafs finished with just six shots, a modern NHL record for the fewest in a game.

MAY 9

LEAFS SWEPT OUT OF THE PLAYOFFS BY THE CANADIENS, 1978

After Toronto knocked off the heavily favoured New York Islanders in the quarterfinals of the 1978 Stanley Cup Playoffs, it set the stage for a matchup against their archrivals the Montreal Canadiens. The last time the two had squared off in the post-season was 11 years earlier when the Leafs defeated the Habs in six games to win the Stanley Cup. While many in the hockey world expected an exciting series that would renew the longstanding rivalry and harken back to the memorable clashes from the Original Six era, it proved to be anything but.

After the Canadiens took the first two games at home, they trounced Toronto 6–1 at Maple Leaf Gardens to take a commanding 3–0 series lead. A few days later, on May 9, 1978, with the blue and white facing elimination, Montreal's Jacques Lemaire scored the opening goal just over seven minutes into the game. It was all the Canadiens would need. They added another tally early in the middle frame to seal a 2–0 victory and sweep the Leafs out of the playoffs.

MAY 10

LEAFS TOP LIGHTNING IN GAME 5, 2022

'll be the first to admit that I didn't have much hope in the Leafs. A few minutes into the second period of the fifth game of Toronto's opening-round playoff series against Tampa Bay, the Buds were down by two and had registered only four shots on net. Meanwhile, the Lightning, the two-time defending Stanley Cup champions, had already scored two goals in the first period in a span of 52 seconds and had four times as many shots as their opponents, so things were not looking good.

But on Toronto's fifth shot of the game, captain John Tavares scored his first of the post-season to ignite the comeback. With the Leafs finally coming to life, they started getting more shots on the Lightning and added two more goals in the final frame to take a 3–2 lead. Although the Bolts tied the game just before the halfway mark in the third, Auston Matthews broke the deadlock with just over six minutes remaining to give Toronto a 4–3 victory and a 3–2 series lead.

KYLE DUBAS NAMED GM, 2018

n 2014, Kyle Dubas was the general manager of the Soo Greyhounds of the Ontario Hockey League, but just four years later, he was GM of one of the greatest hockey franchises in the world. On May 11, 2018, Dubas, who had been assistant general manager for the past four years — duties that included overseeing the Leafs' American Hockey League affiliate, the Toronto Marlies, who would win the Calder Cup a month later — was appointed Leafs GM. A couple of weeks earlier, former general manager Lou Lamoriello was shifted to a senior adviser position, opening up the spot for a new GM to take the helm.

It came down to Dubas and his fellow co-assistant GM, Mark Hunter, but Leafs president Brendan Shanahan made the decision to offer the position to the 32-year-old Dubas, making him the second-youngest general manager in the NHL. Although some questioned the move, insisting Dubas "hadn't played the game" and was too focused on analytics, he made an immediate impact. Less than two months later, he landed highly coveted free agent John Tavares.

LEAFS SIGN BÖRJE SALMING, 1973

B örje Salming was no "chicken Swede." When the rugged Swedish defenceman signed with the Maple Leafs on May 12, 1973, he quickly upended the misguided pejorative within the NHL that European players were soft and could not handle the rougher North American game. But even as Salming soon proved he was as hard as a coffin nail patrolling the Toronto blue line, including hanging tough against "the Broad Street Bullies" in just his second game, the perception still persisted.

Salming's good friend, Inge Hammarström, who signed with the Maple Leafs the same day, could not shake the misconception, even from his owner, Harold Ballard. The curmudgeonly Toronto executive, who was never known to mince words, infamously said that Hammarström "could go into the corner with a dozen eggs in his pocket and not break any of them." Even though it wasn't true, Ballard's remark followed Hammarström around for the rest of his career. But as Salming continued to take everything the league threw at him, he gradually changed the way European players were viewed and paved the way for others.

MAY 13

LEAFS COLLAPSE, 2013

" can't believe the Leafs are going to the second round. This is so exciting," is what I remember writing in an email to my uncle Don. I can't recall exactly what I said because I never sent it. Early in the third period in a do-or-die seventh game against the Boston Bruins, the Leafs had what many believed to be a commanding 4–1 lead. If they could hold it, it would give Toronto its first playoff series victory since 2004.

As a lifelong Maple Leafs fan, I knew it wasn't over until the final buzzer sounded, so I decided to hold off on sending anything to my uncle just yet. With my proposed email sitting in my drafts folder, I watched in disbelief as the Bruins scored three goals in the final 10 minutes of regulation to force overtime. Six minutes into sudden death, Patrice Bergeron scored his second of the night to complete the improbable comeback. Shattered, I fished my phone out of my pocket and deleted that cursed email.

MAY 14

LEAFS DEFEAT SHARKS, 1994

Wendel Clark brought Maple Leaf Gardens to its feet. On May 14, 1994, less than halfway through the first period of Toronto's seventh game against the San Jose Sharks, the Maple Leafs captain wired a shot from the right faceoff circle past goaltender Artūrs Irbe to give the blue and white a 1–0 lead. In the second frame, Clark did it again, recording his eighth goal in 13 games; only Vancouver's Pavel Bure had more tallies so far in the post-season (nine).

After Mark Osborne made it 3–0 early in the final stanza, Igor Larionov finally got the Sharks on the board, but it was too late. Seven minutes later, Clark assisted on a Doug Gilmour goal to make it 4–1 and put the game all but out of reach. But in the dying seconds, with the fans celebrating in the stands, defenceman Sylvain Lefebvre accidentally put the puck into the Toronto net on a clearing attempt. Luckily, it didn't matter on the scoresheet, and the Leafs were off to the conference final for the second straight year.

LEAFS DEFEAT THE BLUES IN SEVEN, 1993

Wendel Clark was home alone. After Glenn Anderson got the puck up to the Leafs captain deep in the St. Louis zone, iconic play-by-play announcer Bob Cole twice declared that Clark was "home alone" before he fired a shot past goaltender Curtis Joseph. But if anyone was actually home alone it was Joseph, whose defencemen had seemingly abandoned him for Toronto's fourth goal of the first period in their decisive seventh game on May 15, 1993.

Things didn't get any better in the second period for Joseph, who was the chief reason the Blues had been able to make the series go the distance. After Kent Manderville scored more than halfway through the frame to make it 5–0, Doug Gilmour extended the lead a few minutes later, recording his third point of the evening to bring his playoff total to 22 points, surpassing Darryl Sittler's benchmark to establish a new franchise record. The only player with more points than Gilmour that post-season was Wayne Gretzky, whom the Maple Leafs would take on next in the conference final.

MAY 16

PETER ZEZEL WINS IT IN OVERTIME, 1994

Just a few minutes into overtime on May 16, 1994, in the first game of Toronto's conference final series against Vancouver, Mark Osborne fired the puck into the Canucks' zone. As Leafs winger Bill Berg went to retrieve the disc, goaltender Kirk McLean came out of the net "for reasons that only he knows," according to colour commentator Harry Neale. But McLean was unable to gather up the loose puck and Toronto's Peter Zezel, who had already scored in the third period that night, pounced on it and fired it past the stranded goalie, way outside his crease, to give the Leafs a 3–2 victory and take the opening game.

Although Zezel was more known for his two-way play than his scoring touch centring Toronto's rugged checking line with wingers Berg and Osborne, coach Pat Burns was more than happy with the additional contributions. "Any goals that line gets are gravy on the potatoes," Burns said after the game. But the gravy soon thinned out because it was the last time the line put up points in the series.

MAY 17

GARRY VALK SENDS LEAFS TO CONFERENCE FINAL, 1999

What a difference a year can make. Just a season earlier, Garry Valk was a member of the Pittsburgh Penguins, but a year later, he snuffed out his former team's playoff hopes as a member of the Maple Leafs. On May 17, 1999, less than two minutes into overtime of the sixth and potentially deciding game of Toronto's semifinal series against the Penguins, Yanic Perreault, who had been so clutch for the Leafs in the faceoff circle, won a defensive zone draw and got the puck back to defenceman Sergei Berezin.

The Russian blueliner got a shot off that was initially stopped by Tom Barrasso, but the Penguins goaltender lost it in between his pads and a diving Valk was able to tap the loose puck into the net to give Toronto a 4–3 overtime victory and take the series. While Valk and the Leafs were off to the conference final for the first time since 1994, uncertainty loomed for his former team. With the Penguins going through bankruptcy proceedings, it remained unclear what the future would hold.

MAY 18

LEAFS ACQUIRE JACQUES PLANTE, 1970

There was no doubt about it. If Jacques Plante hadn't been wearing a mask, the goaltender believed he was as good as dead. In the opening game of the 1970 Stanley Cup Final, Plante, who was tending the twine for St. Louis, took a screaming shot from Boston's Fred Stanfield right in the face. Although Plante's mask protected him from a far worse fate, he left the game and was done for the series. The goaltender told reporters there was no question the mask saved his life. "Did you ever see how they kill cattle? They use a sledgehammer," he said. "That's how the shot felt when it hit me. Without a mask I wouldn't be here today."

On May 18, 1970, a couple of weeks after his death-defying encounter, the Blues traded Plante to the Maple Leafs for cash. He played three seasons in Toronto before being sent to the Bruins in 1973 as part of a deal that included a first-round draft pick the Leafs would use to select Ian Turnbull.

MAY 19

MAYORS SHAKE ON IT, 2021

To commemorate the Leafs and the Canadiens facing off in the playoffs for the first time in more than four decades, the mayors of the two cities shook on it. On May 19, 2021, it was announced that the two leaders had agreed on a friendly wager that centred around culinary offerings. If the Leafs lost, Mayor John Tory would be offering up peameal bacon sandwiches — not necessarily the first thing that comes to mind when I think of Toronto food, but hey, it's called Hogtown for a reason — and if the Canadiens came up short, Mayor Valérie Plante would send smoked meat sandwiches the other way.

In addition to these tasty terms, which also included some cold beers, the two politicians agreed to donate $500 to charity, with the loser kicking in an extra $500. And, of course, the losing mayor would also raise the winning team's flag at city hall. If you've picked up this book by choice, you're probably a Leafs fan, which means you already know which flag ended up flying above Nathan Phillips Square a few weeks later.

MAY 20

LEAFS HIRE MIKE BABCOCK, 2015

t's a bird, it's a plane, it's Mike Babcock. When the head coach failed to come to terms on a new agreement with the Detroit Red Wings in early May 2015, he became the biggest acquisition target of the off-season. While many considered Buffalo to be the front-runner for landing Babcock's services, Toronto's chances suddenly took off when Leafs Nation blogger Jeff Veillette astutely noticed some unusual activity with the private jet belonging to Maple Leaf Sports & Entertainment.

On May 20, 2015, Veillette reported on Twitter that the aircraft was scheduled to arrive in Detroit and return for Toronto within minutes of arrival, sparking speculation that the Leafs were fetching their new bench boss. Sure enough, later that same day, Toronto announced they had signed Babcock to an eight-year, $50 million contract, making him the highest-paid coach in NHL history. It was exciting news at the time, but in the coming years, many Leafs fans might have wished the team's plane had picked up a different passenger.

MAY 21

HARRY LUMLEY TRADED TO
THE BLACK HAWKS, 1956

After just four seasons with the Maple Leafs, Harry Lumley, affectionately known as "Apple Cheeks," was traded back to the Black Hawks, along with Eric Nesterenko, in exchange for cash on May 21, 1956. Lumley was set to battle Al Rollins for the starting netminder position in Chicago when the new season started, but Lumley ended up leaving training camp, which was held in St. Catharines, Ontario, over a contract dispute and returned home to Owen Sound.

The issue was eventually resolved and Lumley inked a new deal with the Black Hawks organization in early October, but he wasn't going to be playing in Chicago. While Rollins had nabbed the number one spot, Lumley agreed to report to the club's American Hockey League affiliate, the Buffalo Bisons. He spent the next two seasons in the AHL until he was traded to a battered Boston Bruins team that was in desperate need of goaltending in January 1958. Lumley played parts of three campaigns with the Bruins before finishing his career in the minors.

MAY 22

LEAFS ACQUIRE EDDIE JOHNSTON, 1973

A couple of months after the Maple Leafs sent Jacques Plante to the Boston Bruins, the trade was completed on May 22, 1973, when the future considerations heading back to Toronto turned out to be goaltender Eddie Johnston. Originally from Montreal, Johnston made his NHL debut for the Bruins in 1962. A couple of years later, he played in every minute of Boston's 70-game schedule in the 1963–64 season, a feat that is unlikely to ever be matched again in the NHL.

A few years after that incredible achievement, Johnston took a slapshot to the side of his head from teammate Bobby Orr during warm-up for a game on Halloween; the blow put him in a coma and kept him in the hospital for weeks. He recovered from his injury and went on to win two Stanley Cups with the Bruins, splitting time in the crease with Gerry Cheevers. Johnston would play just one campaign with the Leafs before finishing his career with the St. Louis Blues and a final stopover with the Chicago Black Hawks.

MAY 23

LEAFS ACQUIRE PIERRE PILOTE FROM CHICAGO, 1968

Pierre Pilote was in shock. On May 23, 1968, the veteran Black Hawks defenceman was traded to the Maple Leafs in exchange for winger Jim Pappin. But instead of learning about the transaction from Chicago, where he had won three Norris Trophies and the Stanley Cup, he first heard it from Toronto sports reporter Red Burnett. Pilote was initially so upset with how the Black Hawks handled the situation that he actually contemplated retirement.

After playing 20 games for Chicago in 1955–56, Pilote never missed a day of work for the next five years, suiting up for every game. By the time his tenure with the Black Hawks came to a sudden conclusion, he had played 821 regular-season games, more than any other player in franchise history. After the dismay of being traded wore off, Pilote decided he still had more hockey in him. The 37-year-old played in all but seven games for Toronto that season before hanging up his skates following the 1969 Stanley Cup Playoffs. Six years later, he was inducted into the Hockey Hall of Fame.

TRADER CLIFF FIRED, 1997

The Cliff Fletcher era in Toronto was over. On May 24, 1997, the Leafs announced they had fired Fletcher as general manager, president, and chief operating officer. He had two years remaining on his contract, and the club had offered him the chance to stay on solely in the capacity of president, but he declined. Although the Leafs missed the post-season and finished near the bottom of the standings in his final season in Toronto, Fletcher, who came by the nickname "Trader Cliff" honestly, was best remembered as the architect of some of the most transformative moves in franchise history.

Not long after joining the Leafs in 1991, Fletcher acquired Doug Gilmour in a blockbuster deal with the Calgary Flames. Five years later, he orchestrated the move that brought Mats Sundin to Toronto, where the Swede would serve as captain for the next decade. But that wasn't the last of Trader Cliff. Following the firing of John Ferguson Jr. in 2008, the Leafs named Fletcher interim GM. His second stint, however, would not be remembered as fondly.

MAY 25

GLENN ANDERSON NETS
OT WINNER, 1993

Glenn Anderson lived for the big playoff moments. After winning five Stanley Cups with the Edmonton Oilers, he was traded to the Maple Leafs on September 19, 1991, along with Grant Fuhr and Craig Berube, in exchange for Vincent Damphousse, Peter Ing, Scott Thornton, and Luke Richardson — one of Cliff Fletcher's first shrewd moves as GM. But the Leafs didn't qualify for the post-season in Anderson's first campaign with the blue and white.

The following year, however, Anderson had the chance to live up to his billing as a clutch playoff performer. On May 25, 1993, in the fifth game of Toronto's conference final series against the Los Angeles Kings, the Leafs managed to force overtime after trailing by two goals late in the second period. With just 40 seconds remaining on the clock in the first sudden-death session, Anderson tapped a bouncing puck past goaltender Kelly Hrudey to give the Leafs a 3–2 victory and a 3–2 series lead. Two nights later, Anderson would open the scoring less than a minute into the sixth game.

MAY 26

DAN MALONEY NAMED
HEAD COACH, 1984

N
ot long after the Leafs missed the playoffs, the club sacked head coach Mike Nykoluk. Toronto owner Harold Ballard was disappointed the team had failed to qualify for the post-season and wanted a different voice behind the bench. The crabby owner felt that Nykoluk, who was revered as a player's coach, was too nice to be an NHL bench boss. Ballard wanted someone who was uncompromising, and he knew just the guy.

Dan Maloney had spent the past two seasons serving as an assistant coach with Nykoluk. A former hard-hitting player who had one of the fiercest right-hand punches of his era, Maloney's fearsome reputation on the ice was exactly what Ballard wanted behind the bench. On May 26, 1984, the Leafs named Maloney head coach, the seventh in the last seven years. In his first season behind the bench, the Leafs continued to struggle and the new coach clashed with captain Rick Vaive, eventually stripping the three-time 50-goal scorer of the *C* on his sweater after he slept in one day and missed practice.

MAY 27

WAYNE GRETZKY HIGH-STICKS KILLER, 1993

I still haven't forgiven Kerry Fraser. Just 39 seconds into overtime, with the Kings on the verge of elimination against the Leafs on May 27, 1993, Wayne Gretzky clipped Doug Gilmour in the face with his stick. The infraction, however, went undetected by Fraser, the referee that game, along with both linesmen. While Gilmour pleaded his case with blood dripping down his chin, the officials conferred. It was a pivotal moment in the game.

If Gretzky had been called for high-sticking, the Leafs would be on the power play in sudden death with the Kings' most valuable player in the box, giving them a golden opportunity to punch their ticket to the Stanley Cup Final. But there was no penalty. Although Gilmour needed eight stitches between his jaw and neck, the game went on. Less than a minute later, Gretzky, who should have still been in the sin bin, took a pass from Luc Robitaille in front of the Leafs' net and buried the puck past Félix Potvin to give the Kings a 5–4 victory and force a decisive seventh game.

MAY 28

MATS SUNDIN SCORES TYING GOAL, 2002

Mats Sundin gave his team a glimmer of hope. With time winding down in the sixth game of Toronto's Eastern Conference Final series against the Carolina Hurricanes on May 28, 2002, and the club's post-season on the line, the Maple Leafs captain scored the tying goal with 21.8 seconds remaining on the clock to force overtime, sending the Air Canada Centre faithful into bedlam. When sudden death commenced, the Buds, seemingly rejuvenated by their captain's heroics, came out flying.

Not long into the extra session, Sundin set up countryman Jonas Höglund on the rush, but the Swedish winger was stymied by goaltender Artūrs Irbe, a critical difference-maker for the Hurricanes throughout the entire series. But just before the halfway mark of overtime, Carolina's Martin Gélinas, who would fittingly earn the nickname "the Eliminator" a couple of years later in the playoffs, tipped in a centring pass from Josef Vašíček to clinch a 2–1 victory, sending the Hurricanes to the Stanley Cup Final for the first time in franchise history.

PAT BURNS NAMED MAPLE LEAFS BENCH BOSS, 1992

Just hours after resigning as head coach of the Montreal Canadiens, on May 29, 1992, Pat Burns inked a four-year, $1.6 million contract to become the bench boss for the Maple Leafs. After making his NHL coaching debut in 1988 with the Habs, Burns won the Jack Adams Award in his first season and then guided the club to the Stanley Cup Final before coming up a couple wins short against the Calgary Flames.

While Burns continued to find success in Montreal over the next few years, he said he could no longer take the intense media focus that came with the job. And if anyone could handle the pressure, it was Burns. Before working his way up to the NHL coaching ranks from junior hockey, he had been an officer with the Gatineau Police Force for nearly two decades. While the Toronto gig would not come with much less scrutiny, Burns was ready for a change. In his first season with the Leafs, he recorded 44 wins and earned his second Jack Adams.

MAY 30

FORBES KENNEDY SOLD
TO PENGUINS, 1969

Forbes Kennedy went out with a bang. In the first game of Toronto's 1969 playoff series against the Boston Bruins, which is remembered notoriously for Pat Quinn knocking out Bobby Orr, Kennedy had been feuding with goaltender Gerry Cheevers all night. After finally getting into a dust-up with the Bruins netminder, Kennedy hit linesman George Ashley when the official attempted to separate the two. When the fracas was broken up, the scrappy centre, who racked up a combined 219 penalty minutes that year with the Philadelphia Flyers and the Maple Leafs, the most in the NHL, received a slew of infractions, including a game misconduct for striking Ashley.

Kennedy was done for the evening, and it would prove to be his last game in the NHL. Following the contest, league president Clarence Campbell suspended him for four games and fined him $1,000. In the off-season, on May 30, 1969, Toronto traded Kennedy to the Pittsburgh Penguins for an undisclosed amount. He would spend the next two seasons in the minors before hanging up his skates.

MAY 31

CANADIENS DEFEAT LEAFS
IN GAME 7, 2021

When the Leafs took a 3–1 series lead against the Montreal Canadiens in their opening-round matchup in the 2021 Stanley Cup Playoffs, I remember my father-in-law, who is a diehard Habs fan, saying to me, "Well, I guess this one is in the bag." I think I just chuckled. As a lifelong Leafs fan, I knew better that it was far from over.

From the missed high stick on Doug Gilmour in 1993 to the monumental collapse against the Bruins two decades later, there was nothing about this franchise that inspired me to believe they would tidily wrap up this series. I hoped I was wrong, but deep down I knew. Sure enough, the Canadiens rattled off two straight wins to force a seventh game. So when the decisive matchup was scheduled for May 31, 2021, I declined my father-in-law's invitation to watch the game together. If it went how I thought it would, I would need to be alone. I made the right call. Montreal won 3–1, handing Toronto its third Game 7 loss in the past four years.

JUNE 1

CONSTRUCTION BEGINS ON
MAPLE LEAF GARDENS, 1931

t was an ambitious project. At the height of the Great Depression in Canada, Maple Leafs owner Conn Smythe wanted a new arena for his team. The club had previously played at the Arena Gardens on Mutual Street, where it had been crowned Stanley Cup champions in 1918, the first in the NHL era, and 1922, but the facility had been built before the First World War, and Smythe believed that a modern, large-capacity venue was the key to drawing in more fans.

He was determined to make his dream into a reality for his club and got shovels into the ground on June 1, 1931, at the corner of Church and Carlton Streets. Just five-and-a-half months after first ground was broken, Maple Leaf Gardens was completed — an incredible feat of engineering and construction. The team would play its first game there on November 12, 1931, against the Chicago Black Hawks and later that season would defeat the New York Rangers to win the first of eight championships in that building.

LEAFS DON'T PLAY IN JUNE, 1918–2023

The Toronto Maple Leafs have never played a game in June. It's an important distinction to make because, beginning with the 1992 Stanley Cup Playoffs, playing games in June means your team is in the final showdown for the rights to the Stanley Cup. Sure, they came pretty close to playing in June in 1993 and, more recently, in 2021, but they lost Game 7 to the Canadiens on the final day of May, despite holding a 3–1 series lead, something we don't need to revisit in detail since we just covered it.

For the most part, however, outside of post-seasons that have been impacted by the Covid-19 pandemic, June is now synonymous with championship hockey. And as Leafs fans know all too well, at the time of this writing, Toronto hasn't won a championship since 1967. This book will be finalized well before the 2023 Stanley Cup Playoffs are concluded, but here's hoping we'll need to stop the presses so I can make some emergency revisions. But if you're reading these words now, that means we'll have to wait another year.

JUNE 3

JOHNNY BOWER PLUCKED IN INTRA-LEAGUE DRAFT, 1958

t would turn out to be one of the greatest pickups in Maple Leafs history. On June 3, 1958, in the NHL's annual intra-league draft, Toronto took goaltender Johnny Bower from the Cleveland Barons for $15,000. Bower made his NHL debut for the New York Rangers in 1953 but had spent most of his time as a minor-leaguer with Cleveland and Providence in the American Hockey League. By the end of the 1957–58 season, he had collected his third Hap Holmes Memorial Award, bestowed annually to the goalie with the best goals-against average, along with his third straight Les Cunningham Award for the most valuable player that season.

It would be the last time Bower would see action in the AHL, and he still holds the record for the most victories in the league with 359. Bower would make his debut for the Maple Leafs the following season and would go on to win two Vezina Trophies and four Stanley Cups in blue and white, while establishing himself as one of the franchise's most beloved players.

TOD SLOAN DEALT TO THE BLACK HAWKS, 1958

Almost every Leafs fan can tell you that Bill Barilko scored the championship-clinching goal in overtime in 1951 because, of course, it was the last goal he ever scored. But few remember it was Tod Sloan who tied the game with 32 seconds left to play to send it to sudden death. Sloan continued to be a dependable centre for Toronto for the next seven seasons, and he even led the team in scoring in the 1955–56 campaign, but he fell out of favour with management for his role in trying to organize the league's first players' union.

Looking to send a message, Toronto sent Sloan to the Chicago Black Hawks in exchange for cash on June 4, 1958. Three years later, in his final NHL season, he won another championship. But although his name was engraved on the trophy as Tod Sloan when he won it with the Leafs, he appeared as Martin A. Sloan with Chicago, a quirk tied to another lesser-known fact about him that he was born Aloysius Martin Sloan.

JUNE 5

CANADIENS TAKE BRAD SELWOOD, 1972

B rad Selwood had already been lured to the upstart World Hockey Association by the New England Whalers, but he was still on the available players list heading into the NHL's annual intra-league draft in 1972. Originally drafted 10th overall by the Maple Leafs in 1968, the blueliner made his debut for Toronto in 1970, suiting up for 28 games, before playing his first, and only, full campaign with the Buds in 1971–72.

Although Selwood had already signed with the Whalers in advance of the WHA's inaugural season, the Montreal Canadiens took a flyer on him in the intra-league draft on June 5, 1972. He would go on to play seven seasons on New England's blue line, which included winning the Avco Cup in his first campaign. When the WHA merged with the NHL in 1979, the Canadiens, which still held Selwood's rights, traded him to the Los Angeles Kings. He played one season with the Kings before finishing his career in the minors. Following his playing days, Selwood got into coaching.

JUNE 6

RANGERS TAKE LARRY CAHAN
FROM THE LEAFS, 1956

t was pretty quiet at the 1956 intra-league draft. Only two players were selected that June 6. Chicago, Boston, and Toronto all opted to forgo their picks, but the New York Rangers nabbed defenceman Larry Cahan from the Maple Leafs, while the Detroit Red Wings took Tom McCarthy from the Rangers. Both players were exchanged for $15,000. Cahan spent parts of seven seasons with New York, as well as some time in the minor-league circuits, before being selected by the newly minted Oakland Seals in the NHL's expansion draft in 1967.

During his inaugural campaign with the Seals, Cahan was involved in a tragic moment in hockey history. On January 13, 1968, during a game against the Minnesota North Stars, he and teammate Ron Harris collided with North Stars forward Bill Masterton. Masterton, who was not wearing a helmet and may have already been suffering from an undiagnosed concussion, fell back and struck his head on the ice. He died two days later. The NHL eventually implemented a rule that made helmets mandatory.

JUNE 7

MAPLE LEAFS ACQUIRE FRANK EDDOLLS, 1940

Toronto acquired Frank Eddolls from the Montreal Canadiens in exchange for the rights to Joe Benoit on June 7, 1940, but it would be another trade involving Eddolls, a few years later, that would forever change the history of the Maple Leafs. Heading into the 1943–44 season, Eddolls was recovering from surgery to repair a knee injury from his younger playing days that had flared up in the summer. The newspapers reported that Eddolls might never play again, but he was still considered a promising young defenceman, especially by Maple Leafs owner Conn Smythe.

The story goes that while Smythe was overseas serving for Canada in the Second World War, his colleague Frank Selke traded Eddolls back to the Canadiens for Ted "Teeder" Kennedy without consulting Smythe. The deal led to a rift between the two executives, and Selke would eventually leave to helm the Canadiens, where he would preside over a dynasty. Meanwhile, in Toronto, Kennedy would go on to become one of Smythe's favourite players, captaining the club for eight seasons and hoisting the Stanley Cup five times.

RED KELLY TRADED TO KINGS, 1967

Not long after winning the Stanley Cup with the Maple Leafs in 1967, Red Kelly already had his next gig lined up. After 20 seasons in the NHL, which included eight championships with the Detroit Red Wings and Toronto, Kelly was hanging up his skates and heading to the West Coast to become the first head coach of the Los Angeles Kings. But when the league held its expansion draft on June 6, 1967, both Kelly and Jack Kent Cooke, the Kings' owner, were taken aback when the Maple Leafs placed him on their list of protected players after the 10th round of selections.

Kelly and Cooke both believed they had a deal with Toronto to ensure the player (soon-to-be coach) was available, but Maple Leafs manager and coach Punch Imlach felt that if the Kings really wanted him, they would need to draft him. Following the draft Kelly and Cooke both filed protests with the league, but the situation was resolved two days later, on June 8, when Toronto sent Kelly's rights to Los Angeles in exchange for Ken Block.

JUNE 9

GERRY CHEEVERS CLAIMED
BY BOSTON, 1965

Punch Imlach thought he might have a buyer for goaltender Gerry Cheevers heading into the NHL's annual intra-league draft on June 9, 1965. Although Toronto's general manager and coach left the goalie unprotected, which meant he could be claimed by any team during the draft, he still figured he could deal him before the draft. Imlach initially approached the New York Rangers about sending Cheevers there, along with Kent Douglas, in exchange for Jim Neilson, but general manager Emile Francis reportedly said, "Make it Douglas and Sawchuk and we've got a deal."

Thinking he might still be able to strike up a deal with the Boston Bruins, Imlach again offered Cheevers and Douglas but was rebuffed by the Bruins' brass, who also insisted on getting Sawchuk instead of Cheevers. And so, having exhausted all his options, Imlach went into the draft without a suitor for his goaltender. Not long after the meeting was called to order, Boston, of course, selected Cheevers from Toronto. He went on to backstop the Bruins to Stanley Cup championships in 1970 and 1972.

JUNE 10

MAPLE LEAFS CLAIM TERRY SAWCHUK, 1964

When Terry Sawchuk found out he had been claimed by the Leafs in the intra-league draft on June 10, 1964, he was reportedly doing yardwork at his home in Union Lake, Michigan. The 34-year-old goalie had spent the past seven seasons with the Detroit Red Wings but was left off the team's protected list to clear the path for up-and-coming netminder Roger Crozier. It wasn't a total surprise to Sawchuk, but he was still taken aback by the move.

Although he said he would report to Toronto, he added that if the team sent him to the minors he would simply retire. But Sawchuk would become a key part of the Maple Leafs. In his first season with the blue and white, he shared the crease with fellow veteran Johnny Bower, and the two combined to win the Vezina Trophy that season. A couple of years later, in 1967, they would both hoist the Stanley Cup. Following that championship, his fourth in the league, Sawchuk was claimed by the expansion Los Angeles Kings.

JUNE 11

MIKE PALMATEER TRADED
TO THE CAPS, 1980

When the Washington Capitals introduced their new goalie, Mike Palmateer, who was acquired from the Maple Leafs on June 11, 1980, in exchange for defenceman Robert Picard and forward Tim Coulis, the netminder sipped on champagne. Palmateer had every reason to celebrate; he was free of coach and general manager Punch Imlach. For the past year, the two had squabbled publicly, including an incident in which Imlach prevented Palmateer and teammate Darryl Sittler from appearing on the TV show *Showdown*. Imlach had also repeatedly refused to sign Palmateer to a multi-year deal, so it was no secret that he wanted out of Toronto.

The Maple Leafs did eventually ink the goaltender to a four-year pact but then immediately sent him to Washington for Picard and Coulis. Palmateer spent two seasons with the Capitals before returning to Toronto in 1982. By that point Imlach was no longer the coach and Palmateer finished his career as a Leaf, hanging up his pads in 1984. Nearly two decades later, the Buds hired him as an amateur scout.

JUNE 12

LEAFS TRADE DANNY MARKOV, 2001

D anny Markov had been one of the Maple Leafs' best defencemen during the 2000–01 season. The Russian blueliner, who was known as "Elvis" for his impersonations of the King of Rock and Roll, was one half of Toronto's top defence pairing, along with fellow countryman Dmitri Yushkevich. Two years earlier, in his first full season in the NHL, Markov made his Stanley Cup Playoffs debut. After the Maple Leafs eliminated the Pittsburgh Penguins in overtime to advance to the conference final for the first time in five years, while the team huddled in celebration around goaltender Curtis Joseph, Markov mocked Penguins superstar Jaromir Jagr by imitating the Czech winger's signature salute.

But after just a handful of seasons with the Maple Leafs, the defenceman was traded to the Phoenix Coyotes on June 12, 2001, in exchange for forwards Travis Green, Robert Reichel, and Craig Mills. In his first campaign in the desert, Markov scored 36 points, a career high. He played two seasons in Phoenix before making stops in Carolina, Philadelphia, Nashville, and Detroit.

JUNE 13

MAPLE LEAFS CLAIM AL ARBOUR, 1961

l Arbour was known as "Radar" because he was one of the few players in NHL history to wear eyeglasses while playing. In fact, even during fights the tough blueliner kept his spectacles on. During a game against the Maple Leafs in 1957, as a member of the Detroit Red Wings, Arbour fought Pete Conacher — and managed to keep his glasses on his face. Following the skirmish both players served their major penalties side by side in the same penalty box; it was still a few years before Maple Leaf Gardens had partitioned sin bins.

Arbour eventually made his way to Chicago, where he won the Stanley Cup with the Black Hawks in 1961. Following the championship Arbour was claimed by the Leafs in the intra-league draft on June 13, 1961. He hoisted Lord Stanley's mug again the next year as Toronto clinched its first of three straight titles. After hanging up his skates in 1971, Arbour went on to become one of the best coaches in NHL history, guiding the New York Islanders to four consecutive championships.

TODD GILL TRADED TO THE SHARKS, 1996

Todd Gill had seen plenty of his teammates come and go through the Maple Leafs dressing room over the years. Drafted 25th overall by Toronto in 1984, Gill made his debut the following season, and by 1996, he was the club's longest-serving active player. By the end of the 1996–97 campaign, the blueliner had worked his way up to 639 career games, the fifth most by a Maple Leafs defenceman.

But on June 14, 1996, it was Gill who finally found himself making his way to another team. That day, he was traded to the San Jose Sharks in exchange for centre Jamie Baker and a fifth-round pick in the upcoming NHL Entry Draft. Not long into his first season with his new club, Gill was named captain, the fourth in franchise history, by head coach Al Sims. Despite playing 79 games, a career high, and picking up 21 assists in his first year in San Jose, Gill failed to score a goal for the first time in 13 NHL seasons.

JUNE 15

WENDEL CLARK DRAFTED FIRST OVERALL, 1985

Heading into the 1985 NHL Entry Draft, Craig Simpson was the consensus number one. The winger had put up 84 points in 42 games at Michigan State and was at the top of the NHL's Central Scouting Bureau's list. But as the draft approached, there were reports that Simpson and his family didn't want him to end up in Toronto, which held the first overall pick after finishing at the bottom of the standings, following some poor meetings with some of the team's brass.

And so, when the draft was held on June 15, many believed Toronto would use the pick on Dana Murzyn, a rugged defenceman from the Western Hockey League. Instead, the Maple Leafs selected another blueliner, Wendel Clark, a tough farm boy from Kelvington, Saskatchewan. Although Clark was ranked three spots behind Simpson, the selection would pay off for the Maple Leafs. The club would move Clark to the wing, and he would go on to become one of the most revered players in franchise history.

JUNE 16

ROB RAMAGE TRADED TO
THE MAPLE LEAFS, 1989

R ob Ramage was apparently the last to know he had been traded. Although it probably wasn't a total shock when he found out, it seemed that everyone else got word before him. The Calgary Flames had just won the 1989 Stanley Cup, but it was no secret that Ramage wanted a bigger role on another team. Going into the off-season, Flames general manager Cliff Fletcher told Ramage's agent, Bill Watters, that he would try to move him somewhere else if he could.

But when Calgary sent Ramage to Toronto on June 16, 1989, in exchange for a second-round draft pick to be used the following day, the defenceman was unreachable. The Flames tried leaving word at hotels they believed he was staying at in either Florida or California, but it turned out Ramage learned the news when he called his friend Craig Hartsburg, who played for the Minnesota North Stars, from San Diego. Craig's wife answered the phone and asked Ramage what he thought of the deal, to which he responded, "What deal?"

LEAFS ACQUIRE WAYNE THOMAS, 1975

With Ken Dryden back between the pipes for the Montreal Canadiens for the 1974–75 season, goalie Wayne Thomas did not get much playing time. In fact, he didn't get any. Thomas made his NHL debut two years earlier, recording a shutout in his first game, and started eight more games down the stretch of the 1972–73 campaign. The following season when Dryden was clerking at a Toronto law firm, Thomas saw more action, suiting up for 42 games.

When Dryden returned, however, Thomas was relegated to third-string position, behind Dryden and Michel "Bunny" Larocque. Although the Canadiens carried three goalies that year, Dryden started most of the games, with Larocque serving as his backup. At the end of the season, on June 17, 1975, Thomas was traded to the Leafs in exchange for a first-round draft pick. In his first season in Toronto, he played 64 games, a career high. He spent another year with the Leafs before being claimed by the New York Rangers in 1977.

COACH DAN MALONEY
CALLS IT QUITS, 1986

Dan Maloney felt he had earned a raise. After guiding the Maple Leafs to an upset against the Chicago Black Hawks in the preliminary round of the playoffs and then taking the St. Louis Blues to seven games, the Toronto bench boss was looking for a new two-year contract with a higher salary. But team owner Harold Ballard, who had often made Maloney the object of cheap shots, refused. Instead, he offered his coach a one-year contract at the same salary he was already receiving.

After getting nowhere with general manager Gerry McNamara as well, Maloney had had enough. On June 18, 1986, he resigned from the Maple Leafs. Even Rick Vaive, who had his share of battles with Maloney, including having his captaincy stripped for sleeping in for a road practice, took his coach's side. Vaive said he didn't blame him for leaving and felt it would set the team back. Maloney, however, wasn't out of work for long. Two days later, he was named head coach of the Winnipeg Jets.

LEAFS ACQUIRE ZACH HYMAN, 2015

Before Zach Hyman had ever played an NHL game, he already had two children's books to his name. Hyman, originally drafted 123rd overall by the Florida Panthers at the NHL Entry Draft in 2010, went on to play college hockey at the University of Michigan. After leading the Big Ten conference in points with 54 in his final season, earning him a finalist nomination for the Hobey Baker Award, Hyman had still not agreed to a contract with the Panthers.

In advance of his becoming a free agent, Florida traded his rights to the Maple Leafs for Greg McKegg and a conditional 2017 seventh-round draft pick on June 19, 2015. Four days later, Hyman, a Toronto native, signed a two-year entry-level contract with the Maple Leafs. He made his NHL debut on February 29, 2016, against the Tampa Bay Lightning. Over the next six seasons, Hyman established himself as a gritty two-way player with plenty of offensive upside to his game. Off the ice in Toronto, he penned his third book, *The Magician's Secret*.

FREDERIK ANDERSEN TRADED TO THE LEAFS, 2016

During the 2015–16 regular season, Anaheim Ducks goaltenders Frederik Andersen and John Gibson allowed just 192 goals, the fewest in the league that year, to earn the pair the William M. Jennings Trophy. But with Andersen, who was four years older than Gibson, set to become an unrestricted free agent in just over a week, the team traded him to the Maple Leafs on June 20, 2016, for a first-round draft pick in the upcoming draft and a second-round selection in 2017.

Upon arriving in Toronto, Andersen promptly signed a five-year contract. In his first season with the Maple Leafs, he established himself as the club's undisputed starting goaltender, playing in 66 games and racking up 33 victories. The following campaign, he appeared in the same number of games, winning 38 of them, a career high. Two years later, on December 14, 2019, in a game against the Oilers, Andersen recorded his 200th career victory in just his 344th game, tying Chris Osgood as the fourth-fastest goalie in NHL history to reach the milestone.

JUNE 21

LEAFS DRAFT VINCENT DAMPHOUSSE SIXTH OVERALL, 1986

With the sixth overall pick at the 1986 NHL Entry Draft, on June 21, the Maple Leafs took Vincent Damphousse from the Laval Titan of the Quebec Major Junior Hockey League. In his final season of junior, he recorded 45 goals and 155 points, an impressive enough total until you remember that Guy Rouleau, who split time with the Longueuil Chevaliers and the Hull Olympiques that year, scored 91 goals and 191 points in 62 games. But then again, the skillful Rouleau, who was small by hockey standards, was never drafted by an NHL team.

Damphousse on the other hand, made the Leafs roster out of junior and scored 46 points in his first season. By his fourth campaign in Toronto, he had established himself as one of the club's best players, recording 94 points. The following year, Damphousse was named to his first NHL All-Star Game, where he scored four goals, becoming just the fourth player in NHL history to accomplish the feat, to earn the MVP award. Before the start of the next season, Damphousse was part of the trade that brought Grant Fuhr to Toronto.

JUNE 22

LEAFS TRADE SERGEI BEREZIN
TO THE COYOTES, 2001

t's fair to say Phoenix Coyotes general manager Cliff
Fletcher knew what he was getting when he acquired Sergei
Berezin from the Maple Leafs in exchange for Mikael
Renberg on June 22, 2001. Back when Fletcher was GM for
Toronto, he selected Berezin 256th overall at the 1994 NHL
Entry Draft. In his first season with the Maple Leafs, Berezin
scored 25 goals, and two years later, during the 1998–99 cam-
paign, he found the back of the net 37 times, a career high
that would go unmatched.

Although Fletcher was excited about his reunion with the
Russian winger, he wasn't in the desert for very long. After just
41 games with the Coyotes, in which he scored seven goals and
16 points, a disgruntled Berezin, who had requested a trade,
was dealt to the Montreal Canadiens for a third-round draft
pick, future considerations, and Brian Savage. Meanwhile, in
Toronto, Renberg returned to the NHL after playing for a
year in Sweden and scored 52 points in 71 games playing on
a line with countryman Mats Sundin.

JUNE 23

LEAFS ACQUIRE JVR FROM PHILLY, 2012

During his tenure as GM of the Maple Leafs, Brian Burke had a number of misses, but he pulled off a master stroke of trading when he acquired James van Riemsdyk from the Philadelphia Flyers in exchange for Luke Schenn on June 23, 2012. While both players had been top first-round picks — the Flyers took van Riemsdyk second in 2007, and the Maple Leafs nabbed Schenn with the fifth overall pick the following year — they had yet to live up to their billing with their respective clubs.

It was becoming increasingly clear that Schenn was never going to be that high-impact defenceman the Leafs hoped he would become. In Philadelphia, after scoring 21 goals and 40 points in his second NHL season, van Riemsdyk inked a six-year contract extension. But after injuries limited him to just 43 games in the 2011–12 campaign, he became the subject of trade rumours. While Schenn floundered in Philadelphia, van Riemsdyk flourished in Toronto. Over the next six seasons, he scored 20 goals or more four times and reached the 30-goal mark twice.

JUNE 24

LEAFS TRADE TUUKKA RASK
TO THE BRUINS, 2006

n what would turn out to be one of the most lopsided trades in Maple Leafs history, on June 24, 2006, Toronto traded Finnish goaltender Tuukka Rask, who had been drafted 21st overall by the club the previous year, to the Boston Bruins in exchange for netminder Andrew Raycroft, who won the Calder Trophy in 2004 as the league's top rookie. Although the move initially paid off for the Buds, with Raycroft recording 37 victories in his first season in Toronto, matching a club record, the deal would come back to haunt the team.

Following his stellar debut for the blue and white, Raycroft struggled; after stints in Colorado, Vancouver, and Dallas, he was out of the league by the end of 2011. Meanwhile, in Boston, Rask became an NHL regular in 2009–10 and then took the reins as the Bruins' starting goaltender in the 2013–14 season, recording 36 victories and winning the Vezina Trophy. He spent his entire career in Boston, retiring in 2022 as the all-time franchise leader in wins with 308.

JUNE 25

ANAHEIM DUCKS DRAFT JOHN GIBSON IN THE SECOND ROUND, 2011

Heading into the 2011 NHL Entry Draft, the Maple Leafs acquired the Anaheim Ducks' first-round pick, 22nd overall, in exchange for the 30th overall pick, which originally belonged to the Boston Bruins, and a second-round draft pick. Toronto used the newly acquired pick to select Tyler Biggs, a big winger from the U.S. National Team Development Program, on June 24, the first day of the draft. Closing out the first round, Anaheim used the 30th overall pick from Toronto to take Rickard Rakell.

The next day, using the second-round pick from Toronto, Anaheim took goaltender John Gibson. Although Biggs would never crack an NHL roster, Rakell would record back-to-back 30-goal seasons with the Ducks, while Gibson would become a bona fide starter and a key reason why teammate Freddie Andersen was expendable and traded to the Leafs in 2016. While Toronto had five good seasons with Andersen, they could have had Gibson from the start. As of this writing, the last goalie the Maple Leafs have truly drafted and developed into a cornerstone in the crease was Félix Potvin, who was taken in 1990.

JUNE 26

PAT QUINN INTRODUCED
AS HEAD COACH, 1998

Whenever I think of Pat Quinn, fondly known as "the Big Irishman," the first image that always pops into my mind is of him chomping on a cigar at his introductory press conference when he was named head coach of the Maple Leafs on June 26, 1998. As he accepted his jersey from team president Ken Dryden, Quinn kept his stogie in his hand. At the time, many Leafs fans hoped it would be the first of many victory cigars to come as Quinn looked to lead the club out of a Stanley Cup drought of more than three decades.

Quinn, who had spent the last nine years with the Vancouver Canucks in roles that included head coach, GM, and president until he was fired not long into the 1997–98 campaign, took over for Mike Murphy, who failed to qualify for the playoffs in two seasons behind the bench in Toronto. In his first campaign with the Leafs, Quinn guided the team to 45 regular-season wins and an appearance in the Eastern Conference Final.

PAT QUINN STEPS DOWN AS GM, 2003

Another indelible image from the Big Irishman's tenure was him behind the Maple Leafs' bench sporting two black eyes. During a pre-season game against the Detroit Red Wings in 2005, the 62-year-old Quinn was hit by a puck and cut above his right eye. Two weeks later, when the Leafs took on the Ottawa Senators, he was once again hit by a puck, leaving him with two shiners. Things went downhill from there that season. Quinn missed the playoffs for the first time in seven years in Toronto and was fired by general manager John Ferguson Jr. a couple days after the season finished.

But before he got those shiners, Quinn had served as both bench boss and GM for the Maple Leafs for four years until it was announced on June 27, 2003, that the Big Irishman would relinquish his GM duties as part of an ownership restructuring to the club. A couple of months later, Quinn's new boss, Ferguson Jr., was hired, which ultimately marked the beginning of the end of the Pat Quinn era in Toronto.

JUNE 28

WENDEL CLARK TRADED
FOR MATS SUNDIN, 1994

Much of Leafs Nation was in an uproar when they heard the news. On June 28, 1994, captain Wendel Clark, Sylvain Lefebvre, Landon Wilson, and a first-round draft pick were sent to the Quebec Nordiques for Mats Sundin, Garth Butcher, Todd Warriner, and a first-round draft pick. Ever since he was selected first overall in 1985, Clark had been the heartbeat of the Maple Leafs with his ability to put the puck in the back of the net and his bone-crushing physical play.

Don Cherry, host of "Coach's Corner," even went as far as saying it must be April Fool's Day because it would have to be a joke to trade Clark for Sundin. But Sundin and the Leafs got the last laugh, as the Swedish centre would go on to become one of the greatest players in franchise history. In all but one of his 13 seasons in Toronto, Sundin led the team in scoring and set franchise records for goals (420) and points (987), both of which still stand as of this writing.

JUNE 29

WAYNE SIMMONDS RE-SIGNS WITH THE LEAFS, 2021

"The Wayne Train" was staying in Toronto. On June 29, 2021, Wayne Simmonds signed a two-year deal to remain with his hometown team. The Scarborough, Ontario, native was originally drafted 61st overall by the Los Angeles Kings in 2007; he had spent the bulk of his career with the Kings and Philadelphia Flyers, along with stops in Nashville, New Jersey, and Buffalo, before signing as a free agent with the Maple Leafs in advance of the 2020–21 season.

Although Simmonds was no longer the offensive threat he was earlier in his career, the two-time 30-goal scorer was still a fearsome player who added depth and grit to Toronto's bottom six. In his first season with the Buds, he potted seven goals in 38 games. By staying with the Leafs, Simmonds had the opportunity to celebrate a milestone that few players reach, let alone in their own backyard. On March 5, 2022, Simmonds appeared in his 1,000th career game in front of the Toronto faithful as the Maple Leafs hosted the Vancouver Canucks.

JUNE 30

LEAFS DRAFT THE GOAT
21ST OVERALL, 2013

F rédérik Gauthier was set to play NCAA hockey for Harvard University when a telephone call from Sidney Crosby made him change his mind. Before Crosby took the NHL by storm, he played junior for the Rimouski Oceanic of the Quebec Major Junior Hockey League. Gauthier had been drafted by Rimouski in 2011, and Crosby wanted him to reconsider his collegiate route and suit up for the Oceanic. Whatever the Penguins superstar said must have been convincing because the young player decided to join the QMJHL instead of pursuing an Ivy League education.

In Gauthier's rookie season with the Oceanic, he scored 22 goals and 60 points in 62 games and was rated by NHL Central Scouting as the eighth-best North American skater heading into the entry draft. On June 30, 2013, Gauthier, a six-foot-five centre who was projected to pull second-line duty in the NHL, was taken 21st overall by the Maple Leafs. He played parts of five seasons with the Buds, but "the Goat" never lived up to his billing, instead pulling fourth-line duty in Toronto.

JULY 1

JOHN TAVARES SIGNS SEVEN-YEAR DEAL, 2018

"Not everyday you can live a childhood dream." Those are the words John Tavares tweeted out, along with a picture of himself as a young boy sleeping in a Maple Leafs blanket, not long after it was announced that he had signed a seven-year, $77 million contract with Toronto on July 1, 2018. As someone who had that exact same bedspread when I was younger, it certainly hit home.

While I never realized my dream of suiting up for the Buds, it was hard not to get carried away by the news. I recall being so excited that I went out onto my deck and tried to chug two beers at the same time for a video I was going to post on social media. I didn't succeed in downing both brews, but it didn't matter — John Tavares was a Toronto Maple Leaf. It was the club's biggest free-agent signing in as long as I could remember, but it felt like much more than that. It was a homecoming, and the start of a new era.

JULY 2

ED BELFOUR SIGNS WITH
THE LEAFS, 2002

"The Eagle" had landed. On July 2, 2002, exactly five years after signing with Dallas as a free agent, goaltender Ed Belfour, who sported an iconic mask adorned with a screaming bald eagle, inked a two-year contract with the Maple Leafs. Although he had backstopped the Stars to a Stanley Cup in 1999, the 37-year-old netminder had been struggling on and off the ice the past few seasons.

Near the end of the 1999–2000 campaign, Belfour was arrested at a Dallas hotel for misdemeanour assault and resisting arrest and reportedly offered police officers a $1 billion bribe not to take him to jail. Two years later, he posted 27 losses and registered a save percentage of .895, the lowest in his career since a brief stint with the abysmal San Jose Sharks five years earlier. But GM and coach Pat Quinn, who had Belfour on his team when Canada won Olympic gold in Salt Lake City in 2002, believed the goalie would rebound. Quinn's hunch paid off. In Belfour's first season in Toronto, he recorded 37 victories, a franchise record.

JULY 3

LEAFS SIGN ALEXANDER MOGILNY, 2001

Alexander Mogilny was exactly the type of skilled winger the Leafs had been hoping to have flank captain Mats Sundin for quite some time. After the Russian sniper was unable to come to terms with the New Jersey Devils, where he had played the last two seasons and won a Stanley Cup in 2000, he signed a four-year, $22 million deal with Toronto on July 3, 2001. GM and bench boss Pat Quinn, who had coached Mogilny for a season in Vancouver, said, "He's one of the more talented players I've ever had the privilege of coaching."

Mogilny made an immediate impact with his new team. In his first game with the blue and white, he scored a pair of goals. A couple of games later, he notched two more tallies to reach the 400-goal mark, becoming the first Russian-born player in NHL history to reach the milestone. Mogilny finished the regular season with 24 goals and 57 points, and in the playoffs, he led the team in goal-scoring in the run to the Eastern Conference Final.

GARY ROBERTS SIGNS WITH MAPLE LEAFS, 2000

When Gary Roberts attended his first training camp with the Calgary Flames not long after the club drafted him 12th overall in 1984, it was an eye-opener. At the time, Roberts's off-ice conditioning consisted of playing lacrosse in the summer, so when he could muster only two chin-ups, head coach "Badger Bob" Johnson let him have it. Although Roberts was embarrassed, it had a huge impact on his career. Following that humbling experience, he purchased a chin-up bar and began taking his training seriously.

By the time Roberts signed a three-year, $8 million contract with the Maple Leafs on July 4, 2000, he had been in the NHL for 13 seasons and established a reputation as a fearsome competitor who was committed to fitness. After scoring a team-leading 29 goals in his first campaign in Toronto, he ended up playing nearly another decade in the league, a testament to his conditioning. After Roberts hung up his skates in 2009, he established Gary Roberts High Performance Training to train the next generation of hockey players.

JULY 5

LEAFS SIGN DAVID CLARKSON, 2013

knew exactly where I was. Well, maybe not exactly where, but I was somewhere between Sudbury and Ottawa on a bus headed east, refreshing my Twitter feed and repeating to myself, *Please don't sign David Clarkson. Please don't sign David Clarkson.* It was the opening of free agency, and all signs pointed to the Maple Leafs inking Clarkson, a one-time 30-goal scorer, to a significant deal.

In my younger days, Clarkson would have been a player I rooted for. He was a local guy from Mimico, he had grown up worshipping Wendel Clark, and just like his boyhood idol, he could score and wasn't afraid to drop the gloves. But Clarkson had just turned 29 years old, and the one time he had reached the 30-goal mark, he did so on an unsustainably high shooting percentage, with nearly a third of his tallies coming on the power play. Not exactly a player you wanted to lock up long term. But sure enough, on July 5, 2013, the Leafs signed Clarkson to a whopping seven-year, $36.75 million contract.

JULY 6

LEAFS SIGN FRANÇOIS BEAUCHEMIN, 2009

rançois Beauchemin missed most of the 2008–09 season with a knee injury, but the Maple Leafs knew that when the defenceman was healthy, he could shut down the league's top players. In the 2007 Stanley Cup Playoffs, as a member of the Anaheim Ducks, he was logging an average of 30 minutes a night and was a critical part of the club's first-ever championship that year. So when Beauchemin became a free agent, the Leafs were keen to add him to the blue line.

On July 6, 2009, they signed the steady rearguard to a three-year, $11.4 million contract. Although Beauchemin initially struggled adjusting to Toronto's system and a defence corps that was much more porous than the Anaheim group, which boasted future Hall of Famers Scott Niedermayer and Chris Pronger, he eventually became the kind of top-pairing defenceman the Leafs were looking for. But halfway through his second campaign, Beauchemin was traded back to the Ducks in exchange for Joffrey Lupul, Jake Gardiner, and a fourth-round draft pick, in what would prove to be a shrewd move for Toronto.

LEAFS SIGN KRIS KING, 1997

K ris King liked playing under the desert skies in Arizona with the Coyotes, but at heart, he was an Ontario boy. And after his six-year-old son wanted snow for Christmas one year, King knew it was time to come home. When free agency opened, he drew interest from many clubs seeking his hard-nosed brand of hockey, but he had only one team in mind.

And so, on July 7, 1997, King signed a four-year deal with the Maple Leafs, an early Christmas present for him and his family. This year, he wouldn't need to gather up snow from the arena for his son — there would be plenty of it in Toronto. While King was happy to be coming home, many wondered if it meant Tie Domi, who was in need of a new contract, would have to look elsewhere. But the following month, Domi signed a five-year deal, reuniting him with King. The two had played together in Winnipeg, where they once combined for a colossal 552 penalty minutes in a single season.

JULY 8

LEAFS ACQUIRE LARRY MURPHY, 1995

Philadelphia head coach Fred Shero once joked that he was considering putting earmuffs on defenceman Tom Bladon to try to drown out the taunts he endured from the Flyers faithful at the Spectrum. Many years later, if the Maple Leafs had known Larry Murphy would be subjected to similar treatment from his home crowd, they might have considered getting a pair of earplugs thrown into the deal they made on July 8, 1995.

When the Leafs acquired Murphy from the Pittsburgh Penguins in exchange for Dmitri Mironov and a second-round draft pick, they were getting a skilled, playmaking defenceman who had been an integral part of back-to-back Stanley Cups. But in Toronto, where Murphy was one of the highest-paid players, he became the scapegoat for the club's struggles and was often booed mercilessly at Maple Leaf Gardens. Despite finishing third in team scoring in his first season with the blue and white, the heckling continued. But before the end of his second campaign in Toronto, Murphy was traded to Detroit, where he would once again win consecutive championships.

JULY 9

JAY HARRISON SIGNS WITH HURRICANES, 2009

Jay Harrison travelled a long and winding road to the NHL. After being taken first overall in the 1998 Ontario Hockey League Priority Selection, he was drafted in the third round by the Maple Leafs a few years later. But despite his junior pedigree, which included two appearances on the Canadian national team for the World Junior tournament, Harrison spent the next six years with Toronto's American Hockey League affiliate. Although he had made a handful of NHL appearances over those seasons, he just couldn't stick around with the big club.

In 2008, instead of starting another campaign in the minors, Harrison decided to play in Switzerland. But before season's end, he returned to Toronto and suited up for seven games with the Maple Leafs down the stretch. In the off-season, on July 9, 2009, Harrison moved on from the Buds again, signing with the Carolina Hurricanes. After splitting the next season with the Hurricanes and its AHL club, the Albany River Rats, Harrison finally became an NHL regular, playing the next five seasons in Carolina and Winnipeg.

JULY 10

TROY BODIE BECOMES A
MAPLE LEAF, 2013

When a young Troy Bodie found out the Jets were relocating to Phoenix, Arizona, he was devastated. Growing up in Portage la Prairie, Manitoba, not far from Winnipeg, the Jets were his life. And when Bodie discovered there was a fundraiser to keep the team in the province, he pleaded with his parents, John and Shirley, to let him donate whatever savings he had to the cause. Although Bodie had to say goodbye to the Jets, they weren't gone forever.

Not long after Bodie made his NHL debut in 2009, there were rumblings that big-league hockey might return to Winnipeg. Two years later, the Jets touched down again when the Atlanta Thrashers were relocated to Manitoba, but with Bodie playing in the minors at the time, he didn't get to face the reincarnation of his beloved childhood team. But after signing a one-year two-way contract with the Maple Leafs on July 10, 2013, Bodie would get his chance. Later that season, in his first game in Winnipeg as an NHLer, he scored his eighth career goal.

JULY 11

DARRYL SITTLER MEETS TERRY FOX, 1980

S ometimes you forget that, before he became a Canadian hero, Terry Fox was once just a regular kid. Before embarking on the Marathon of Hope on just one leg to raise money for cancer research and awareness, he had his own heroes. One of them happened to be Maple Leafs star Darryl Sittler. So when the Marathon of Hope brought Fox to Toronto, he got the chance to meet his idol.

When Fox arrived at Nathan Phillips Square on July 10, 1980, he had already run 3,300 kilometres. Although Fox was in awe meeting the Leafs legend, the same could be said for Sittler, who said he had never encountered any athlete with as much courage. When Fox was forced to halt his crusade later that summer when his cancer spread to his lungs, Sittler offered to finish the route, but Fox declined. It was something only he could do. Although he was unable to complete the Marathon of Hope, Fox inspired countless people and remains one of the greatest Canadians our country has ever known.

JULY 12

STUMPY RETURNS TO TORONTO, 1998

The story goes that when Steve Thomas first strolled into the Maple Leafs dressing room after being called up from the team's American Hockey League affiliate, the St. Catharines Saints, in 1984, veteran forward Bill Derlago took one look at the rookie and said he looked like a stump. It didn't take long before Thomas became known as "Stumpy" to his teammates. Even after he was traded to Chicago a few years later, following a 35-goal season with the Leafs, the nickname followed him throughout his career.

But after spending more than a decade with the Blackhawks, the Islanders, and the Devils, Stumpy returned to Toronto. On July 12, 1998, he inked a deal with the Leafs, rejoining the club that had initially signed him as an undrafted free agent 14 years earlier. In his first season back with the Buds, Thomas would clinch the club's first victory at the Air Canada Centre with an overtime goal against the Canadiens, and finish the regular season with 28 goals, his most productive goal-scoring campaign in five years.

JULY 13

ERIK WESTRUM SIGNS WITH MAPLE LEAFS, 2006

E rik Westrum scored the game-winning goal in the shoot-out to clinch the bronze medal for the Americans in the 2004 World Championship. A few years later, he found himself on a different sort of international team. The 2007 American Hockey League All-Star Game was held at Ricoh Coliseum in Toronto and featured two squads: Canada and another known as PlanetUSA, a geographically confounding group made up of the league's top players born outside of Canada.

Westrum, who was captain of the Toronto Marlies after signing a two-year two-way contract with the Maple Leafs on July 13, 2006, found himself on PlanetUSA along with fellow Americans Ryan Callahan and Dustin Byfuglien and Europeans that included Jaroslav Halák and Henrik Lundqvist's twin brother, Joel. In front of the home crowd, Westrum scored a goal and added an assist in a 7–6 victory over the all-Canadian team. After finishing the season as the Marlies' leading scorer, Westrum, who managed two games for the Maple Leafs, his final appearances in the NHL, signed on to play in Switzerland.

JULY 14

COACH QUINN BECOMES GM, 1999

Pat Quinn was going to be doing double duty. On July 14, 1999, the Maple Leafs added to their head coach's plate by naming him general manager. The extra workload wasn't anything new for Quinn. He had served in both roles when he was with the Vancouver Canucks, but it wasn't exactly a standard portfolio in the NHL anymore. Quinn was the first person to wear both hats for the Leafs since Punch Imlach last did it almost two decades earlier, and following the firing of Tampa Bay's Jacques Demers just the day before his appointment, he became the only current executive in the league with both jobs.

The GM position in Toronto had become available in the off-season when team president Ken Dryden, who had been hired two years earlier, relinquished the duties. But when associate general manager Mike Smith abruptly left the club at the end of June following a public feud with Dryden, Quinn was tapped to take the reins. He maintained both roles until the Leafs named John Ferguson Jr. GM in 2003.

JULY 15

LEAFS LAND CUJO, 1998

The Leafs' crease was looking pretty crowded. On July 15, 1998, the club signed goaltender Curtis Joseph to a four-year, $24 million deal. Joseph, who had spent the past three seasons in net for Edmonton, joined Félix Potvin and Glenn Healy between the pipes. Prior to joining Toronto, Cujo appeared to be destined for New York, but when talks broke down, he inked a contract with the blue and white. With Joseph's arrival, the Leafs had three bona fide NHL goaltenders, something head coach Pat Quinn quickly noted was not an ideal situation.

So it all but spelled the end of Potvin's tenure in Toronto. Potvin, who was at his cottage near Montreal when the news broke, had already been linked to the Canadiens in a trade to clear the crease, but those rumours were quickly dispelled. Although many thought Potvin's departure would be imminent, it didn't happen until January 9, 1999, when he, along with a sixth-round pick, was finally traded to the Islanders for former Calder Trophy–winning defenceman Bryan Berard and a sixth-round pick.

JULY 16

JAMIE LUNDMARK SIGNS
WITH LEAFS, 2010

A decade after being selected ninth overall by the New York Rangers in the draft, Jamie Lundmark was still fighting for a spot in the NHL. Following a promising first professional season in the American Hockey League, he spent the next two campaigns with the Rangers. But after opening the 2005–06 campaign on Broadway, Lundmark was dealt to the Coyotes after just three games. Following 38 games in Phoenix, he was sent to the Flames, his third NHL team that season.

After splitting the next year in Calgary and Los Angeles, Lundmark went to Russia before making his way back to the AHL and, eventually, the NHL. Following parts of two seasons with the Flames, he was picked up on waivers by the Leafs in 2010. He dressed for 15 games for Toronto that year and later signed with the club as a free agent on July 16, 2010. Lundmark, however, spent the next season in the American Hockey League before returning to Europe, where he put together a strong career for the next seven years.

JULY 17

LEAFS ACQUIRE JARED McCANN, 2021

ootage of a flying fish made Leafs fans think Jared McCann might be sticking around. No, you read that correctly. A few days after Toronto acquired McCann from Pittsburgh in exchange for Filip Hållander and a seventh-round draft pick on July 17, 2021, just before the deadline for the NHL's expansion draft, a video leaked from Seattle's Pike Place Market that seemed to indicate the league's new team was going to pluck Alexander Kerfoot from the Leafs.

But when the clip went viral, the Kraken threw cold water on the idea by saying the video was just one of several versions the team had completed. So when the draft was held, Leafs fans were left scratching their heads when Seattle took McCann. A few months later, however, we learned it was all part of the plan. In an episode of *The Leaf: Blueprint*, the club's brass revealed their thought process behind acquiring McCann was to expose him, along with Kerfoot, in order to protect a fourth defenceman, Justin Holl, and entice the Kraken to select either forward.

JULY 18

LEAFS TRADE DMITRI YUSHKEVICH, 2002

"The most honest person in the organization is Carlton the Bear because he never says anything" is what a disgruntled Dmitri Yushkevich told the media not long after he was abruptly traded to the Florida Panthers for fellow blueliner Róbert Švehla on July 18, 2002. Yushkevich had plenty of reasons to be upset. After missing the end of the 2001–02 campaign, along with the opportunity to represent Russia at the Winter Olympics, because of a blood clot in his right leg, Yushkevich, who had another year on his contract, was looking forward to getting back in the lineup.

In the off-season he was asked to undergo a physical for what he believed was insurance purposes. But not long after the medical examination, he was dealt to Florida. While the Panthers had shown interest in the Russian defenceman for quite some time, Yushkevich felt the Leafs had not been entirely forthcoming with him. However, he got the last laugh. In his first game back in Toronto, he picked up an assist in a 4–1 Florida victory.

JULY 19

MIKE KOSTKA LEAVES FOR
THE WINDY CITY, 2013

The Maple Leafs got a good look at Mike Kostka. In the 2012 Calder Cup Final, the Toronto Marlies squared off against the Norfolk Admirals, where he patrolled the blue line. It was actually Kostka who put a dagger in Toronto's chances of winning the American Hockey League championship that year. In the third matchup of the series, he scored the only goal of the game, a fluky shot in overtime from centre ice that bounced off the glass and into the back of the net, to the dismay of the home crowd at Ricoh Coliseum.

Kostka's goal gave the Admirals a commanding 3–0 series lead. A couple of days later, Norfolk completed the sweep to earn the first Calder Cup in franchise history. Less than a month after that, Kostka signed with Toronto. But after splitting the season with the Leafs and Marlies, he inked a one-year deal with the Blackhawks on July 19, 2013. In his second game with Chicago, Kostka scored his first NHL goal against who else but the Leafs.

FLOYD SMITH BECOMES HEAD COACH, 1979

loyd Smith didn't mince words at his introductory press conference. On July 20, 1979, the new Maple Leafs head coach said, "If you can't skate, you can't play hockey," a clear indication of his current assessment of the team's abilities. For Smith, strong and aggressive skating was key to winning a Stanley Cup, and that would be one of the areas he would focus on. But he wouldn't even get a full season behind the Toronto bench.

One night in March while heading home from a practice, Smith got into a head-on collision on the Queen Elizabeth Way. Both passengers in the other vehicle, Anna Joint and Donald Osinski, were killed and Smith was taken to hospital with a smashed kneecap. Following the crash, he was charged with criminal negligence causing death and impaired driving. While Smith recovered from his injuries, GM Punch Imlach and Dick Duff took over his coaching duties. A year later, Smith was acquitted on both charges. He stayed on with the Leafs as a scout and eventually served as general manager for a pair of seasons.

JULY 21

KEITH AUCOIN SIGNS WITH LEAFS, 2012

Keith Aucoin was never drafted to the NHL but that didn't stop him from winning a Stanley Cup. After finishing up his collegiate career with Norwich University, Aucoin initially turned pro in 2001. By the 2005–06 campaign, he had become an AHL regular with Carolina's affiliate, the Lowell Lock Monsters. Later that year, in the Stanley Cup Playoffs, Aucoin was added to the Hurricanes roster as a "black ace," serving as a replacement if needed. Although never called into action, he was with the club for the historic run and got to hoist Lord Stanley's mug.

While Aucoin may not have contributed directly to Carolina's title, he played an integral role in helping the Hershey Bears, Washington's farm team, win back-to-back Calder Cup championships a few years later. Following his time in Hershey, he signed a one-year deal with the Leafs on July 21, 2012. But Aucoin never played a game for Toronto. When the Buds reassigned him to the minors before the shortened NHL season started, he was scooped up on waivers by the Islanders.

JULY 22

DAVID BOOTH SIGNS WITH LEAFS, 2014

While Canucks fans would have loved to see the team take down the Bruins in 2011, many felt David Booth went too far the next year. Following his first season in Vancouver, where he scored 16 goals and 29 points in 56 games and then made his first career appearance in the playoffs, Booth came under fire when he posted a video in which he hunted and killed a black bear in Alberta.

Although Booth might have thought he had support for bagging what he called a "Chara-sized bruin," many in and outside the hockey world were critical of the activity, particularly that he had baited the bear, a practice that, while legal in some jurisdictions, is not permitted in provinces such as British Columbia. Following the controversial video, which he later removed, Booth spent two more seasons with the Canucks before signing a one-year, $1.1 million deal with the Leafs on July 22, 2014. In his one and only season in Toronto, the former 30-goal scorer and big-game hunter scored seven goals and 13 points in 59 games.

LEAFS ACQUIRE DAVID CLARKSON'S CONTRACT, 2019

never thought the Leafs would be able to trade David Clarkson. Before the ink had even dried on his massive seven-year, $36.75 million dollar deal, it seemed unlikely. And then, after he finished his first campaign in Toronto with just five goals and 11 points, it seemed an impossibility. But 58 games into his second season, the Leafs managed to move Clarkson to the Blue Jackets for Nathan Horton, who had been placed on long-term injured reserve (LTIR) with a degenerative back condition.

Clarkson played just 23 games for Columbus in 2015–16, and he, too, struggled with back issues that forced him to hang up his skates early. After he was dealt to the Golden Knights as part of the 2017 expansion draft, Clarkson made his way back to Toronto, at least on paper, when he was traded there, along with a fourth-round pick, for goaltender Garret Sparks on July 23, 2019. Although Clarkson's time with the Leafs came full circle, he was never expected to play and was soon placed on LTIR.

JULY 24

PONTUS AND MOLLY ÅBERG
SIGN WITH TORONTO, 2019

For a single dad like Pontus Åberg, the Maple Leafs organization was a perfect fit. Although other NHL teams had shown interest in the soon-to-be 26-year-old Swedish winger, he chose Toronto because if he was called up to the Leafs from the Marlies, the club's American Hockey League affiliate, he wouldn't need to uproot his three-year-old daughter, Molly. So on July 24, 2019, Åberg signed a one-year, two-way contract with Toronto.

Åberg started the campaign with the Marlies but was called up for a few games in December and a pair of contests in February. When he was with the Marlies, he was one of the team's top scorers. Before the campaign was suspended by the Covid-19 pandemic, Åberg had racked up 20 goals and 44 points in 55 games. The only Marlies player with more points was Kenny Agostino. Following his year in Toronto, Åberg opted to spend the next season in the Kontinental Hockey League before returning to the AHL to lace up for the Belleville Senators.

JULY 25

LEAFS HIRE ROGER NEILSON, 1977

One of my favourite Roger Neilson stories took place when he was head coach of the Peterborough Petes of the Ontario Hockey Association. During a game against the Toronto Marlboros on September 26, 1968, Neilson replaced his goaltender with defenceman Ron Stackhouse to stop a penalty shot. As soon as the Toronto player crossed the blue line, Stackhouse skated out from his crease and halted his opponent's advance. Neilson's well-earned reputation for shrewdly exploiting weaknesses in the game's rulebook eventually caught the attention of NHL executives.

Following a season behind the bench of Toronto's minor-league affiliate in Dallas, Neilson was tapped by Leafs owner Harold Ballard on July 25, 1977, to take over the club's bench. Although he was in Toronto for only two seasons, his impact was far reaching. Over the next two decades, Neilson coached at the NHL level, and his innovative thinking changed the game. He continued to employ inventive tactics on the ice and became a pioneer in using video to scout opposing teams and players, earning him the nickname "Captain Video."

JULY 26

LEAFS SIGN TREVOR MOORE, 2016

The Leafs have done well signing undrafted free agents coming out of the University of Denver. In 2009, they inked Tyler Bozak, who would go on to play nearly a decade with the Buds, recording 365 points. Seven years after landing Bozak, on July 26, 2016, Toronto added another Denver alum, Trevor Moore, to its ranks. Although Bozak was still with the team when Moore agreed to terms, the two never crossed paths.

Moore spent his first two seasons with the organization in the AHL with the Marlies, where he won a Calder Cup in 2018. By the time Moore made his NHL debut in 2018, Bozak was on to his next chapter with the St. Louis Blues, where he would win a Stanley Cup later that year. After spending parts of two campaigns with the Leafs, Moore, who was from Thousand Oaks, California, was traded to his hometown Los Angeles Kings, along with a third-round pick and a conditional pick, in exchange for goaltender Jack Campbell and forechecking winger Kyle Clifford.

JULY 27

LEAFS ACQUIRE WAYNE PRIMEAU, 2009

On July 27, 2009, Wayne Primeau was on the ice at his annual hockey school in Hanover, Ontario, where he and his family made their off-season home, when his wife, Leanne, suddenly appeared. When she finally got her husband's attention, she told him that Darryl Sutter, the GM of the Calgary Flames, where Primeau had been playing for the past three seasons, was trying to get a hold of him. When the hulking centre eventually connected with the club, he learned he had been traded to the Leafs, along with a second-round pick, in exchange for Anton Stralman, Colin Stuart, and a seventh-round pick.

Primeau's time in Calgary had been sidelined by injuries, and he suited up for a combined 94 games. But in Toronto, he managed to stay relatively healthy, logging 59 games, the most for him in a single season since he appeared in a career-high 72 contests with the San Jose Sharks in 2003–04. The following year, the Leafs signed Primeau to a professional tryout but ended up releasing him before the 2010–11 season started.

JULY 28

LEAFS SIGN MICHAEL BUNTING, 2021

When the Leafs signed Michael Bunting as a free agent on July 28, 2021, it's safe to say most of the fans did not figure the club was signing a top-line winger. Bunting, who was drafted 117th overall by the Coyotes in 2014, had spent most of his career in the minors up to that point. And since he had appeared in only 26 games combined for Arizona over the past few seasons, he was still technically a rookie by the NHL standard.

Leafs GM Kyle Dubas was familiar with Bunting from his time with the Soo Greyhounds, but even he couldn't have predicted what the winger would do in his first season in Toronto. Finding instant chemistry on the top line with stars Auston Matthews and Mitch Marner, Bunting went on to score 23 goals and 63 points in 79 games and was named a finalist for the Calder Trophy. Although some bemoaned Bunting's consideration as the league's top rookie because he was significantly older than his peers, it was tough to argue against his performance.

JULY 29

LEAFS SIGN MIKE CRAIG, 1994

The Leafs selected Grant Marshall 23rd overall in the 1992 NHL Entry Draft, but the winger would never appear in a game for the blue and white. Just over two years later, after Toronto signed Dallas Stars winger Mike Craig on July 29, 1994, Marshall and Peter Zezel were later sent to the Lone Star State as part of the compensation the Leafs owed the Stars because Craig was classified as what was known as a Group 1 free agent.

Although Craig remained in Toronto for the next few seasons, scoring a modest 50 points in 172 games, he spent the rest of his career in the minor leagues before eventually playing in Europe. Meanwhile, in Dallas, Marshall became a reliable depth contributor. After winning the Stanley Cup with the Stars in 1999, Marshall played an integral part in New Jersey's championship run a few years later. He scored the conference semifinal series–clinching goal in triple overtime and added a pair of goals in the Stanley Cup Final against the Mighty Ducks.

JULY 30

ONDŘEJ KAŠE SIGNS WITH TORONTO, 2021

remember when Ondřej Kaše first came on my radar. I was participating in my father-in-law's annual hockey draft. I had been attending for a few years by then, and as I came to know the group, I recognized that they often mispronounced the names of players. So when it was my next turn to make a selection, I shouted out Kaše exactly how it is written in the NHL's pronunciation guide: KAH-sheh. Everyone looked at me befuddled, so I blurted it out again but sheepishly said it like "case," to which most of them replied, "Oh, Kase."

While my brief lesson on how to properly pronounce the Czech winger's name went over like a lead balloon, Kaše ended up scoring 20 goals that season. Although it worked out well for me in the standings, I didn't think about Kaše again until he signed with the Leafs on July 30, 2021. He played one season in Toronto, recording 27 points in 50 games, before inking a deal with the Hurricanes as a free agent.

NICK RITCHIE SIGNS WITH LEAFS, 2021

really wanted Nick Ritchie to work out in Toronto. On July 31, 2021, the big centre signed a one-year deal with the club. Seven years earlier at the NHL Entry Draft, when the Leafs took William Nylander eighth overall, there were some who lamented that the club didn't use the selection to draft Ritchie, who was taken two spots later by the Anaheim Ducks. But the Leafs had unequivocally made the right choice. By the time Ritchie made it to Toronto, Nylander had racked up 263 points to his 137 with the Ducks and Bruins.

While Nylander was unquestionably more skilled, Ritchie had just recorded 15 goals with the Bruins, five of which came on the man advantage, so there was some merit to the idea of putting a big body like Ritchie in front of the net and hoping the puck went in. The experiment, however, didn't work. After Ritchie scored just two goals in 33 games, he was traded to the Coyotes, along with a conditional pick, for Ryan Dzingel and Ilya Lyubushkin.

AUGUST 1

BUBBLE HOCKEY, 2020

They called it bubble hockey. After the NHL, along with the rest of the world, was upended by the onset of the Covid-19 pandemic in March 2020, the league resumed operations in late July when it proceeded with the post-season. Since the regular season was never completed, the league expanded the pool to 24 teams instead of the usual 16. While the top four teams in each conference squared off in a short round-robin tournament to determine seeding, the remaining 16 teams played a best-of-five series in a qualifying round.

Although these 16 teams were in the post-season, according to the NHL, it was not technically the playoffs just yet. And because the pandemic was still raging, all the games would be played in two hub cities in order to avoid the typical travel schedules. The Western Conference teams played in Edmonton, while the Eastern Conference clubs played at the Scotiabank Arena in Toronto. There would be no fans in the arenas, and the players would be confined to their respective bubbles for the duration of the playoffs.

AUGUST 2

LEAFS DROP FIRST GAME TO BLUE JACKETS, 2020

The Leafs got their first taste of bubble hockey on August 2, 2020, against the Columbus Blue Jackets. Although Toronto played an exhibition game a few days earlier against the Canadiens, this marked the beginning of the team's qualifying round, with a ticket to the Stanley Cup Playoffs on the line. It was not exactly the start the Leafs were hoping for. After two scoreless periods, Cam Atkinson found the back of the net just over a minute into the final frame to put Columbus ahead.

It was all the Blue Jackets would need. Alexander Wennberg sealed the victory with an empty-net goal with 19 seconds remaining. The Leafs could not solve goaltender Joonas Korpisalo, who made 28 saves to record the first-ever post-season shutout for Columbus, a team that had been in the league for nearly two decades. Remember what I've said about milestone moments happening against the Leafs? Well, add this one to the list. A couple of days later, however, Toronto turned the tables, shutting out the Blue Jackets with a 3–0 win to even the series.

AUGUST 3

DOMINIC MOORE CELEBRATES HIS BIRTHDAY, 1980

The fact that we've made it this far into the book without highlighting a birthday is a testament to how much Leafs history there is each and every day. I made a point to not lean on birthdays too much in the Hockey 365 series, but since we're drawing from a shallower pool for this one, we will need to make a few exceptions, so please be sure to wish Dominic Moore a happy birthday.

Moore, who was born in Thornhill, Ontario, on August 3, 1980, had two separate stints with the Buds. Originally drafted 95th overall by the Rangers in 2000, Moore was claimed off waivers by Toronto on January 11, 2008, when he was with the Minnesota Wild. He played parts of two seasons with the blue and white before he was dealt to the Buffalo Sabres. Moore returned to the Leafs for a second tour of duty on July 1, 2017, when he signed a one-year deal. He scored six goals and 12 points in 50 games that season, his final appearances in the NHL.

AUGUST 4

DOUG SHEDDEN AIMS FOR 400, 1988

D oug Shedden thought he would never hit the 400-game mark. Although he was just eight games shy, after suffering a pair of knee injuries over the past few seasons, the milestone looked out of reach. But it wasn't just about hitting a benchmark. If Shedden were to appear in 400 NHL games, he would be eligible to receive a $250,000 pension when he turned 55 years old. After spending much of the 1987–88 campaign with the Baltimore Skipjacks of the American Hockey League, where he recorded 88 points in 80 games, he signed with the Leafs on August 4, 1988.

Although Shedden started the season in the minors with the Newmarket Saints, he was called up to the Leafs for a game in December. But in just his second shift, he tore the ligaments in his left knee. He missed the rest of the year, and doctors told him he may never play again. Shedden, however, was relentless. He returned to the Leafs a couple of years later and secured his pension on November 23, 1990.

AUGUST 5

LEAFS SIGN JOSEPH DUSZAK TO ONE-YEAR CONTRACT, 2021

After leading his team in scoring as a defenceman, Joseph Duszak had caught the eye of Leafs scouts. Originally from Franklin Square, New York, Duszak recorded 47 points in 37 games in his final season with Mercyhurst University in the NCAA. After the team's 2018–19 campaign was finished, Toronto signed the offensively skilled blueliner. He soon turned pro, appearing in two games with the Marlies in the American Hockey League. The next season, Duszak split his time between the Marlies and the Newfoundland Growlers of the ECHL.

Following another stint with the Marlies, Duszak signed a one-year two-way contract extension with the Leafs on August 5, 2021. Although he started the next season in the minors again, he quickly demonstrated he had elevated his game. But after collecting 37 points in the first 37 games, it was reported that Duszak was looking for an opportunity to play elsewhere to get a shot at the NHL. While he finished the year with the Marlies, recording 52 points in 61 contests, he signed with Dinamo Minsk of the KHL in the off-season.

AUGUST 6

NICK ROBERTSON SCORES FIRST NHL GOAL, 2020

Nick Robertson did something that hadn't happened in nearly eight decades. Just before the halfway mark of the second period in the third game of Toronto's qualifying series against the Blue Jackets, on August 6, 2020, he scored to give Toronto a 3–0 lead. Robertson, who was a month away from reaching the legal drinking age in Ontario, became just the third 18-year-old in Maple Leafs history to record a point in the post-season.

The last time it happened was on March 28, 1944, when Ted Kennedy scored Toronto's lone goal against Montreal. It was the last tally the Leafs recorded that post-season. A couple of nights later, the blue and white were shellacked 11–0 and eliminated from the playoffs. Perhaps it was a historical omen. After the rookie's milestone, Toronto allowed four un-answered goals to lose 4–3 in overtime and fall behind 2–1 in the series. It should have been a unique page in the team's history, but it ended up being a story Leafs fans know all too well: blowing third-period leads.

AUGUST 7

LEAFS MOUNT COMEBACK, 2020

won't lie to you, dear reader. I missed one of the most exciting third periods of Leafs hockey. I watched most of the game, but when Columbus went up 3–0 with less than six minutes remaining, I figured I knew how this one would end. While the Leafs had a well-earned reputation of coughing up leads in the third period, they weren't exactly known for multi-goal comebacks in the final frame.

So I let my inner pessimist get the better of me and switched over to *Selling Sunset*, a ridiculous reality TV show about a high-end real estate brokerage in Los Angeles that I knew would take my mind off hockey. But as I was watching Amanza navigate inter-office politics, my phone was buzzing. When I finally had a look, it turned out the Leafs had scored three straight goals to force overtime. Although I missed the comeback, I wasn't going to snooze on OT. The Oppenheim Group could wait. Just over halfway through the extra session, Auston Matthews scored to even the series at two games apiece.

KAREL PILAŘ SIGNS WITH ATLANTA THRASHERS, 2007

K arel Pilař had a promising start to his career with the Leafs. After he was called up from the minors in the 2001–02 campaign, the Czech defenceman played a prominent role on the blue line in the playoffs. But the next season, after a game on the road against the Oilers, Pilař woke up not feeling well. Doctors eventually diagnosed him with viral myopathy, a condition that stiffens the heart. After missing nearly a year of hockey to undergo treatment, he returned to the Leafs in 2003, suiting up for 50 games.

Pilař returned home to play during the 2004–05 lockout, but he was sidelined by his heart condition the next year. After stepping away from hockey again for nearly two years, he appeared in 10 games for the Toronto Marlies down the stretch of the 2006–07 season. Eyeing a return to the NHL, Pilař signed with the Atlanta Thrashers on August 8, 2007. Although a big-league comeback was not in the cards, he remained healthy enough to continue playing in Europe for another decade.

AUGUST 9

BLUE JACKETS ELIMINATE LEAFS, 2020

W hen the NHL regular season was suspended, the Leafs had scored 237 goals. The only team that tickled the twine more times than Toronto was Tampa Bay. But when the Leafs needed their scoring the most, they couldn't find the back of the net. After making an improbable comeback against the Blue Jackets two nights earlier, scoring four unanswered goals to stave off elimination, the Leafs once again could not get any pucks past Joonas Korpisalo, who made 33 saves to record his second shutout of the series.

After Zach Werenski scored just over six minutes into the first period, Liam Foudy notched his first NHL goal to make it 2–0. And then, with 23 seconds remaining in the game, Nick Foligno, whose dad once played for the blue and white, added an empty-netter, putting the final nail in the coffin. While the Blue Jackets punched their ticket to the Stanley Cup Playoffs, the Leafs would need to wait another year for an elusive post-season series victory.

AUGUST 10

LEAFS TRADE JUSTIN POGGE, 2009

After backstopping Canada to a championship at the World Juniors in 2006, Justin Pogge's stock was on the rise. Drafted 90th overall by the Leafs in 2004, Pogge was soon regarded as one of the team's top prospects following his golden performance. But just three years later, he was out of the organization. After recording just one victory in six starts with the Leafs in the 2008–09 season, Pogge was traded to Anaheim on August 10, 2009, for a conditional draft pick in 2011.

While he was unlikely to dress for many games in Toronto as the third-string goaltender, he didn't fare much better with the Ducks. Slotted behind Jonas Hiller and Jean-Sébastien Giguère on the depth chart, Pogge started the next campaign in the ECHL. Although he worked his way back up to the American Hockey League, he never returned to the NHL. Later that season, he was traded to Carolina as part of a deal for Aaron Ward. Pogge played a few more years in the AHL before embarking on a long career between the pipes in Europe.

AUGUST 11

GORD STELLICK RESIGNS AS GM, 1989

J ust over a year into his job as general manager of the Leafs, Gord Stellick had had enough. On August 11, 1989, he tendered his resignation to club owner Harold Ballard. It was hardly a surprise. The two had been quarrelling throughout the season, but Stellick believed they reached the point of no return when he fired head coach John Brophy against Ballard's wishes.

Even before Stellick quit, the crotchety owner, who never shied away from using the newspapers to take shots at his adversaries, said that his GM's days were numbered and that he already had a successor waiting in the wings. When Stellick spoke with the media in the wake of his departure, he addressed his relationship with Ballard and said, "I thought public floggings were illegal in Canada." Although Stellick tried to stick it out, he realized it was best for him and the club to step aside. He wasn't out of work for long, however. A few days later, he was hired by the New York Rangers as an assistant general manager.

LEAFS SIGN MARIÁN ŠŤASTNÝ, 1985

When Peter and Anton Šťastný were preparing to defect from behind the Iron Curtain, they thought it was too dangerous to have their older brother, Marián, join them. Marián would be leaving behind a family, and they believed the risk was just too great. So when Peter and Anton made their daring escape while playing for the Czechoslovakian team in Innsbruck, Austria, in August 1980, Marián stayed behind.

But a year later, he defected and reunited with his younger brothers on the Quebec Nordiques, where they eventually all played together on a line. Marián would go on to play 252 games for the Nordiques, scoring 98 goals and 241 points. After Quebec granted him an unconditional release in the 1985 off-season, he signed with the Maple Leafs on August 12. While Marián struggled in his final season with the Nordiques, tallying just seven goals and 21 points, he rebounded with the Leafs, collecting 23 goals and 53 points in what would be his only campaign with the blue and white and his last in the NHL.

PANTHERS SIGN JUMBO JOE, 2021

After nearly two decades in the NHL, Joe Thornton was still chasing a Stanley Cup. Although the former Hart Trophy winner had come close with the San Jose Sharks in 2016, coming up two wins short to the Pittsburgh Penguins, it still eluded him. While Thornton still had the same passion for the game that he did when he made his NHL debut as a teenager, time was not on his side. Looking to add a championship to his collection before hanging up his skates, the 41-year-old signed a one-year contract with the Leafs in 2020.

In 44 regular-season games with the Buds, Thornton recorded 20 points, but his dream of hoisting Lord Stanley's mug was dashed in a heartbreaking seven-game series against the Montreal Canadiens. Thornton, however, wasn't ready to throw in the towel just yet. On August 13, 2021, he signed a one-year contract with the Florida Panthers. But again, it wasn't meant to be. While a Cup escaped Thornton's grasp, he is destined for the Hall of Fame.

AUGUST 14

BIG NICKEL HOSTS GEORGE ARMSTRONG'S HOMECOMING, 2016

George Armstrong's banner was coming home. As part of the celebrations for the Maple Leafs' centennial anniversary, all of the 18 tapestries for the club's honoured players were being returned to their hometowns before new ones were unveiled during the milestone 2016–17 season. On August 14, 2016, Armstrong's banner arrived in Sudbury. The ceremony, which I was lucky enough to attend, took place at Dynamic Earth, the site of the Big Nickel, a giant replica of the Canadian five-cent piece. Standing more than nine metres tall and tipping the scales at nearly 30,000 pounds, it's the largest coin in the world and was the perfect backdrop to honour Armstrong, a larger-than-life figure who captained the Leafs to their last, as of this writing, Stanley Cup in 1967.

Following the ceremony, Armstrong's banner was taken to Garson Arena, where it proudly hangs to this day. No matter how many times I've been there to play hockey or just go for a skate with my family, I can't help but look up and smile as Armstrong oversees the ice.

AUGUST 15

GEORGE ARMSTRONG DISMISSED
AS HEAD COACH, 1989

I almost felt bad putting a story about George Armstrong getting fired as head coach of the Maple Leafs right after one about his banner returning home, but the truth is, he never wanted the job in the first place. In fact, when Armstrong was dismissed on August 15, 1989, he was actually relieved. It was no secret that he didn't want to be a bench boss. When head coach John Brophy was fired in December, Armstrong, who was serving as an assistant GM and scout, was asked to step into the breach.

He dutifully agreed even though, by his own admission, he had no interest in coaching. With Armstrong at the helm, the Leafs went 17-26-4 and missed the playoffs. While the former Leafs captain did the best he could under the circumstances, he felt the team was better off with someone else behind the bench and was quite happy to return to his role as scout. Following Armstrong's sacking, interim GM Floyd Smith, who was appointed after Stellick's resignation, named Doug Carpenter coach.

AUGUST 16

LEAFS SIGN DAVE MANSON, 2000

Not long into his NHL career, Dave Manson got into a fight with Sergio Momesso. During the brawl, Manson caught a punch to the throat, which permanently damaged his vocal cords. He hoped to get the injury repaired after he eventually hung up his skates, but until then he was forced to speak softly while patrolling the blue line. But make no mistake, while Manson may have had to settle for talking in a raspy whisper, the crushing defenceman was one of the league's toughest customers.

Originally drafted 11th overall by the Chicago Black Hawks in 1985, Manson quickly earned a reputation for bone-crunching hits and never being afraid to drop the gloves. In his third season with the Black Hawks, he racked up 352 penalty minutes, the third most in the league that year. But as Manson became more established, he spent less time in the penalty box and more on the ice. When he signed a two-year deal with the Leafs on August 16, 2000, it wasn't long before he became one of team's most trusted and reliable defencemen.

AUGUST 17

SCOTT SABOURIN SIGNS WITH THE SENATORS, 2021

Scott Sabourin played only one game with the Maple Leafs, but he will always be linked to the team by an incident that happened to him as a member of the Ottawa Senators. During a pre-season game in 2019, the 27-year-old Sabourin, who had spent the last seven seasons in the minors and had yet to dress for a regular-season NHL matchup, started jawing at Auston Matthews, who was coming off his third straight 30-goal campaign.

Instead of chirping back, Matthews simply looked over both of Sabourin's shoulders as if he were trying to get a better look at his nameplate, implying he had no idea who his opponent was. The moment quickly went viral. Although some criticized Matthews as being disrespectful, it was all part of the game. Besides, Sabourin got the last laugh. Two weeks later, in his NHL debut, he scored his first career goal against the Leafs. And the next year, the two were briefly teammates until Sabourin signed a one-year deal to return to the Senators on August 17, 2021.

AUGUST 18

KILLER GETS THE C, 1994

Wendel Clark was the heart and soul of the Maple Leafs and one of the franchise's most beloved captains. After Clark was traded to the Quebec Nordiques in the off-season, the club had a significant leadership position to fill. But if anybody was up to the challenge, it was Doug Gilmour. Affectionately known as "Killer," Gilmour endeared himself to Toronto fans, when he arrived two years earlier, with how he played the game. Despite being one of the league's most skilled players, he approached every shift as though it may be his last.

Although Gilmour was unquestionably Toronto's best player, his lunch-pail work ethic also made him a fan favourite. Who better to succeed Clark than Killer? And so, on August 18, 1994, during a luncheon at the Hockey Hall of Fame in Toronto, Gilmour was presented with his captain's sweater while some of the greatest leaders in Maple Leafs history proudly looked on. Gilmour wore the C with distinction for three seasons until he was traded to New Jersey in 1997.

AUGUST 19

BIG SAVE DAVE MAKES HIS WORLD DEBUT, 1992

He was known as "Big Save Dave," and he was born in Jihlava, Czechoslovakia (now the Czech Republic), on August 19, 1992. Although David Rittich went undrafted to the NHL, the goaltender was eventually signed by the Calgary Flames in 2016. After spending the season with Calgary's AHL affiliate, the Stockton Heat, Rittich made another memorable debut down the stretch, relieving Brian Elliott in the third period of the Flames' final game of the year.

Rittich started the next year in the minors but was called up to Calgary in November and suited up for 21 games that season. For the next three years, he was a Flames regular, sharing the crease with Mike Smith. But with his contract set to expire at the end of the 2020–21 season, Calgary dealt the Czech goalie to the Maple Leafs for a third-round draft pick on April 11, 2021. Rittich's time with the Buds, however, was fleeting. He appeared in four games and earned one victory. Following his brief stint in Toronto, Rittich signed with Nashville.

LEAFS ACQUIRE SYLVAIN LEFEBVRE, 1992

Following Ric Nattress's brief stint with the Leafs in 1991–92, an arbitrator determined the defenceman's salary was below the league average for that season. This determination classified Nattress as a Group 5 free agent. Although it is still in the current NHL collective bargaining agreement, it is a bit of a relic in today's game. But back then, a Group 5 classification applied to players who had 10 years of NHL experience but earned a salary below league average, which made them eligible to become an unrestricted free agent one time in their careers.

For Toronto, this meant Nattress could sign anywhere without the team receiving compensation in return. After he invoked the clause and inked a deal with the Flyers, the Leafs needed to shore up their back end. So on August 20, 1992, they acquired Sylvain Lefebvre from Montreal for a third-round pick. Lefebvre patrolled the Toronto blue line for two seasons until he was traded to the Quebec Nordiques as part of the deal for Mats Sundin.

AUGUST 21

LEAFS TRADE FOR BRAD MAXWELL, 1985

Legend has it that Brad Maxwell was traded to Minnesota because Phil Esposito, general manager of the New York Rangers, lost a card game to his colleague Lou Nanne, GM of the North Stars. The two executives had supposedly been gambling on players and when Esposito came up short, he forfeited Maxwell, whom he had only recently acquired before the 1987 deadline. For Maxwell, it was a return to where his professional hockey career started nearly a decade earlier and his last NHL stop.

But before that final trade, the defenceman had been part of another deal, two years earlier, that was not determined by the shuffle of a deck, at least that we know of. On August 21, 1985, Maxwell, who had been shipped to the Quebec Nordiques earlier that year from Minnesota, was dealt to the Leafs for John Anderson, who had recorded four straight 30-goal seasons playing with Rick Vaive and Bill Derlago. Maxwell patrolled the Toronto blue line for one season before making his way back to the North Stars in that card game.

LEAFS SIGN JHONAS ENROTH, 2016

Although Jhonas Enroth's time with the Leafs didn't work out the way he had hoped, the team would always have a place in his heart. Six years before signing a one-year deal with Toronto on August 22, 2016, the Swedish goaltender, as a member of the Buffalo Sabres, recorded his very first NHL victory against the Leafs. Enroth stopped 23 shots in regulation and all but one in the shootout to secure a 3–2 win. As the saying goes, you never forget your first.

Enroth spent the next four seasons in the Buffalo crease and then made stops in Dallas and Los Angeles before signing on with Toronto to back up Frederik Andersen. While Enroth got his first triumph against the Buds, he didn't have the same luck wearing the uniform. He went winless in six appearances for the Leafs and was then waived just three months into the season. After playing three games for the Marlies in the American Hockey League, Enroth was traded to Anaheim for a seventh-round draft pick.

AUGUST 23

LEAFS ADD HAYLEY WICKENHEISER, 2018

When the Leafs first added Hayley Wickenheiser to the front office, she was already overqualified. One of the most decorated players in women's hockey history, Wickenheiser became the assistant director of player development on August 23, 2018. At the time, she was still going to medical school at the University of Calgary. While working toward her degree, Wickenheiser would oversee prospects the club had developing in the Western Hockey League.

Wickenheiser was a quick study. Three years later, not only was she Dr. Wickenheiser and an honoured member of the Hockey Hall of Fame, but she was also elevated to senior director of player development. Working with her former Canadian Olympic teammate Danielle Goyette, who had been hired as a director, Dr. Wickenheiser served in the role for a year until she earned another promotion. On July 5, 2022, she was named assistant general manager, becoming just the fourth woman in league history to hold the portfolio. Hopefully, it won't be too long before Dr. Wickenheiser adds NHL GM to her already sterling resume.

LEAFS ACQUIRE JOHNNY POHL, 2005

B efore he helped lead the Minnesota Golden Gophers to an NCAA title in 2002, Johnny Pohl was Mr. Hockey. Four years earlier, Pohl, who racked up 107 points in 28 games in his final season with his high school team the Red Wing Wingers, was given the Mr. Hockey Award, bestowed annually to the most outstanding senior high school boy's hockey player in Minnesota. Following his standout campaign, Pohl was drafted 255th overall by the St. Louis Blues.

After graduating from the University of Minnesota with a championship under his belt, Pohl turned pro and spent the next three seasons in the minors until he was traded to the Leafs on August 24, 2005, for future considerations. Although he started his tenure in Toronto with the Marlies, he was called up in December and scored his first career NHL goal on New Year's Eve against the Devils. Pohl would play 114 games with the Leafs over the next few years. After hanging up his skates in 2010, he went back to school to become a teacher.

AUGUST 25

LEAFS TRADE KASPERI KAPANEN, 2020

Kasperi Kapanen was drafted 22nd overall by Pittsburgh in 2014, but before he ever appeared in a Penguins uniform, he was on the move. Barely a year later, Kapanen, along with Nick Spaling, Scott Harrington, and a pair of draft picks, was traded to the Leafs in exchange for Phil Kessel, Tyler Biggs, Tim Erixon, and a second-round pick. While Kessel would go on to win back-to-back Stanley Cups in Pittsburgh, including narrowly missing out on the Conn Smythe Trophy in 2016, Kapanen spent the next few years with the Marlies in the AHL until he earned a regular spot with the Leafs in the 2018–19 season.

With William Nylander out to start that campaign because of a contract dispute, Kapanen got the opportunity to play on the top line alongside superstar Auston Matthews. After finishing the season with 20 goals in 78 games, Kapanen signed a three-year, $9.6 million extension in the off-season. But just one year into his new deal, he was traded back to Pittsburgh as part of a six-player deal on August 25, 2020.

AUGUST 26

LEAFS SIGN TREVOR KIDD, 2002

When Curtis Joseph broke a bone in his hand toward the end of the 2001–02 season, the Leafs had inquired about Trevor Kidd. Although the team ended up acquiring Tom Barrasso instead, their interest in Kidd did not wane. After signing Ed Belfour in the off-season to replace Joseph, who left in free agency, Toronto was still looking for a reputable backup. Meanwhile, Kidd, who had been recently bought out by the Panthers, was in search of a new gig.

Although Kidd still had a year remaining on his contract in Florida, he wanted out. With Roberto Luongo beginning to play the lion's share of the Panthers' games, the opportunities for Kidd to tend the twine would be few and far between. So on August 26, 2002, following his buyout, Kidd inked a multi-year contract with the Leafs. In his first season in Toronto, he made 19 starts and recorded six victories. He played one more campaign with the Leafs, his final in the NHL, before finishing his career in Germany with the Hannover Scorpions.

AUGUST 27

LEAFS ACQUIRE MATT LASHOFF, 2010

I f hockey didn't work out for Matt Lashoff, he might have made a career in music. When the defenceman first left home to pursue his hockey dreams, he also began honing his skills as a songwriter. While he developed on the ice, his guitar was never far away. After Lashoff was drafted 22nd overall by Boston in 2005, he turned pro the following year. Although he spent most of that campaign in the minors, he played 12 games for the Bruins that season.

But over the next four years, Lashoff, who was traded to Tampa Bay in 2009, struggled to find a regular spot in the big leagues. While his future in the NHL was uncertain, music was still an important part of his life. Before he was traded to Toronto from Tampa Bay on August 27, 2010, he spent the off-season recording his debut album, *Living on Heart*. While Lashoff played only 11 games for the Leafs, his final NHL appearances, he continued playing pro for another six years while still pursuing his passion for music.

AUGUST 28

LEAFS SIGN CLARKE MACARTHUR, 2010

Atlanta's loss turned out to be Toronto's gain. Following the 2009–10 season, restricted free agent Clarke MacArthur, who was coming off a 35-point campaign split between the Buffalo Sabres and the Thrashers, filed for salary arbitration. After the hearing, MacArthur was awarded a one-year, $2.4 million contract, a considerable raise from what he'd earned the previous season. But Atlanta chose to walk away from the arbitrator's decision, making MacArthur an unrestricted free agent.

Just over a month later, on August 28, 2010, he inked a one-year deal with the Leafs. In his first season in Toronto, playing on a line with Mikhail Grabovski and Nikolay Kulemin, MacArthur recorded 21 goals and 62 points, both career highs, in 82 games. In the off-season, he elected once again to go to salary arbitration, for the third time in his career, but before the hearing took place, he agreed to a two-year, $6.5 million deal with the Leafs. MacArthur reached the 20-goal mark again the next season, but following the lockout-shortened campaign in 2012–13, he signed with the provincial rival Senators.

AUGUST 29

LEAFS NAME JOHN
FERGUSON JR. GM, 2003

This is one chapter that many Leafs fans would still like to forget. On August 29, 2003, Toronto named John Ferguson Jr. general manager. Although he had a strong hockey pedigree — his father, John Sr., had been a hard-nosed winger for the Montreal Canadiens who, after his playing career, went on to serve as an NHL executive — many felt John Jr. was too inexperienced. Although he had served as vice president and director of hockey operations for the St. Louis Blues, he had big shoes to fill in Toronto.

Ferguson took over the GM duties from Pat Quinn, who remained with the club as head coach. Although the Leafs advanced to the conference semifinals in Ferguson's first season, it proved to be the only bright spot in his tenure. Following the 2004–05 NHL lockout, the club missed the playoffs for the next two years. While Ferguson is notoriously remembered for trading Tuukka Rask to the Boston Bruins, he also dismissed Quinn, who was beloved and missed the playoffs only once in his seven seasons behind the Toronto bench.

AUGUST 30

LEAFS ACQUIRE DMITRI YUSHKEVICH, 1995

When Dmitri Yushkevich was asked why the Flyers had traded him, his reply was simple: "Because I wanted a good contract and big money." That might have been part of the reason for the Russian blueliner's exodus to Toronto on August 30, 1995, but it wasn't the whole story. The truth was that things had been rocky between Yushkevich and the Flyers for a while. During the 1993–94 campaign, he was benched for several games by head coach Terry Murray, and the following year, when the lockout-shortened schedule began in January, Yushkevich, much to the dismay of the team's brass, showed up to camp overweight and out of shape.

While Yushkevich also divulged he had been happy at times in Philadelphia, he was pleased to be going to a team that wanted him. Over the next few seasons, he became a top-pairing defenceman with the Leafs and was an integral part of a few deep playoff runs. Although Yushkevich's tenure in Toronto started off with a bang, his departure, covered in the last chapter, was a bust.

AUGUST 31

LEAFS SIGN TONY SALMELAINEN, 2007

Less than two months after signing a contract with the Leafs, Tony Salmelainen's time with the organization came to a sudden halt. After inking a one-year two-way contract with the club on August 31, 2007, Salmelainen, who played 57 games with the Chicago Blackhawks the previous year but was traded to Montreal in the off-season before free agency opened, began the season with the Marlies in the American Hockey League. But after just two games in the minors, he abruptly left the team and returned home to Finland.

Citing personal reasons for his departure, Salmelainen was soon suspended by the Leafs for violating the terms of his contract. However, he had no intention of returning to North America. He quickly found another gig and played the rest of the campaign with Lokomotiv Yaroslavl of the Russian Superleague. Following his stint in Russia, Salmelainen moved to Switzerland, where he played for the next five seasons. In 2013, he returned to Finland, signing with HIFK of the Liiga, where his professional hockey career had begun nearly two decades earlier.

SEPTEMBER 1

SALMING KICKS OFF CANADA CUP, 1981

By the time the Canada Cup was hosted in 1981, Börje Salming had already been in the league for nearly a decade, defying the misguided "chicken Swede" narrative and demonstrating he was one of the toughest players in the game. But when one of the first games of the tournament was held on September 1, Team USA captain Robbie Ftorek experienced just how rough Salming could be. Although the Americans took a 2–0 lead in the first period, Sweden outshot them and demonstrated their determination to pry the puck loose from the corners the entire game.

While Sweden ended up losing 3–1, Salming sent a message at the end of the game. After he and Ftorek exchanged pleasantries, the Leafs defenceman angrily slammed his stick into the back of Ftorek's head. Players streamed off of both benches, but the officials were able to keep the situation from escalating further. It would be the only time the two teams would meet in the tournament. Although the Americans made it to the semifinals, Sweden failed to advance beyond the round-robin stage.

SEPTEMBER 2

MIKE VAN RYN BECOMES A LEAF, 2008

Mike Van Ryn knew for a while he was coming to Toronto. The only thing that stopped the future Leafs blueliner from taking up new residence was that the deal was not official. A trade had been in the works for weeks but because Bryan McCabe, who was going the other way to Florida, was due to receive a $2 million bonus on September 1, the Panthers preferred to wait. And so, a day after McCabe was paid out, on September 2, 2008, the Leafs traded him, along with a fourth-round pick, to Florida for Van Ryn.

While Van Ryn hoped to shake off his injury woes with the Panthers — he appeared in only 20 games the previous campaign because of a wrist injury — he didn't fare much better in Toronto. Following a solid start, he missed five weeks with a concussion and a broken bone in his hand and suited up for just 27 games that season. The next year, after knee surgery in October, Van Ryn sat out the entire campaign before retiring in July 2010.

SEPTEMBER 3

OLCZYK AND SECORD DEALT
TO TORONTO, 1987

Blackhawks general manager Bob Pulford said it was the most difficult trade he ever had to make. On September 3, 1987, he sent Eddie Olczyk, along with Al Secord, to the Leafs for Rick Vaive, Steve Thomas, and Bob McGill. A hometown kid, Olczyk, who grew up in the suburbs of the Windy City, had been drafted third overall by Chicago a few years earlier. Following a solid rookie season in which he recorded 20 goals and 50 points, Olczyk followed that up with a 79-point campaign that included 29 tallies.

But after his production dropped off in his third season, the team decided to move on. It did not take long for Olczyk to make the Blackhawks regret the deal. In his first season in Toronto, he racked up 42 goals. The next year, he scored 90 points, a career high. But after another solid year with the Leafs, Olczyk was traded again early in the 1990–91 campaign, this time to Winnipeg along with Mark Osborne, for Dave Ellett and Paul Fenton.

SEPTEMBER 4

SUMMIT SERIES SHIFTS TO MAPLE LEAF GARDENS, 1972

Following a deflating 7–3 defeat to the Soviets in the opening game of the Summit Series at the Forum in Montreal, Canada looked to avenge the loss when the series moved to Maple Leaf Gardens on September 4, 1972. While it was just the first matchup in an eight-game series that would eventually shift to Moscow, it felt more devastating than a typical loss. For many Canadians, it shattered the myth of the country's unquestioned superiority in hockey and upended their belief in everything they held dear.

But by the second game, some of that faith had been restored. Canada put on a much better performance, grinding down the free-wheeling Russians with tight checking. Following a scoreless first period, Phil Esposito found the back of the net to give the Canadians the lead. The final frame was punctuated by four goals, including one by former Leaf Frank Mahovlich, as Canada secured a 4–1 victory. While it evened up the series, it would prove to be the only win the Canadians would get on home soil.

SEPTEMBER 5

MATS SUNDIN MEETS WITH
THE LEAFS, 2008

t looked as though Mats Sundin might be coming back to the Leafs for a final curtain call. After infamously refusing to waive his no-trade clause leading up to the 2008 trade deadline despite the club being well outside the playoff picture, Sundin became a free agent in the off-season when his deal expired. While he continued to explore his options, Sundin wasn't even sure if he would be returning to the NHL.

But on September 5, 2008, the Swedish star, along with his agents, J.P. Barry and Claes Elefalk, met with Leafs GM Cliff Fletcher and his assistant, Joe Nieuwendyk. Although many Leafs fans had wanted Sundin to waive his no-trade clause to allow the club to recoup some assets from a team looking to make a post-season run, they still welcomed a reunion with the long-time captain. But it wasn't meant to be. When he hadn't signed with a club before the start of the regular season, he returned home to Sweden. Finally, a few months later, he signed a one-year deal with Vancouver.

SEPTEMBER 6

JAKE GARDINER SIGNS WITH CANES, 2019

Jake Gardiner was as good as gone. After eight seasons on the Leafs blue line, which included a 52-point campaign, the defenceman was due for a new contract. No matter what salary cap gymnastics the Leafs could do, given what Gardiner would fetch on the open market, there was no way the club would be able to retain his services. It was just as well for many Leafs fans. Gardiner could pile up the points, but he could be a frustrating player.

While every player makes mistakes, Gardiner's blunders often seemed to come at the worst possible moment. In Toronto's seventh game against the Bruins in the 2019 playoffs, he coughed up the puck behind the Leafs' net, which led to Boston scoring a goal with just over two minutes remaining in the first period to take a 2–0 lead. The Leafs went on to lose 5–1, the team's second straight Game 7 loss to the Bruins. Gardiner officially found his new home on September 6, 2019, when he signed a four-year, $16.2 million contract with Carolina.

SEPTEMBER 7

LEAFS FANS SALUTE SALMING, 1976

Börje Salming may have been on the opposing team, but the Leafs faithful gave him a warm welcome just the same. When Sweden squared off against Canada on September 7, 1976, as part of the round-robin tournament for the Canada Cup, Salming received a roaring standing ovation from the home crowd at Maple Leaf Gardens. The moment was something that stayed with him for the rest of his life. "I'll never forget our game in Toronto," he said later. "The fans gave me a standing ovation during the introductions. I was representing my country and Canadian fans gave me a standing ovation. Sometimes hockey has no country."

In the three years that Salming had been patrolling the blue line for the Leafs, he had endeared himself to the fans for his skill and toughness, so even though he was wearing the wrong colours that night, he was still a Leaf. But it was Salming's teammates Darryl Sittler and Lanny McDonald who stole the show. Their line, which included Bob Gainey, combined for two goals in a 4–0 victory.

SEPTEMBER 8

LEAFS ADD DAVE SEMENKO, 1987

The Leafs were adding a heavyweight to their lineup. On September 8, 1987, the team acquired Dave Semenko from the Hartford Whalers in exchange for Bill Root. Semenko, who threw some of the toughest punches in the league, was known for serving as Wayne Gretzky's bodyguard during his tenure with the Oilers. Semenko's fighting prowess was such that he once had a charity boxing match against the legendary Muhammad Ali in Edmonton.

But by the time Semenko made his way to Toronto, his passion for the sport had waned. Although he was playing in every Leafs game, he was no longer being relied upon the way he had been in his glory days with the Oilers. After travelling with the team to Vancouver for a game in late March 1988, Semenko took off and returned to his home in Edmonton. When he was eventually reached for comment, he said he had simply had enough. After hanging up his skates, Semenko, who was born and raised in Winnipeg, was inducted into the Manitoba Hockey Hall of Fame.

SEPTEMBER 9

LEAFS SIGN JOE NIEUWENDYK, 2003

t was John Ferguson Jr.'s first major move as GM of the Leafs. On September 9, 2003, he signed Joe Nieuwendyk to a one-year deal. Nieuwendyk, who turned 37 the day after inking his deal with the Leafs, was just coming off his third Stanley Cup with the New Jersey Devils and was highly regarded for his play on both sides of the puck. During his time with the Flames, he recorded back-to-back 51-goal seasons and had reached the 30-goal mark six more times during his time in Calgary and later with Dallas.

Slotting in behind Mats Sundin in Toronto, Nieuwendyk centred a line with Alexei Ponikarovsky and Nik Antropov that became known as "the Skyline" because each member of the trio towered well above six feet. Nieuwendyk scored 22 goals in the regular season and added six more in the playoffs, including the series winner against Ottawa. The Leafs re-signed him for the 2004–05 campaign but when that was wiped out by the lockout, Nieuwendyk returned to the NHL with Florida for his final stop.

SEPTEMBER 10

FRANK EDDOLLS'S ON-ICE
FUTURE UNCERTAIN, 1943

Frank Eddolls's hockey career was in jeopardy. After injuring his knee during his junior hockey days in Verdun, the Maple Leafs prospect, who was currently playing in the Quebec Senior Hockey League as a member of the Royal Canadian Air Force, aggravated his nagging joint while playing lacrosse in the summer. The injury was significant enough that, on September 10, 1943, newspapers reported he would need surgery and it was uncertain whether he would ever be able to play hockey again. But while Eddolls was recuperating from his operation, the Leafs traded his rights to Montreal for Ted Kennedy.

As we covered a few chapters back, the story goes that Frank Selke, who was acting manager for the Leafs while Conn Smythe served in the Second World War, made the swap without approval from his owner. While Smythe was initially upset over the deal, Kennedy quickly became one of his favourite players. Meanwhile, Eddolls made a full recovery, winning a Stanley Cup with the Canadiens in 1946 and later captaining the New York Rangers.

SEPTEMBER 11

FRENCH'S CHALLENGE IS
CONTESTED, 1993

You could say this game was a cut above the mustard. On September 11, 1993, the Leafs and Rangers squared off at Wembley Arena in London, England, in what was billed as the French's Challenge, a series of exhibition games sponsored by the company best known for its condiments. It was the NHL's second attempt at a British invasion. After starting the 1992–93 campaign with a pair of contests between the Canadiens and Blackhawks, the league returned again to grow the game across the pond.

After the Leafs dropped the first matchup 5–2, Wendel Clark and Mike Krushelnyski were tasked with putting on hockey demonstrations in bustling Covent Garden, but newspapers reported that few turned out for those showcases. While Toronto hoped to head home with a series split, they were defeated 3–1 the next day in the last game. Leafs fans, however, were spared from watching their team get its London broiled. Because of a scheduling conflict with coverage of soccer and the Italian Grand Prix on TSN, the games were not broadcast in Canada.

SEPTEMBER 12

HARRY WATSON CALLED TO THE HALL, 1994

There was a time when the Hockey Hall of Fame had a unique category for veteran players. Established in 1988, it was meant to recognize players who had been out of the game for years and missed out on the regular induction process. Rather than competing with contemporary players on the ballot, this slot allowed the Hall of Fame to induct notable players who might have been overlooked in the past.

On September 12, 1994, two players got the nod in this category: Harry Watson and Lionel Conacher. Watson spent 14 years in the NHL, winning four Stanley Cups with the Leafs, before retiring in 1958. Conacher, whose brother Charlie was part of the Leafs' first championship in 1932, was one of the best athletes in Canadian history but passed away four decades earlier. Known as "the Big Train," Lionel Conacher excelled on both the ice and the gridiron and is just one of three players to win the Stanley Cup and the Grey Cup. Before the Hall of Fame eliminated the veterans category in 2000, Conacher's younger brother, Roy, was the last player to be honoured that way.

SEPTEMBER 13

LEAFS ACQUIRE GARRY MONAHAN, 1978

Garry Monahan was the first player ever drafted to the NHL. When the league introduced the amateur draft in 1963, Monahan was selected first overall by the Montreal Canadiens. After spending the next few years with the Peterborough Petes of the Ontario Hockey Association, Monahan made his NHL debut in 1967, but he had trouble staying on a deep Canadiens roster. A couple of years later, he was sent to the Detroit Red Wings as part of a trade for Pete Mahovlich, who would win four Stanley Cups in Montreal.

But after struggling in the Motor City, Monahan was dealt again, this time to the Kings, before making his way to the Leafs as part of another trade. In Toronto, however, Monahan found his footing and established himself as an NHL regular. Following four seasons in the blue and white, he was dealt to Vancouver but was eventually traded back to Toronto on September 13, 1978, for cash. After one final campaign with the Leafs, Monahan moved to Tokyo and played three years in the Japan Ice Hockey League.

SEPTEMBER 14

LEAFS OPEN TRAINING CAMP, 2018

When the Leafs opened their training camp in Niagara Falls, Ontario, on September 14, 2018, they made sure the players had the opportunity to play tourist. Following the first set of on-ice sessions and scrimmages, the club headed to the falls for a voyage on the *Maid of the Mist*. As the name of the ship implies, sightseers get a little wet on the tour, so the club made sure everyone was outfitted in special Leafs ponchos.

While it was a fun ride, particularly for Mitch Marner, who was featured on Twitter smiling from ear to ear with his slicker cinched tightly beneath his chin, there was a notable absence on the boat. William Nylander, a restricted free agent who was coming off his second straight 61-point campaign, had not accompanied the team to Niagara Falls because he was in the middle of a contract dispute. As the saga unfolded, Nylander would miss training camp, the entire pre-season, and nearly a third of the regular season before signing a six-year contract extension at the eleventh hour on December 1, 2018.

SEPTEMBER 15

DARRYL SITTLER WINS THE CANADA CUP, 1976

Just over halfway through overtime in the second game of the Canada Cup Final, on September 15, 1976, Darryl Sittler caught a pass from linemate Marcel Dionne just before centre ice. As Sittler skated into the Czechoslovakian zone, goaltender Vladimír Dzurilla came way out of his net to challenge the Leafs captain. With a golden opportunity on his stick, Sittler moved to his left to evade the Czech netminder and put the puck into the wide-open net to clinch the inaugural championship for Canada.

While the win netted Sittler and his teammates $5,000 each for their efforts, he didn't care about the money. "What will remain with me forever is playing with the greater players ever assembled for the greatest country in the world," he later told reporters. As time passed, it meant even more to Sittler. Although he would play nearly another decade in the NHL, Sittler never got the chance to hoist the Stanley Cup. But for him, being on that Canada Cup team and leading his country to victory was the highlight in a Hall of Fame career.

SEPTEMBER 16

SALMING GETS THE CALL, 1996

The King was going to the Hall. On September 16, 1996, Börje Salming, who earned the royal sobriquet from his teammates for his exceptional talent, got the call that he would be inducted into the Hockey Hall of Fame. Regarded as one of the best defencemen of his era, it was an easy decision for the selection committee, which voted unanimously to send Salming to hockey's pantheon of greatness.

Among the other players considered on the ballot that day were goaltender Roger Crozier, who won the Conn Smythe in a losing effort in 1966 with Detroit; netminder Rogie Vachon, winner of the Vezina in 1968; and Doug Wilson, who patrolled the Chicago blue line for more than a decade and earned the Norris in 1982, but the King reigned above them all. While those players did not make the cut, Salming would be joined by Bobby Bauer in the veteran players category; former Islanders bench boss Al Arbour, who was inducted as a builder; and legendary broadcaster Bob Cole, who received the Foster Hewitt Memorial Award.

SEPTEMBER 17

LEAFS ACQUIRE MICHAEL GRABNER, 2015

As the Leafs approached the start of the 2015–16 season, the team was sitting just below the 50-contract limit. Looking to find some manoeuverability, the club made a move with the New York Islanders on September 17, 2015, sending Taylor Beck, Carter Verhaeghe, Matt Finn, Tom Nilsson, and Christopher Gibson to Long Island for Michael Grabner. By dealing a handful of minor-league players, Toronto not only found room on paper but also gained a former 30-goal scorer in Grabner, although Verhaeghe would become a 40-goal scorer for the Florida Panthers.

Originally drafted 14th overall by the Canucks in 2006, Grabner was traded to New York a few years later, where he recorded back-to-back 20-goal seasons. An injury-plagued campaign in 2014–15 limited him to just 34 games, and the Leafs hoped he could regain his scoring touch. But the puck simply didn't go his way in Toronto. Grabner scored just nine goals in 80 contests, but he would go on to record consecutive 20-goal seasons with the Rangers after leaving via free agency in 2016.

SEPTEMBER 18

LEAFS ACQUIRE PHIL KESSEL, 2009

Nice guy. Tries hard. Loves the game. That's Phil Kessel's Twitter bio, and it's tough to argue with. Kessel had speed and a blistering shot and made both look effortless. And despite enduring criticism from fans and the media, sometimes about his physique, he never lost his passion for the sport and continued filling the back of the net with a quiet confidence.

Drafted fifth overall by the Boston Bruins in 2006, Kessel had his rookie campaign interrupted when he was diagnosed with a rare form of testicular cancer, but he returned to finish the year, winning the Masterton Trophy in 2007. But when the winger needed a new contract in 2009, he and the Bruins were at an impasse. Looking to bring his services to Toronto, the Leafs acquired the sniper for first- and second-round picks in 2010 and another first-rounder in 2011, on September 18, 2009, and then promptly signed him to a five-year deal. Although the price proved to be steep, the Buds got four 30-goal seasons out of Kessel and a player who was easy to root for.

SEPTEMBER 19

LEAFS ACQUIRE GRANT FUHR, 1991

G rant Fuhr had known he was the subject of trade rumours for weeks. Despite knowing his time with Edmonton, where he won five Stanley Cups, was coming to an end, it didn't make it any easier when he finally found out he had been dealt. A few days after facing the Maple Leafs in a pre-season game, Fuhr was traded to Toronto on September 19, 1991, as part of a seven-player deal. Although a tearful Fuhr was sad to leave Edmonton behind, he was looking forward to starting a new chapter in Toronto.

In his first season with the Buds, Fuhr earned 25 victories. But after playing 29 games to start the next campaign, he was dealt to Buffalo, along with a fifth-round pick, for Dave Andreychuk, Daren Puppa, and a first-round pick that the Leafs would use to take defenceman Kenny Jönsson 12th overall in 1993. A couple of years later, Toronto dealt Jönsson to the Islanders, where he would adeptly patrol the blue line for nearly a decade, to bring back Wendel Clark.

LEAFS SIGN CODY DONAGHEY, 2014

Cody Donaghey was one step closer to the NHL. After getting passed over in the 2014 draft, a few months later, the defenceman from St. John's, Newfoundland, was invited to the Leafs' rookie camp. The team evidently liked what they saw in the young blueliner and, on September 20, 2014, signed him to a three-year entry-level contract. For Donaghey, who grew up a Leafs fan, it was a dream come true. After his first brush with the Buds, he was sent back to the Quebec Remparts of the Quebec Major Junior Hockey League.

But not long into the season, Donaghey injured his knee, tearing his ACL, and was out for the rest of the campaign. The following year, however, his time with the Leafs came to an end. On February 9, 2016, he was part of the nine-player deal that sent Toronto captain Dion Phaneuf and his $7 million cap hit to Ottawa. Although Donaghey wasn't with the Leafs organization for long, he will always be part of a significant moment in franchise history.

SEPTEMBER 21

LANNY McDONALD GETS THE CALL TO THE HALL, 1992

I f Lanny McDonald knocks on your door, chances are you're letting him in. When the former Leaf, who later capped off his career with a Stanley Cup in Calgary, was in Toronto for his Hockey Hall of Fame induction ceremony, it was reported that he and his family spent some time checking out his old stomping grounds. Before the ceremony McDonald and his family even stopped by his old house in Mississauga. Recognizing the newly minted Hall of Famer, the family who lived there invited them in for a tour and even managed to show off some of their own Lanny memorabilia, a pop-up poster of the former Leaf.

After taking a stroll down memory lane, McDonald was formally inducted on September 21, 1992. In the years that followed, he became a fixture with the Hall of Fame. After serving on the selection committee for nine years, McDonald was appointed as chairman of the board in 2015 and is often the voice on the other end of the telephone line delivering the good news to inductees.

SEPTEMBER 22

SUMMIT SERIES KICKS OFF IN MOSCOW, 1972

When the Summit Series shifted to Moscow, many people remember Phil Esposito taking a tumble during the player introductions or Canada squandering a 4–1 lead, but most forget that Paul Henderson suffered a concussion that could have, and probably should have, kept him out of the lineup. After scoring just over halfway through the second period to make it 3–0 for Canada, the speedy Leafs winger was tripped up and slid backward into the boards, hitting his head so hard he was knocked unconscious.

While Henderson initially left the game, he eventually returned, against the advice of the team's medical staff, and notched another goal in the final frame just over a minute after the Soviets broke Tony Esposito's shutout bid. Despite Henderson's best efforts, the Canadians allowed four unanswered goals in just over five minutes and lost the game 5–4. With Team Canada on the brink two days later, Henderson scored his first of three straight game-winning goals. How different would hockey history be if Henderson hadn't been able to dress for that pivotal sixth game?

SEPTEMBER 23

PHIL KESSEL VS. JOHN SCOTT, 2013

P hil Kessel wanted nothing to do with John Scott. And who could blame him? At six-foot-eight and tipping the scales at 260 pounds, Scott was one of the biggest players in the league. After the two exchanged pleasantries near centre ice before a faceoff in a pre-season game on September 23, 2013, Scott threw off his gloves in preparation to fight Kessel. But the four-time 30-goal scorer knew better than to engage with the Sabres' enforcer.

As Kessel quickly skated away, he got in a couple whacks at Scott's skates as though he was trying to chop down the lumbering giant with his stick. As a melee ensued, David Clarkson, who had recently signed a seven-year, $36.75 million deal with the Leafs, jumped over the boards to protect the star goal scorer and his new teammates. But by leaving the bench, Clarkson earned an automatic 10-game suspension and missed nearly the first month of the regular season. He finally made his Leafs debut against the Blue Jackets on October 25, 2013, finishing minus-1 in a 5–2 loss.

SEPTEMBER 24

SPLIT-SQUAD DOUBLEHEADER, 2022

t was a Leafs doubleheader. On September 24, 2022, the blue and white played two split-squad games in the same venue on the same day for the first time in franchise history when they hosted the Ottawa Senators for a pair of preseason games. The first matchup began in the afternoon. After Ottawa's Tim Stützle, drafted second overall in 2020, opened the scoring, the Leafs scored four unanswered goals to take the matinee 4–1.

One of those goals came from Denis Malgin, who signed a one-year deal with the Leafs a few months earlier. For Malgin, on his second tour of duty with the team since he was originally traded there a couple of years earlier, it was an important audition. After playing eight games for the Leafs in the 2019–20 campaign, he spent the next two seasons in Switzerland before returning to Toronto. While Malgin made a strong case to stick around, another newcomer, Calle Järnkrok, also impressed in his debut, scoring both goals in a 4–2 loss as the Leafs split the series.

SEPTEMBER 25

IMLACH PUNCHES TICKET TO THE HALL, 1984

One of the most enduring images of Leafs coach Punch Imlach was taken right after the club's second straight championship in 1963. Sitting down with his feet resting on a table that is holding the Stanley Cup, Imlach is casually sipping champagne. Next to him on a blackboard, scrawled in chalk, are the words *No Practice Tomorrow*. The juxtaposition is perfect because if the Leafs had failed to hoist Lord Stanley's mug, the bench boss may very well have scheduled a session the following day. Imlach was notoriously hard on his players and, by his own admission, was not the easiest to get along with.

But he got results. The next season, Imlach guided the Leafs to a third consecutive title. He would add another in 1967 before heading to Buffalo to build the upstart Sabres. Following his time in Buffalo, where he served as GM and coach, Imlach returned to Toronto in 1979 to finish out his career. Five years later, on September 25, 1984, he was inducted into the Hockey Hall of Fame as a builder.

SEPTEMBER 26

MONSTER MAKES LEAFS DEBUT, 2009

Jonas Gustavsson was known as "the Monster" because of his imposing frame. The Swedish goaltender, who towered at six-foot-four between the pipes, went undrafted to the NHL but signed with the Leafs as a free agent in July 2009. Although Gustavsson aimed to steal the net from incumbent Vesa Toskala, he missed most of training camp while he recovered from surgery to correct an accelerated heart rate.

After he was cleared to return to the crease, Gustavsson made his debut for the Leafs in a pre-season game against Detroit on September 26, 2009. He stopped all 15 shots he faced and was elated to be back on the ice. Despite his condition, Gustavsson succeeded in wrestling the top job from Toskala. In his first season in Toronto, the Swede made 39 starts, recording 16 victories. After appearing in just 23 games the next year while missing time to undergo two more heart procedures, Gustavsson made 36 starts in the 2011–12 campaign, his last with the Leafs. That off-season, he signed a two-year deal with the Red Wings.

SEPTEMBER 27

LEAFS SIGN BRAD BOYES, 2015

B rad Boyes, Brad Boyes, whatcha gonna do, whatcha gonna do when he scores on you? If you're of a certain vintage, you probably have the theme song to the TV show *Cops* stuck in your head; if you're not, you are probably wondering what I'm going on about. But a shrewd hockey mind will remember this was often the refrain when Boyes lit the lamp.

Originally drafted 24th overall by the Leafs in 2000, Boyes, who grew up in neighbouring Mississauga, nearly missed the chance to suit up for his local team. Not long into his professional career, he was dealt to San Jose as part of the trade that brought Owen Nolan to Toronto. But after more than a decade in the NHL, which included a 43-goal campaign, Boyes finally became a Leaf when he signed a one-year contract on September 27, 2015. And then, on November 2, 2015, just 5,609 days after he was drafted by Toronto, Boyes scored his first goal as a Leaf. Brad Boyes, Brad Boyes …

SEPTEMBER 28

PAUL HENDERSON WINS THE SUMMIT SERIES FOR CANADA, 1972

t was more than a kid from Kincardine could ever have dreamed of. After scoring a pair of goals, including the game-winner, against the Russians in the sixth game of the Summit Series, Paul Henderson, despite sustaining a concussion in the previous contest, continued to shoulder the load for his team and the nation. For this wasn't simply a hockey tournament. It was a battle for on-ice global supremacy and the collision of two competing political ideologies at the height of the Cold War. Canada was transfixed.

The next game, with the Canadians once more on the verge of losing the series, Henderson did it again; he scored the game-winning goal with just over two minutes remaining in regulation to keep a country's dream alive. So when the decisive game was held on September 28, 1972, all eyes were once again on the kid from Kincardine. With just 34 seconds remaining in the game, Henderson scored what proved to be the game-winning tally, capping off an incredible hat trick of game-winning goals, to clinch the Summit Series for Team Canada.

SEPTEMBER 29

LEAFS RE-SIGN MUSHROOM-FORAGING BLUELINER, 2022

To take his mind off contract negotiations, Leafs defenceman Rasmus Sandin went foraging for wild chanterelle mushrooms in the woods near his home in Sweden, as one does. Sandin, who was drafted 29th overall by Toronto in 2018, was a restricted free agent and in need of a new deal as the 2022–23 season approached.

But as the campaign neared, several key injuries to the blue line provided a timely opportunity for Sandin and the Leafs to finally reach an agreement. On September 29, 2022, it was announced that the team had signed him to a two-year, $2.8 million extension. With a new contract in hand, Sandin left Sweden to join the Leafs for the tail end of the pre-season. Teammates such as Mitch Marner were impressed by how great the blueliner looked on the ice despite missing all of training camp. Perhaps it was all the fungi. In Toronto's home opener a couple of weeks later against the Washington Capitals, Sandin assisted on Auston Matthews's game-winning goal to give the club its first victory of the season.

SEPTEMBER 30

LEAFS NAME MATS SUNDIN
CAPTAIN, 1997

After Doug Gilmour was traded to the Devils during the 1996–97 campaign, the Leafs needed a new captain. Although the club decided not to name a replacement during the season, it wasn't much of a contest when it was time to make a new appointment. It would be Mats Sundin. The Swedish centre, who had a quiet confidence and led by example on the ice, had been the team's leading scorer since arriving by trade from the Nordiques a few years earlier. While it would be tough to fill Gilmour's shoes, if anyone could, it was Sundin.

The Leafs made it official at a press conference on September 30, 1997, naming him the 16th captain in franchise history and the first non-Canadian to hold the title. Although Sundin joined countrymen Lars-Erik Sjöberg and Thomas Steen, who each led their teams during their time in the big leagues, captaincies in the NHL were still largely held by Canadians. Between smiles, Sundin was quick to point out that it would be big news back home. And it was.

OCTOBER 1

LEAFS ACQUIRE CORY CROSS, 1999

With it looking like Dmitri Yushkevich would miss the start of the 1999–2000 campaign because of a contract dispute, the Leafs needed to shore up their blue line. On the eve of the regular season, October 1, 1999, Toronto traded Swedish winger Fredrik Modin to the Tampa Bay Lightning for defenceman Cory Cross and a seventh-round draft pick in 2001. The hulking Cross, who was listed at six-foot-five and 225 pounds, missed most of Tampa's training camp while he, too, waited for a new contract. After he agreed to a one-year extension, he was traded promptly to the Leafs a few days later.

In the playoffs the following year, Cross, who was not exactly known for his goal-scoring prowess, scored perhaps the biggest goal of his NHL career. In the third game of Toronto's opening-round matchup against Ottawa, the second-highest-seeded team in the Eastern Conference, he notched the overtime winner to give the Leafs a 3–0 series lead. Toronto would go on to complete the sweep in a stunning upset against their provincial rivals.

OCTOBER 2

LEAFS ACQUIRE BRYAN McCABE, 2000

A year after Dmitri Yushkevich missed training camp and a few games to start the season because of a contract dispute, the Leafs had another disgruntled Russian defenceman on their hands. Restricted free agent Alexander Karpovtsev had patrolled the Toronto blue line for the past two seasons, but when the two sides reached an impasse on a new deal during the off-season, he stayed in Russia and started the 2000–01 campaign with his former team in the KHL, Dynamo Moscow.

With the NHL season less than a week away, on October 2, 2000, the Leafs traded Karpovtsev and a fourth-round pick to the Blackhawks for blueliner Bryan McCabe. McCabe, who had spent the past five seasons in New York, Vancouver, and Chicago, finally found a home in Toronto. Over the next seven years with the Leafs, McCabe was a regular on the team's lethal power play. In the 2005–06 season, he racked up 68 points, third most in the NHL that year among defencemen, behind only future Hall of Famers Nicklas Lidström and Sergei Zubov.

OCTOBER 3

LEAFS SNAG BRAD MARSH, 1988

Heading into the NHL's annual waiver draft in 1988, the Flyers had defenceman Brad Marsh on their list of protected skaters. But before we go any further, some of you might be thinking, *What is the waiver draft?* Well, from 1977 to 2003, the league held a draft before the start of the regular season, in which teams could pluck players from other clubs for a fee, while protecting 18 skaters and two goalies from selection. Where things got interesting was that when a team selected a player from another club, they were forced to remove a player from their own protected list.

So, on October 3, 1988, after Philadelphia snagged Doug Sulliman from New Jersey, they needed to expose a player, which happened to be Marsh. Now suddenly available, he was scooped up by the Leafs in the next round. Marsh made his debut for the Buds a few days later. He spent the next two seasons on the Toronto blue line until he was traded to the Red Wings for an eighth-round draft pick on February 4, 1991.

OCTOBER 4

LEAFS NEARLY SELL FRANK
MAHOVLICH, 1962

Many of us have had nights when we drank too much and did something we regret, but unless you are Harold Ballard, you probably never sold your team's star player. When the Leafs owner sat down for dinner with his Chicago counterpart, James Norris, on the evening of October 4, 1962, they chatted about league business, but as the night turned into the early morning hours, they struck a deal. Norris offered to purchase star Frank Mahovlich for $1 million, an unprecedented sum for a professional athlete at the time. Ballard accepted.

The two clinked glasses, shook hands, and outlined the terms of the deal on a stationery pad from the Royal York Hotel, which included both of their signatures. But when Black Hawks GM Tommy Ivan arrived at Maple Leaf Gardens the next morning with a cheque, Toronto president Stafford Smythe was incensed. He had not been consulted and refused to honour the owners' agreement. Fortunately for Leafs fans, Smythe nixed the deal and Mahovlich went on to win four Stanley Cups in Toronto.

OCTOBER 5

LEAFS LOSE FIRST NHL SHOOTOUT, 2005

With just 62 seconds remaining in a game on October 5, 2005, Senators captain Daniel Alfredsson scored his second of the night against the Leafs to force overtime. But when neither club scored in the extra session, Toronto and Ottawa became the first set of teams in NHL history to head to the shootout. Prior to the 2004–05 lockout, regular-season games that were not solved in OT ended in a tie. But in an effort to bring more excitement to the game, especially after shutting out the fans for a year, the league introduced the shootout.

Taking the first shot in the exhibition was Ottawa's Alfredsson. He beat Leafs goaltender Ed Belfour to give the Senators the lead. After Jason Allison had the puck poke-checked away by Dominik Hašek, Martin Havlát was stopped by Belfour. Up next was Toronto newcomer Eric Lindros, but he missed the net. With the game on his stick, Dany Heatley, making his Senators debut, found the back of the net to seal the win. As usual, the Leafs were a part of hockey history, just not on the right side.

OCTOBER 6

DAVE KEON FINALLY MAKES
LEAFS DEBUT, 1960

Dave Keon thought he was about to make his NHL debut. Following another standout season with the Toronto St. Michael's of the Ontario Hockey Association, Keon got a call from the Leafs. They wanted him ready for the team's playoff series against the Montreal Canadiens. But before he could suit up, Toronto was swept out of the playoffs. Although the Leafs' season was over, the club still wanted to give Keon some pro experience, so they sent him to Sudbury to join the Wolves in their playoff match-up against the Montreal Royals for the Eastern Professional Hockey League title.

Keon made an immediate impact, scoring two goals and an assist in his first game, but was used sparingly as the series wore on. Although Sudbury lost the championship, it was an important moment in Keon's development. The next season, he returned to Sudbury, but as a member of the Leafs as part of a pre-season exhibition game. And then, finally, on October 6, 1960, he hit the ice for his first game in the big leagues.

OCTOBER 7

AUSTON MATTHEWS VS. PATRICK KANE, 2018

t was an incredible back-and-forth by two of the best American players in the game. With just over a minute remaining on the road against the Blackhawks, on October 7, 2018, Auston Matthews scored his second goal of the night to give the Leafs a 6–5 lead. While the tally had unquestionably quieted the United Center faithful, Matthews raised a cupped hand to his ear to be sure. But just 33 seconds later, Patrick Kane, who had tied the game for Chicago just 22 seconds before Matthews scored the go-ahead goal, potted another to even the score once again, stunning the Leafs.

Against a roaring backdrop, Kane mimicked Matthews's earlier gesture by raising his hand to his ear and dismissively tossing his arm down to his side. As the young Toronto star sat on the bench while Chicago celebrated, he couldn't help but smile. Although he knew Kane had gotten the better of him, Matthews and the Leafs got the last laugh. Just 19 seconds into overtime, Morgan Rielly scored the game-winner to give Toronto a 7–6 victory.

OCTOBER 8

ALEXANDER MOGILNY SCORES
HIS 400TH CAREER GOAL, 2001

After scoring his 400th career goal, becoming the first Russian-born player to accomplish the feat, Alexander Mogilny was pretty nonchalant about the achievement. "I guess I go for No. 500 now," he told reporters after a 6–1 victory against the Mighty Ducks of Anaheim on October 8, 2001. While Mogilny acknowledged that the milestone was not a big deal for him personally, it was a significant part of Toronto's win that evening.

Before Mogilny made history, he opened the scoring just 53 seconds into the game to give the Leafs a 1–0 lead. Before the first period came to a close, he picked up an assist on a Robert Reichel goal that made it 3–0. And then just over a minute into the middle frame, Mogilny found the back of the net again to reach the 400-goal mark and give his team a commanding 4–0 victory. Although he was already looking ahead to 500, he would fall just short. Following two more seasons in Toronto and a final stop in New Jersey, Mogilny finished his NHL career with 473 goals.

OCTOBER 9

LEAFS SIGN T.J. BRODIE, 2020

Before the Leafs eventually traded Nazem Kadri to the Avalanche in 2019, the centre reportedly vetoed a deal that would have sent him to Calgary as part of a package that would have brought T.J. Brodie to Toronto. Although that deal never came to pass, a year later, the Leafs still got their guy. On October 9, 2020, Toronto signed the defenceman to a four-year, $20 million contract. Brodie, who had spent nearly the last decade patrolling the Flames' blue line, was exactly what the Leafs were looking for on the back end.

While Brodie could rack up points, it was his defensive play in his own end, including a well-earned reputation for prying the puck off of his opponents' sticks, that had him on Toronto's radar for quite some time. Although the original deal between the Leafs and Flames fell through, things have a way of working themselves out. After Kadri won the Stanley Cup with the Avalanche in 2022, he ended up signing a seven-year, $49 million contract with the Flames late in the off-season.

OCTOBER 10

LEAFS GET KING CLANCY, 1930

t was a king's ransom. On October 10, 1930, the Leafs acquired Frank "King" Clancy from the Ottawa Senators for Art Smith, Eric Pettinger, and $35,000. While it proved to be a great bet for Toronto — Clancy was one of the era's best defencemen and would play an integral part of the team's first Stanley Cup at Maple Leaf Gardens — the story about how the trade came together is even better.

After getting into thoroughbred horse racing a year earlier, owner Conn Smythe entered his horse, Rare Jewel, in the 1930 Coronation Futurity Stakes at Woodbine. With odds of 106-to-1 to win, it was a long shot. But the young filly pulled it out, earning Smythe $14,000 on the race. The extra cash came in handy, and he put most of it down to complete the trade with Ottawa. Smythe remained involved with the sport for the rest of his life, and just like his team on the ice, he had a winning track record. His horses would go on to win 131 stake races and two Queen's Plates.

OCTOBER 11

LEAFS TRADE "BUILDER LEGO," 1985

I was just a few months old when the Leafs traded Bill Derlago to Boston for Tom Fergus on October 11, 1985, but I know that if I had been older while he was still in Toronto, he would have been one of my favourite players. I think this not because of his playing style, although he did record four 30-goal campaigns with the Leafs, but simply because of his name.

I had never thought about it much until I read Sean McIndoe's *The Down Goes Brown History of the NHL*. In the book, McIndoe recounted how when he was a child, he thought Derlago's name was actually "Builder LEGO." As a young kid obsessed with both LEGO and the Leafs, you could understand why he would want to make that connection. While I never got to witness the "Builder LEGO" era in Toronto, as an adult who has rediscovered my passion for the little Danish building blocks, Derlago will always have a special place in my heart.

OCTOBER 12

AUSTON MATTHEWS SCORES FOUR IN ELECTRIFYING DEBUT, 2016

For Leafs fans, it has already entered into the lore of "Where were you when it happened?" On October 12, 2016, Auston Matthews, making his NHL debut in a game against Ottawa, scored four goals, establishing a modern-era record for the most goals in a rookie debut. I know I'll never forget where I was; I was at home with my wife, Chantal, and two-week-old daughter, Zoe. As Matthews continued to rack up goal after goal, Chantal, who isn't much of a hockey fan, said something along the lines of "Is this normal?" I told her emphatically that it was not and that we were watching something historic.

Although Zoe slept through the whole game in her tiny Maple Leafs pajamas that were still a couple sizes too big, holding her as we shared an unforgettable moment in hockey history is something I will cherish forever. While the Leafs ended up losing in overtime, something every Senators fan is always so quick to point out, it's probably a game that holds special meaning for you as well.

OCTOBER 13

WENDEL CLARK MAKES NHL DEBUT, 1985

When Wendel Clark was selected first overall by the Leafs at the 1985 NHL Entry Draft, he was a defenceman. In his final season of junior patrolling the blue line for the Saskatoon Blades, Clark had scored 87 points while racking up 253 penalty minutes. But a few months later, when he arrived for his first training camp with the Leafs, Clark was shifted up front to left wing. Although the change initially caught the tough Kelvington, Saskatchewan, native off guard, the move worked out well for him and the team.

When he played his first NHL game on October 13, 1985, the newly minted winger scored two goals in a 5–1 victory against the Chicago Black Hawks. It was the first of many goals he would score for the Buds throughout his career. Clark wrapped up his inaugural campaign with 34 goals, a team record that stood until Auston Matthews made his debut three decades later, and finished runner-up to defenceman Gary Suter for the Calder Trophy as the league's top rookie.

OCTOBER 14

MATS SUNDIN SCORES
500TH GOAL, 2006

t was quite the way to reach a milestone. Less than a minute into overtime, with the Leafs still killing a penalty that Darcy Tucker earned in the dying seconds of the third period, Mats Sundin blasted a shot from just above the left faceoff circle to beat Calgary goaltender Miikka Kiprusoff and complete his hat trick. A short-handed overtime game-winner. But that wasn't all. It was Sundin's 500th career goal, making him the first Swedish player in league history to accomplish the feat.

Following the game, he told reporters it was a special way to reach the benchmark, and it was something he would remember for the rest of his life. While Sundin undoubtedly stole the show that night, October 14, 2006, against the Flames, on the other side of the ice, Mark Giordano scored his first pair of NHL goals. He would go on to play 14 seasons on the Calgary blue line, winning the Norris as the league's top defenceman in 2019, before he was traded to the Leafs by Seattle in 2022.

OCTOBER 15

NATHAN PERROTT SIGNS WITH MARLIES, 2006

Nathan Perrott was a tough customer. During his only full season with the Leafs, in 2003–04, Perrott got into 16 fights, including one against Ottawa's Chris Neil in which he unloaded a flurry of lefts to easily take the match. So it's no surprise that after Perrott hung up his skates, he picked up boxing gloves. After starting the 2005–06 campaign with the Leafs, he was traded to the Stars for a fifth-round pick.

Following another eight donnybrooks with Dallas, Perrott spent the next season in the AHL with the Toronto Marlies after signing a contract on October 15, 2006. But after appearing in only eight games for the Marlies over the next two seasons, he spent some time in Russia before finishing his hockey career in the Central Hockey League for the 2009–10 season. During that final season, Perrott also started boxing professionally. He earned a technical knockout in his first bout and competed in two more that year. Nearly a decade later, at the age of 40, Perrott made a comeback to the ring.

OCTOBER 16

LANNY McDONALD SCORES HAT TRICK IN LESS THAN THREE MINUTES, 1976

L anny McDonald didn't need much time to score three goals. In the first period of a game against the Flyers on October 16, 1976, the Leafs winger opened the scoring just before the halfway mark. Sixty-one seconds later he scored again. And then less than two minutes after that, McDonald potted another to complete the hat trick. All told, McDonald needed just two minutes and 54 seconds to accomplish the feat, surpassing Babe Dye by a single second to establish a new club record for the fastest three goals.

On December 27, 1924, with the St. Patricks trailing Ottawa 4–0 with just a few minutes remaining, Dye notched three straight power-play goals. But despite Dye's swift efforts, Toronto fell one tally shy of forcing overtime. Five decades later, McDonald's feat was overshadowed by the fact that the Leafs nearly blew it. Despite leading 4–0 after the first period, the club surrendered five straight goals to Philadelphia. Luckily, Jim McKenny potted his first of the season with less than four minutes left to salvage a tie.

OCTOBER 17

TIE DOMI SUSPENDED EIGHT GAMES, 1995

With just over a minute remaining in a game against the Rangers in mid-October, Leafs pugilist Tie Domi unexpectedly punched New York defenceman Ulf Samuelsson in the face. The Swedish blueliner fell backward, hitting his head on the ice, and was knocked unconscious. He lay there motionless for what felt like an eternity. Although Samuelsson, who famously said, "You don't make friends on the ice," had a well-earned reputation as one of the dirtiest players in the game, including a previous incident in which he speared Domi, it's never something you want to see happen.

Following the game, Samuelsson was diagnosed with a concussion and needed four stitches to close the gash on the back of his head. While Domi earned a game misconduct for his actions that night, he also faced supplementary discipline from the league. Domi claimed he believed Samuelsson was going to drop his gloves and argued that he wasn't known for suckerpunching opponents. A few days later, on October 17, 1995, he received a stiff eight-game suspension, along with a $1,000 fine.

OCTOBER 18

PATRICK MARLEAU PLAYS 1,500TH GAME, 2017

As Patrick Marleau skated out onto the ice to take on Detroit on October 18, 2017, he made history. Marleau, who had signed a three-year contract with the Leafs a few months earlier, was playing in his 1,500th career game, becoming the 18th player in NHL history to reach the milestone. Not long after inking his deal with Toronto, he turned 38 years old. And while he had a few more grey hairs than his teammates, he could still put the puck in the back of the net and brought veteran leadership to a young core that was looking to take the next step.

It didn't take long for players like Mitch Marner and Auston Matthews to gravitate toward him. While Marleau may have been the elder statesman, he got off to a hot start with his new team, recording five points in his first five appearances. Although he couldn't maintain that pace, he continued to collect milestones with the Leafs. A year later, Marleau suited up for his 1,600th game, once again joining some illustrious company.

OCTOBER 19

BOB NEVIN SCORES FIRST GOAL, 1960

Bob Nevin kept his eye on the puck. Just over halfway through the third period in a game against the Canadiens on October 19, 1960, the Leafs rookie caught a pass from Frank Mahovlich and put it into the back of the net to score his first career NHL goal. Nevin would add 20 more tallies that year to finish runner-up for the Calder Trophy, as the league's top rookie, to teammate Dave Keon.

The following season, in a matchup against the Black Hawks, everyone was looking out for Nevin. Early in the second period, he was drilled by Chicago's Dollard St. Laurent. As Nevin was falling, St. Laurent reportedly landed a quick left hook. In a heap on the ice, Nevin, who was one of the first players in NHL history to wear contact lenses, realized he was missing one of his lenses. Teammates, officials, and the opposition came to his aid, scouring the ice on their hands and knees to try to find Nevin's contact lens, but they were never able to locate it.

NICK ROBERTSON MAKES MORE OBSCURE HISTORY, 2022

Nick Robertson isn't far into his NHL career, but obscure history seems to follow him. After making his big-league debut in 2020, he became the first 18-year-old Leafs player to score a post-season goal in more than seven decades. After spending most of the next year with the Marlies in the AHL and starting there to begin the 2022–23 campaign, he made his season debut on October 20, 2022, squaring off against Dallas and his older brother, Jason. The younger Robertson, who arguably earned a roster spot out of camp but was sent down because he was waiver exempt, made the most of the opportunity.

Less than two minutes into the third period, he scored to give the Leafs a 2–1 lead. After the Stars forced overtime, Robertson scored the game-winner, becoming just the second player in NHL history to score his first career regular-season OT goal in a game opposite his brother in more than a century. The last time it happened, it was also a Toronto player, Corb Denneny, who got the better of his older brother, Cy.

OCTOBER 21

GUSTAV NYQUIST SCORES ON PENALTY SHOT IN OT, 2019

Just over two minutes into overtime against the Leafs on October 21, 2019, Blue Jackets forwards Alexander Wennberg and Gustav Nyquist were advancing into the Toronto zone. As Wennberg passed the puck over to his teammate, Mitch Marner hooked his stick around Nyquist's pants. It seemed like an innocuous play, but at the next whistle, Nyquist was awarded a penalty shot. Marner was incensed. As Nyquist approached the puck at centre ice, Scotiabank Arena erupted into a chorus of boos.

Against that backdrop, Nyquist skated in on goaltender Frederik Andersen and fired a shot that beat the Danish netminder glove-side. Although it gave the Blue Jackets the victory, it held significance for both teams. Not only was it the first time in franchise history that Columbus scored an overtime penalty shot goal, it also marked the first time the Leafs gave up a penalty shot goal in an extra session. While it seems that plenty of teams set records against the Leafs, at least this time the Buds set one of their own.

OCTOBER 22

DALE McCOURT SIGNS
WITH THE LEAFS, 1983

For the first time in his career, Dale McCourt was a free agent. Originally drafted first overall by Detroit in 1977, McCourt finished his inaugural campaign in the Motor City with an impressive 72 points in 76 games. But after the Red Wings signed Kings goaltender Rogie Vachon that following off-season, an arbitrator ruled that McCourt would be awarded to Los Angeles as compensation. But McCourt refused to go along. Instead, he sued the league, the National Hockey League Players' Association, the Red Wings, and the Kings.

Although the matter was resolved the next year, McCourt, who led the Wings in scoring in the two seasons that followed, was traded to Buffalo on December 2, 1981. Following one full year with the Sabres, he was put on waivers and released just five games into the 1983–84 season, hitting the open market. After mulling over several offers, McCourt, nephew of legend George Armstrong, signed with the Leafs on October 22, 1983. But after one season in Toronto, he moved to Switzerland, where he played for nearly a decade.

OCTOBER 23

STEVE SULLIVAN CLAIMED OFF WAIVERS, 1999

When my family moved to Timmins, Ontario, in 1997, I struggled with the change. The silver lining was that when we settled into the small gold-mining town, it turned out we were living on the same street as Leafs forward Steve Sullivan, who grew up in the community and stayed there in the off-season. When my mom discovered this, she wrote him a letter explaining my situation and left it in his mailbox. Later, when Sullivan was signing autographs at the local mall, she mentioned the note to him and he signed a picture for me that said, "Keep your head high."

At the time I didn't understand the significance of the message, but now as a parent myself, I appreciate the time he took to try to lift my spirits. While Doug Gilmour was always my mom's favourite Leaf, I think she found extra room in her heart that day for Sullivan, so we were both a little blue when he was claimed by the Blackhawks on October 23, 1999, after being waived by Toronto.

OCTOBER 24

TED KENNEDY SCORES IN EIGHT SECONDS, 1953

B
ull riders are judged by how they perform in the first eight seconds after coming out of the gate. While Ted Kennedy may never have been in a rodeo holding on to a bucking bull for dear life, that's all the time he needed to find the back of the net. On October 24, 1953, just eight seconds after the opening puck drop in a matchup against Boston, Kennedy beat Bruins goaltender "Sugar Jim" Henry. At the time it was believed to have tied an NHL record for the fastest goal from the start of a game, matching the benchmark originally set by the New York Americans' Ron Martin more than two decades earlier.

But later research by hockey historians discovered this was not accurate. On February 6, 1932, Toronto's Charlie Conacher scored on Boston in only seven seconds, and even better, on December 29, 1926, Montreal Maroon Merlyn Phillips needed just five seconds to score against Chicago. Phillips's mark was later equalled by Doug Smail, Bryan Trottier, and Alexander Mogilny and remains the gold standard.

OCTOBER 25

MATS SUNDIN SCORES 300TH
GOAL WITH TORONTO, 2003

Mats Sundin might have had a slow start to the season, but the slump didn't last for very long. After going scoreless in the first five matchups of the 2003–04 campaign, the Leafs captain picked up an assist in each of the next two contests before reaching a significant milestone in a game against the Capitals on October 25, 2003.

After helping to set up Bryan McCabe's first tally of the season early in the second period, just over four minutes later, Sundin recorded his 300th career goal with Toronto, becoming just the fourth player in franchise history to accomplish the feat, joining Dave Keon, Ron Ellis, and Darryl Sittler. Sundin would add 30 more goals that season to close out the campaign with 330 career goals with Toronto, just two back from Ellis's total. In the years following the 2004–05 lockout, Sundin continued to bulge the twine and rewrite the Leafs' record books. And finally, just five games into the 2007–08 season, his last with Toronto, he scored his 390th goal, surpassing Sittler for the franchise record.

OCTOBER 26

DARRYL SITTLER NETS BACK-TO-BACK HAT TRICKS, 1980

t seemed as though Darryl Sittler's days in Toronto were numbered. At the end of the 1979–80 season, cantankerous owner Harold Ballard exclaimed that "Sittler will never wear a Maple Leafs uniform again" and barred him from attending training camp in September. It was the crescendo of a longstanding public feud between the star centre and Ballard, along with GM Punch Imlach, which included an incident in which Sittler cut off the *C* from his jersey after the team traded away Lanny McDonald.

Despite Ballard's threat, Sittler said he still intended to be at training camp, noting you had to take the remarks with a grain of salt. Over the course of the off-season, with Imlach in poor health, Sittler and Ballard reportedly made amends. Back in his boss's good graces, Sittler got off to a hot start to the season. After notching his 14th career hat trick on October 25, 1980, he recorded another three-goal performance the very next day. He would add three more hat tricks that season, establishing a franchise record that still stands.

OCTOBER 27

LEAFS TOP BLACKHAWKS IN OT, 2021

The only way David Kämpf could have scripted it any better was if he scored the game-winner. A native of the Czech Republic, Kämpf went undrafted to the NHL but signed with the Blackhawks in 2017. After spending the next four seasons with Chicago, he inked a two-year deal with Toronto on July 28, 2021. A few months later, on October 27, 2021, he returned to the United Center as a visitor. With the Leafs trailing 2–1 with less than eight minutes remaining in the third period, Kämpf backhanded the puck into the net to score his first goal with the blue and white to tie the game.

Kämpf's timely heroics forced overtime against his former team, and his new Buds took care of the rest. Less than two minutes into the extra session, Auston Matthews found a loose William Nylander, who skated into the offensive zone ahead of the Blackhawks and beat goaltender Kevin Lankinen to complete the comeback. When Kämpf faced his former team for an encore in December, he scored again, and this time it *would* be the game-winner.

OCTOBER 28

LEAFS FINALLY WIN AT CHICAGO STADIUM, 1993

T he Leafs were due. It had been more than four years since they'd won at Chicago Stadium. Following a victory on December 22, 1989, Toronto then lost 14 times in a row at "the Madhouse on Madison," a dreary streak that included five shutouts. But there was more on the line than quieting the Blackhawks faithful. Heading into the game in Chicago on October 28, 1993, the Leafs had started the season on a nine-game winning streak and were making history.

Having already surpassed the benchmark of eight straight to open a campaign, originally set nearly six decades earlier, the blue and white were going for double digits. Hitting 10 would not only set a new franchise record for the longest winning streak, it would also establish an NHL record for the longest winning streak from the start of the season. Chicago opened the scoring early in the second period, but the Leafs scored four straight goals to cruise to their 10th straight victory. Although the Sabres matched the feat in 2006, it remains a league record.

OCTOBER 29

MORGAN RIELLY SIGNS EIGHT-YEAR CONTRACT EXTENSION, 2021

Ever since he was selected fifth overall by Toronto at the 2012 Entry Draft, Morgan Rielly had been a stalwart on the Leafs blue line. He had been an alternate captain for six seasons and eventually became the current longest-serving member on the team. Rielly had been everything the team needed him to be, from his play on the ice, which included a 72-point campaign in the 2018–19 season, to his leadership. He may well have been one of the best picks from his draft class.

After the Leafs called Rielly's name from the stage nearly a decade earlier at the draft, NHL commissioner Gary Bettman asked then GM Brian Burke if that's who they wanted, to which Burke replied, "We had him first." History may just prove Burke right, and Rielly will be in a Leafs uniform for a long time. On October 29, 2021, the team signed the 27-year-old defenceman to an eight-year, $60 million contract extension that could keep him in blue and white until he's ready to hang up his skates.

OCTOBER 30

GUS BODNAR MAKES HOT START, 1943

G us Bodnar wasted no time in his first NHL contest. Just 15 seconds after puck drop, on October
30, 1943, the young rookie from Fort William (now
Thunder Bay), Ontario, scored his first goal with the Leafs,
establishing a league record for the fastest goal by a rookie in
his first game, easily eclipsing the mark of 60 seconds originally set by the Montreal Wanderers' Dave Ritchie in one of the
very first NHL games on December 19, 1917.

But Bodnar wasn't done there. He assisted on Lorne
Carr's goal early in the second period, and just a minute into
the final frame, Bodnar found the back of the net again. He
finished the season with 22 goals and 62 points in 50 games,
winning the Calder Memorial Trophy as the league's top
rookie. In the eight decades since Bodnar made NHL history, no other rookie has matched his feat. A few have come
close, such as Buffalo's Danny Gare, who notched his first in
18 seconds, but none as quick as Gus.

OCTOBER 31

DOUG GILMOUR AND MATS SUNDIN SET HALLOWEEN MILESTONES, 1996

t was all treats and no tricks for Doug Gilmour and Mats Sundin on Long Island on October 31, 1996. With just a few minutes remaining in the first period, Sundin scored a short-handed tally to put the Leafs on the board and notch his 200th career goal. Although New York's Ziggy Pálffy scored two goals in 49 seconds in the middle frame to give the Islanders a 2–1 lead, Toronto notched three straight to regain the lead with five minutes remaining in the stanza.

The third marker in that offensive onslaught was scored by Gilmour. Just before the halfway point of the third period, the Leafs captain reached a pair of milestones when he picked up his second goal of the night, his 350th in the league. The goal also marked Gilmour's 400th career point with the Leafs, making him the 16th player in franchise history to reach the benchmark. And since it wouldn't be Halloween without ghosts, Toronto's Kirk Muller, who was making his first return to Nassau Coliseum since being traded last season, received all the boos.

NOVEMBER 1

MIKE PALMATEER RECORDS THIRD STRAIGHT VICTORY, 1976

Less than a week after being called up from the minor league in Dallas, Mike Palmateer was making his presence felt in the NHL. On November 1, 1976, the 22-year-old rookie goaltender recorded his third straight victory. Palmateer might not have been especially busy that night, facing just 21 shots on the road against the lowly Cleveland Barons, but head coach Red Kelly remarked that his new netminder "made the saves when we needed them."

Drafted 85th overall by the Leafs in 1974, Palmateer spent two seasons in the minors before being recalled by the blue and white nine games into the 1976–77 campaign. When he made his debut on October 28, the Leafs were in the midst of a seven-game winless streak, but the young goalie stopped all but one shot he faced from the Detroit Red Wings to snap the skid. After rattling off three straight victories to start his career in Toronto, Palmateer would finish the season with 23 wins and finish fifth in voting for the Calder Memorial Trophy as the league's top rookie.

NOVEMBER 2

GORDIE HOWE SCORES LAST GOAL AGAINST THE LEAFS, 1979

The Leafs thought they had seen the last of Gordie Howe. When he hung up his skates in 1971, Howe had racked up 133 goals against the Leafs. But he didn't stay retired for very long. After a couple of seasons working in Detroit's front office, he joined the rival World Hockey Association and spent five years there, playing with his sons Mark and Marty for Houston and then New England. When the WHA merged with the NHL in 1979, Howe found himself back in the league when the Whalers, rechristened as Hartford, were admitted, along with Edmonton, Winnipeg, and Quebec.

When the Leafs travelled to take on the Whalers at their temporary home in Springfield, Massachusetts, on November 2, 1979, Howe proved he hadn't lost a step. Halfway into the first period, the 51-year-old scored his fourth of the season to give Hartford a 2–0 lead. He would find the back of the net again in the third period, recording his first multi-goal performance in the NHL in nearly a decade, and his last tally against the Leafs.

NOVEMBER 3

PANTHERS PLAY FIRST GAME AGAINST THE LEAFS, 1993

Although Florida opened the scoring at Maple Leaf Gardens, Toronto spoiled the team's first trip north of the border. On November 3, 1993, the expansion club played its first game in Canada. After Jesse Bélanger got the Panthers on the board less than seven minutes into the first period, the Leafs notched six straight goals, including four in the middle frame, to take a commanding lead. Among the offensive onslaught, Dave Andreychuk scored twice to improve to a sterling 12 goals in 13 games to start his first full season in Toronto.

Although the Panthers picked up two goals late in the third period to cut the deficit in half, they were no match for the Leafs. While the two teams squared off again in Canada that season, it would not be in Toronto. As part of an ongoing effort to grow the game, the NHL had been experimenting with a number of neutral-site matchups. On March 23, 1994, the Leafs and Panthers played to a 1–1 tie at Copps Coliseum in Hamilton, Ontario.

EDDIE O SCORES SIX POINTS, 1987

t's tough to say who had a worse night at the office, Jets goaltender Pokey Reddick or linesman Ryan Bozak. After allowing six goals on 13 shots in the first 30 minutes in a game against the Leafs on November 4, 1987, the Winnipeg netminder was mercifully yanked in favour of Daniel Berthiaume, who stopped all but one of the 13 shots he faced the rest of the matchup.

While Reddick was likely able to shake it off, Bozak couldn't say the same. During the first period, the linesman took a puck to the face and suffered a broken cheekbone and was expected to miss the next five weeks. Although things didn't go their way, the same couldn't be said for Eddie Olczyk. Playing in his first season in Toronto, Olczyk, who was traded there from his hometown Blackhawks a couple of months earlier, scored a goal and assisted on five others as the Leafs cruised to a 7–3 victory. He was just one helper away from tying Babe Pratt's franchise record for most assists in a game.

NOVEMBER 5

LEAFS TRADE MIKE FOLIGNO, 1993

t was time for Mike Foligno to move on. After dressing for only four games for the Leafs to start the 1993–94 campaign, the 34-year-old knew the writing was on the wall. With less playing time coming his way, Foligno, who was known for his trademark leaping celebrations after scoring a goal, approached GM Cliff Fletcher about a fresh start elsewhere. The upstart Panthers were dealing with injuries, so Fletcher obliged the request and gave him the opportunity to earn a regular spot in a lineup.

On November 5, 1993, the Leafs sent Foligno to Florida for future considerations. He dressed for 39 games with the Panthers before hanging up his skates at the end of the season. Nearly three decades later, when Foligno's son, Nick, was traded to the Leafs, he appeared before a game wearing a hat his father had been issued during his last full season with the club and said he was bringing "a little bit of old with the new." Nick, however, wouldn't go as far as wearing his dad's old Northland bucket.

NOVEMBER 6

LEAFS TAKE ON BRUINS FOR FIRST TIME IN NEARLY TWO YEARS, 2021

think I speak for many Toronto fans when I say I didn't miss the Boston Bruins. Although it got boring watching the Leafs play the same six teams in the Scotia NHL North Division, a.k.a. the Canadian division, during the pandemic-shortened 2020–21 season, I was not clamouring for them to take on Boston again. The wounds were still fresh from back-to-back Game 7 losses in 2018 and 2019, not to mention the team's monumental 4–1 collapse in 2013.

But despite that trauma, a part of me knows that if the club is going to exorcise its playoff demons, they're going to have to vanquish the Bruins. So when the Leafs faced the Bruins on November 6, 2021, the first matchup in nearly two years, I embraced it. Although there was nothing high stakes on the line, it felt good to watch Auston Matthews and John Tavares each score twice in a 5–2 victory, the club's first win against Boston since October 19, 2019. Now they just need to do it four times in the post-season.

NOVEMBER 7

LEAFS ACQUIRE EDDIE SHACK, 1960

Clear the track, here comes Shack. On November 7, 1960, the Leafs traded Pat Hannigan and Johnny Wilson to the Rangers for Eddie Shack. While Shack made an immediate impact with his new team, recording 14 goals and 28 points, both career highs, his significance to the franchise was long-lasting. Over the next six seasons, and two more in the twilight of his career, Shack became one of the most beloved players in Leafs history.

Known as "the Entertainer" for his rambunctious, physical, and skillful style of play, he always found ways to get the fans out of their seats. After securing his first Stanley Cup with Toronto in 1962, the next year, Shack scored the championship-winning goal. A couple of years later, there was even a song about him. In 1965, Brian McFarlane, who was early into his tenure at *Hockey Night in Canada*, wrote the song "Clear the Track, Here Comes Shack." The song was later recorded by the Secrets and topped the Toronto music charts. Shack passed away in 2020, but his legacy will live forever.

JAMIE MACOUN SUITS UP FOR 1,000TH CAREER GAME, 1997

Jamie Macoun beat the odds. A defenceman at Ohio State University, many believed Macoun didn't have a shot at the NHL, but after finishing his collegiate career, he signed with the Flames. He quickly earned a regular spot in the lineup and became an integral part of the Calgary blue line. But after his fifth campaign with the Flames, his career nearly came crashing down. In the off-season, Macoun rolled his sports car while under the influence. While he waited for first responders to arrive, his left arm was pinned underneath the roof against the pavement. He suffered nerve damage and doctors thought he might never play again.

But after missing the 1987–88 season while he recovered, Macoun returned the next year and played a pivotal role in Calgary's first-ever Stanley Cup. He eventually made his way to Toronto as part of the blockbuster trade that landed Doug Gilmour. A few years later, on November 8, 1997, Macoun suited up for his 1,000th career game, a milestone that wouldn't have seemed possible in college, but especially after his injury.

NOVEMBER 9

WENDEL CLARK SCORES FOUR IN COMEBACK VICTORY, 1996

t was vintage Wendel Clark. With the Leafs trailing 3–1 to the Oilers going into the second period of a game on November 9, 1996, Clark punctuated an offensive on-slaught that saw Toronto mount a determined comeback. After Sergei Berezin and Mike Craig each scored to tie the game, Clark continued to lead the charge.

A minute after Craig's equalizer, Clark tickled the twine to take the lead. He scored two more to close out the team's five-goal period and complete the natural hat trick, his first three-goal performance with the blue and white since he was reacquired in March 1996. But Clark wasn't done just yet. He added a fourth goal in the final frame to give the Leafs a 7–4 victory. It was the first time since his second season in the NHL that he scored four times in a game. While Clark would play two more seasons in Toronto and parts of another a few years later, it would prove to be his final hat trick with the Leafs.

FÉLIX POTVIN VS. RON HEXTALL, 1996

Ron Hextall had a well-earned reputation as one of the meanest goalies in the league. During the 1987 Stanley Cup Final, the Flyers goaltender chopped down Edmonton's Kent Nilsson with a hack to the ankle that earned him an eight-game suspension to start the following campaign. A couple of years after that incident, Hextall attacked Montreal's Chris Chelios in the post-season, netting himself a 12-game ban.

While few wanted to tangle with Hextall, on November 10, 1996, the fiery netminder found out the hard way it's best not to mess with the Cat. In the dying seconds of Toronto's matchup against Philadelphia that night, a number of brawls broke out. As Leafs netminder Félix Potvin looked to approach the fray, Hextall darted out of his crease, throwing away his blocker and trapper as he passed centre ice and entered the Toronto zone. As the two tangled in the corner, they tore off their masks and started trading punches. Potvin yanked Hextall's jersey over his head and, to put it diplomatically, beat the wheels off of him.

LEAFS TRADE IAN TURNBULL, 1981

an Turnbull hadn't been happy with the Leafs for quite some time. The defenceman, who was best known for scoring five goals in a game, an NHL record, felt he had lost his competitive edge in Toronto and was looking for a fresh start elsewhere. After joining the team on a western road trip early in the 1981–82 season, Turnbull was sent home from Denver.

While Turnbull waited, speculation swirled about where the disgruntled defenceman would land. Less than a week after being dispatched, on November 11, 1981, Toronto dealt him to the Kings for Billy Harris and John Gibson. Following the announcement the Leafs said that if they hadn't found a trading partner, they would have sent Turnbull to their farm team. But despite moving to Los Angeles, he found himself in the minors just the same. After playing 42 games for the Kings, Turnbull wound up in the American Hockey League. The NHL veteran didn't mind the demotion. After scoring his first goal in the AHL, he told reporters he was having a blast there.

A TOUCHING TRIBUTE FOR
BÖRJE SALMING, 2022

There was not a dry eye in the house. After announcing in the summer that he was suffering from ALS, Börje Salming made a courageous homecoming to Toronto for the Hockey Hall of Fame's annual induction. He made his first appearance before the Leafs hosted the Penguins on November 11, 2022, alongside former teammate Darryl Sittler and Mats Sundin. It was beautiful but also incredibly heart-breaking to see Salming, who was so fierce on the ice, in such a weakened state. As the crowd gave him a much-deserved standing ovation, both he and Sittler were overcome with emotion. It was one of the most touching moments in Leafs history.

The next night, Salming returned with his family for a tribute and ceremonial puck drop. In honour of Salming and his franchise legacy, head coach Sheldon Keefe's starting line-up for the game was all Swedes. Although Toronto fell behind early in the first period, they came back to earn the victory for the King. Sadly, just two weeks later, Salming passed away. A warrior until the end.

NOVEMBER 13

MORGAN RIELLY SCORES LATE GAME-WINNER, 2021

Two weeks after signing an eight-year contract extension with the Leafs, Morgan Rielly proved, yet again, why he was money in the bank. With just 11.8 seconds remaining on the clock in a game against the Buffalo Sabres on November 13, 2021, Rielly fired the puck through traffic and past goaltender Aaron Dell, who was making his first start for the Sabres, to power the Leafs to a 5–4 victory.

Although Toronto was up 4–2 with just 10 minutes to go in regulation, the Sabres scored two goals in less than a minute to knot it up. But unlike in past moments in which the Leafs squandered multi-goal leads in the third period, they clamped down and prevented the opposition from forcing overtime. Rielly's goal, his first of the season, also ensured that Toronto goalie Joseph Woll, who was making his NHL debut, picked up his first big-league victory. Two games later, when the Leafs hosted the Rangers, Rielly scored the team's only goals in a 2–1 win, giving the blue and white its fifth straight triumph.

NOVEMBER 14

HERB CARNEGIE INDUCTED INTO HOCKEY HALL OF FAME, 2022

eralded as hockey's first Black star, Herb Carnegie is also considered the best Black player to never suit up in the NHL. The son of Jamaican immigrants, he started playing hockey in Toronto and eventually caught the eye of Leafs owner Conn Smythe. The story goes that one morning after practice, Carnegie's coach pulled him aside and told him Smythe was watching from the stands. He added that Smythe was interested in adding him to his team if only he could find a way to turn Carnegie white.

Although Carnegie had experienced racism before, he was in disbelief. It felt like his hockey dreams had been dashed. He went on to be one of the top players of the Quebec Senior Hockey League, winning the MVP award in three straight seasons, but never got a fair shake at the NHL. While Carnegie was inducted posthumously into the Hockey Hall of Fame as a builder on November 14, 2022, he might have been voted in as a player, but he never got the chance to prove himself on the game's biggest stage.

NOVEMBER 15

LEAFS RACK UP 154 PENALTY MINUTES, 1986

Brad Smith set the tone early. Just three seconds after puck drop in a game against the Red Wings on November 15, 1986, the Leafs winger went after Gerard Gallant. For Smith, it was payback from a couple of weeks earlier when Gallant fought Dan Daoust, leaving the Toronto forward with a broken left foot and putting him on the shelf for a few months. After the initial retaliatory skirmish lit the powder keg, things were just getting started.

There were three more fights in the middle frame, followed by an explosive final stanza. In the last session, after Wendel Clark scored to make it 5–0 Toronto, Smith was at it again, this time fighting Basil McRae in a spirited tilt. After the linesmen broke it up, Detroit's Tim Higgins lunged at Smith and the pair fought until they were both shown the gate. After a few more donnybrooks, officials doled out nearly a dozen misconduct penalties that period. When the final buzzer sounded, the Leafs had racked up 154 penalty minutes, a franchise record that still stands.

NOVEMBER 16

LEAFS BEAT HAWKS YET AGAIN, 1986

The Blackhawks just couldn't catch a break. Going back to the end of the last regular season and playoffs, the Leafs had defeated them eight times in a row. Three of those victories were in the post-season when Toronto swept the Norris Division winners in the opening best-of-five series. When they squared off again on November 16, 1986, it was much of the same for Chicago. Although the Blackhawks only trailed 2–1 five minutes into the second period, the Leafs scored four straight to take a commanding 6–1 lead.

Two of those tallies were a pair of short-handed markers scored by Börje Salming and Greg Terrion in a span of 27 seconds, establishing a dubious Chicago record for the fastest two short-handed goals against in franchise history. Although the Blackhawks added two more in the final frame, the Leafs also picked up another to cruise to a 7–3 victory, their ninth straight win against their Windy City rivals. Chicago would finally get a triumph against the Buds at home on January 7, 1987.

NOVEMBER 17

CRAIG SMITH WHIFFS ON
SURE GOAL, 2011

t should have been the easiest goal Craig Smith ever scored. With just over a minute remaining in a game against Nashville on November 17, 2011, Toronto, trailing 3–1, pulled their goalie. As Smith skated in toward the empty net, he caught a pass from Sergei Kostitsyn. With the puck on his stick, all he had to do was slide it into the back of the yawning cage. But the Predators rookie roofed it up high and over the Leafs' net.

With the puck out of sight, the goal horn sounded and the spotlight found Smith as he skated away. Many in the crowd, even those sitting behind the goal, rose to their feet, assuming he had bulged the twine. When Smith returned to the bench he was despondent. As the sullen rookie kept his head down, he was consoled by assistant captain Mike Fisher, who couldn't help but crack a slight smile. If Smith played for the Titans, Nashville's NFL team, it would have been the perfect field goal kick through the uprights.

LEAFS LOSE BIG TO PREDS, 2014

D ion Phaneuf did not hold back. "When you get beat like that in professional sports, it's embarrassing," he told reporters following a humiliating 9–2 loss to the visiting Predators on November 18, 2014. In a word, the Toronto captain called it "unacceptable." After Leafs goaltender Jonathan Bernier gave up three goals on 12 shots in the first period, head coach Randy Carlyle yanked him in favour of James Reimer.

Although Reimer gave up only one goal in the middle session, things really went off the rails for Toronto in the final frame. After Mike Ribeiro scored 53 seconds after puck drop, the Predators added three more goals in just over four minutes to take a commanding 8–0 lead. While Mike Santorelli and Nazem Kadri got the Leafs on the board with a pair of tallies, Nashville added one more for good measure to really rub some salt in the wound. Before the game was even over, a fan was apparently so disgusted by the team's performance they tossed their jersey onto the ice in protest.

NOVEMBER 19

BRUCE HOOD REFS 1,000 GAMES, 1983

t was probably one of the few times in his career that referee Bruce Hood received a round of applause from the crowd. When the veteran official stepped onto the ice at Maple Leaf Gardens on November 19, 1983, he became the first referee in NHL history to oversee 1,000 games. Hood's big-league journey began nearly twenty years earlier in the same building when he refereed his first NHL game as the Leafs hosted the Rangers.

Hood likely would have reached the milestone much earlier had not injuries, both on and off the ice, gotten in the way. He had suffered broken bones in games, but an off-season badminton mishap also kept him out of his stripes for a season. While Hood basked in the ovation before the game that night, the cheers quickly turned to jeers. Just before the first period came to a close, he sent Toronto defenceman Dave Farrish to the box for tripping and heard the disapproval from the crowd. Hood may have made history, but it was just another day at the office.

NOVEMBER 20

LEAFS FIRE MIKE BABCOCK, 2019

The Mike Babcock era in Toronto was over. On November 20, 2019, Babcock, who took the reins as head coach in 2015 after signing a lucrative eight-year contract, was fired the day after the team extended its losing streak to six games. On the surface it seemed as though the bench boss might have been able to extend his shelf life, even if just for a bit, if the Leafs hadn't been robbed by Marc-André Fleury the night before. With Toronto trailing 3–2 late in a game against Vegas, Nic Petan had a golden opportunity to tie it up, but Fleury made an incredible dive across the crease to snare the puck and prevent a sure goal.

Not long after his termination, it was revealed that Babcock, who had a well-earned reputation as a difficult coach, was using controversial tactics on the team's younger players. A few years earlier, he made rookie Mitch Marner rank the team's hardest-working players and then, to Marner's dismay, showed the list to the teammates who were at the bottom.

NOVEMBER 21

LEAFS NAME PUNCH IMLACH GM, 1958

N ot long after Punch Imlach guided the Springfield Indians to their first-ever appearance in the American Hockey League's Calder Cup Final as both manager and coach, he was plucked by the Leafs. The team, which had missed the playoffs for its second straight year, hoped Imlach could come in and turn things around by serving as an assistant general manager with King Clancy.

But just a few months after starting his tenure in Toronto, on November 21, 1958, the Leafs made Imlach the team's GM. In one of his first duties in his new role, just over a week later, Imlach fired head coach Billy Reay and named veteran winger Bert Olmstead a player-coach, but it was clear it was the GM who would be running the bench. The Leafs returned to the post-season in Imlach's first campaign as coach, and then, a few years later, he led the club to its first Stanley Cup in more than a decade. Imlach would pick up three more championships in Toronto as coach and GM.

NOVEMBER 22

LEAFS HONOUR WENDEL CLARK'S NUMBER, 2008

t was one of the proudest moments in Wendel Clark's career. While the adoring fans at the Air Canada Centre (now Scotiabank Arena) fixed their gaze on the former captain, he watched as his No. 17 ascended to the rafters, joining those of other Leafs legends. Clark, a fan favourite for his ability to score and deliver bone-crunching body checks, had racked up 260 goals with Toronto and guided the team to back-to-back conference final appearances while wearing the *C* for three seasons.

Addressing the crowd on November 22, 2008, Clark likened his jersey being honoured to recording a hat trick. "The two proudest moments in my career were being drafted first overall by the Toronto Maple Leafs and, secondly, the day I was named captain of the Toronto Maple Leafs," he told the Leafs faithful from centre ice. "Tonight, the official hat trick. Being honoured and raised to the rafters is a natural hat trick to be able to be in this building and to be in the building forever up there with those great players."

NOVEMBER 23

LEAFS HALT DEVILS' WINNING STREAK AT 13, 2022

All that stood between the Devils and making history were the Leafs. After rattling off an incredible 13 straight victories, New Jersey had the chance to extend their winning streak to a franchise best when they hosted Toronto on November 23, 2022. The Devils opened the scoring in the first period, but the goal was overturned for goaltender interference. Early in the middle frame, with the Leafs leading 2–0, New Jersey appeared to score again but that, too, was waved off.

And then, halfway through the final frame, the Devils seemed to finally get one, but it was called back as well. Although you could quibble with the first pair of calls, there was no getting around that Erik Haula had kicked the puck over the line. While it was the right call, the Devils faithful resorted to pelting the ice with debris in protest. Although they did eventually score, New Jersey lost 2–1. A winning streak halted by a hat trick of disallowed goals is something so improbable you'd think it could only happen to the Leafs.

NOVEMBER 24

TORONTO ACQUIRES JOHN CULLEN, 1992

t was a dream come true for John Cullen. Ever since he was a kid, growing up hearing stories about his father, Barry, playing for the Leafs, he had hoped that one day, he, too, would be able to wear the blue-and-white sweater. That dream became a reality on November 24, 1992, when Toronto acquired him from the Whalers in exchange for a second-round draft pick the following year.

While Cullen was excited to follow in his father's footsteps in Toronto, he was also eager for a fresh start. After beginning his NHL career in Pittsburgh, he was acquired by Hartford as part of the trade for Ron Francis. Although Cullen had put together back-to-back 90-point campaigns with the Penguins, he would always be in the shadow of Francis, who was the heart and soul of the Whalers for nearly a decade. While Cullen and the Leafs hoped he'd return to his scoring ways from his time in Pittsburgh, injuries, including a herniated disc in his neck and a sprained ankle, limited his productivity in Toronto.

NOVEMBER 25

LEAFS BLANK SEALS 11–0, 1972

A lesser writer would have said the Leafs clubbed the Seals, but not me. On November 25, 1972, Toronto trounced the California Golden Seals 11–0. After Garry Monahan opened the scoring just over six minutes into the first period, Toronto added three more to take a 4–0 lead. Although the Seals had reportedly outplayed the Leafs in the middle session, outshooting them 16–10, the blue and white potted two more to extend their advantage. Less than three minutes into the final frame, Rick Kehoe scored his second of the night to make it 7–0.

But not long after Kehoe's tally, Leafs goaltender Jacques Plante, who had stopped all 29 shots he faced that night, was forced to leave the game with a bruised hip. The veteran net-minder, just a couple of months shy of his 44th birthday, was still searching for his first shutout of the season. Meanwhile, substitute Ron Low was perfect in relief and the Leafs added four more with him in the crease, including another by Kehoe to complete his first NHL hat trick.

NOVEMBER 26

BÖRJE SALMING GETS CUT IN
THE FACE BY A SKATE, 1986

Börje Salming could have easily played the villain in a James Bond movie. Let me explain. During a game against the Red Wings on November 26, 1986, the Leafs defenceman was down on the ice in a goalmouth scramble. When Detroit winger Gerard Gallant fell over, he stepped on Salming's face with his skate. Although Salming had started the season wearing a visor after breaking a bone beneath his left eye, he had reportedly ditched the protection a few days earlier after complaining that it hindered his vision.

Salming was rushed to hospital, where he needed more than 200 stitches to close the gash that ran from just above his right eye to the corner of his mouth. He was ruled out indefinitely, but the dogged Swedish rearguard returned to action just a couple of weeks later. While he was recuperating from his injury, there's a photograph of him, with the jagged scar across his face, tenderly holding a kitten, the spitting image of Ernst Stavro Blofeld, James Bond's archnemesis.

NOVEMBER 27

LEAFS RECALL PAT QUINN, 1968

P at Quinn started the 1968–69 season with the Leafs but played just one game before he was sent to the minors. Following a stint in Tulsa, Oklahoma, with the club's affiliate in the Central Hockey League, Quinn was recalled by Toronto and remained with the team for the rest of the campaign. After getting back into the Leafs line-up on November 27, 1968, for a game against the Pittsburgh Penguins, the tough defenceman posted 95 penalty minutes in 40 games.

Quinn played another year for the blue and white before he was claimed by the upstart Vancouver Canucks in the NHL's 1970 expansion draft. Two years later, he was once again plucked in an expansion draft, this time by the Atlanta Flames. In his first four seasons with the Flames, Quinn missed just one game. While he was solid on the blue line, he wasn't much of a skateboarder. During the 1976 off-season, he broke his leg trying his daughter's skateboard and missed the start of the next season while still stuck in a cast.

GERRY JAMES WINS GREY CUP, 1959

After breaking his leg in two places in the fall of 1958, Gerry James would be missing more than just the hockey season. A running back for the Winnipeg Blue Bombers of the Canadian Football League, James, who was known as "Kid Dynamite," was just a year removed from his second Most Outstanding Canadian Award. Beyond his feats on the gridiron, he was also an accomplished hockey player. After making his NHL debut in 1955 with the Leafs, James played the next three campaigns with Toronto until he broke his leg. Although he missed the remainder of the 1958 football schedule and subsequent hockey season, he returned to action the following year.

On November 28, 1959, James won the Grey Cup with the Bombers. A few weeks later, he returned to the Leafs. Later that year, he had the opportunity to pick up another championship, but the Leafs fell short to the Canadiens in the title match. James remains the only person to play in a Grey Cup and Stanley Cup Final in the same season.

NOVEMBER 29

WENDEL CLARK RECORDS 500TH POINT, 1997

endel Clark recorded his 500th career NHL point, but all everybody could do was talk about Mark Messier. With the Leafs hosting Vancouver on November 29, 1997, the Canucks captain was the story because, before puck drop, Team Canada had revealed its men's roster for the upcoming Olympic Winter Games in Nagano, Japan, and Messier's name was nowhere to be found on the list. While Team Canada GM Bobby Clarke had broken the news earlier in the day, Messier, who represented his country with distinction internationally throughout his career, including winning three consecutive Canada Cups, had to put the disappointment out of his mind and focus on his matchup in Toronto.

During the first intermission, with the Leafs up 2–0, Don Cherry railed against the snub during his "Coach's Corner" segment on *Hockey Night in Canada*, calling Messier's omission "a crime." After the Canucks scored twice in the second period, Messier, with the spotlight shining on him that night, delivered the eventual game-winning goal three minutes into the final frame, all but overshadowing Clark's milestone.

NOVEMBER 30

A DAY FOR SCORELESS DRAWS, 1947 AND 1950

The Leafs couldn't seem to find the back of the net on November 30, but they also managed to keep the puck out of their twine as well. On that day in 1947, in a game against Boston, Toronto reportedly directed 26 shots on Bruins goaltender Frank Brimsek — who earned the nickname "Mr. Zero" by stymying opponents throughout his tenure in Boston — but he stopped them all. Even in the final minutes of the third when Toronto threw everything they could at him, Mr. Zero remained unflappable. Meanwhile, at the other end of the ice, Leafs netminder Turk Broda was also perfect and turned aside 15 shots in a 0–0 tie.

Exactly three years later, the Leafs found themselves in a similar spot. Squaring off against the Canadiens on the road, Toronto rookie goalie Al Rollins, who had been undefeated in his first seven starts that season, saved every shot he faced, but so did Montreal's Gerry McNeil, who recorded his fourth shutout of the campaign, tying him with Broda for the league lead, in another scoreless draw.

DECEMBER 1

FRANK MAHOVLICH RECORDS
FIRST NHL HAT TRICK, 1957

When Frank Mahovlich broke into the NHL in 1957, some were already comparing him to Montreal's Jean Béliveau. Mahovlich, who would come to be known as "the Big M" for his height, had some undeniable similarities to Béliveau, referred to as "le Gros Bill," also for his stature. Beyond towering over opponents in their era, they were both smooth-skating forwards with plenty of offensive skill. After racking up 52 goals in 49 games in his final season of junior with the Toronto St. Mike's, Mahovlich, who appeared in three games for the Leafs that season, started the 1957–58 campaign in the big leagues.

After scoring just three goals in his first 20 games, Mahovlich broke through with a three-goal performance against Chicago on December 1, 1957. He would finish the season with 20 goals and 36 points to earn the Calder Memorial Trophy as the league's top rookie. Although Mahovlich may not have lived up to the Béliveau comparisons — few could — the two eventually became teammates in Béliveau's final season, culminating in a Stanley Cup.

DECEMBER 2

ANOTHER SCORELESS AFFAIR, 1950

Two days after a scoreless stalemate with the Canadiens, it happened again to the Leafs. On December 2, 1950, Toronto returned home and hosted the Black Hawks at Maple Leaf Gardens. Although, once again, no goals were scored in the game, it was not without excitement. After stopping everything that came his way in the first period, Leafs goaltender Al Rollins took a shot from Ernie Dickens above his left eye. Rollins, who was coming off his second career shutout in Montreal, was forced to leave the game to get stitches to close the gash. Turk Broda entered the crease in relief and was perfect the rest of the way to preserve the shutout.

At the other end of the ice, Chicago netminder Harry Lumley was also hurt in the middle frame when a blistering shot from Harry Watson broke his nose. Despite the injury, Lumley stayed in the game, but the officials regularly halted play in the final stanza to allow the valiant goalie to wipe away the blood that was still flowing from his battered beak.

DECEMBER 3

MATS SUNDIN GETS 500TH POINT ON INCREDIBLE EFFORT, 1996

B reaking out of his own zone on a short-handed rush, Mats Sundin had two Blues closing in on him as he approached centre ice. Late in the first period on December 3, 1996, Sundin pushed the puck up as he attempted to dodge the pair of hulking opponents — defenceman Igor Kravchuk on his left and forward Jim Campbell on his right. Campbell was initially able to corral the loose puck, but Sundin, who practically had all 215 pounds of Kravchuk draped on his back, was able to get his stick under Campbell's and lift it up to regain possession as they entered the St. Louis zone.

While Sundin had spun Campbell around with his evasive manoeuvre, the big Blues winger stayed with him, attempting to pry the puck loose as they veered toward the net. Although Campbell succeeded in knocking Sundin off balance as they neared the blue paint, the Swedish centre managed to get a shot off. Before Sundin even hit the ice, the puck went through Grant Fuhr's pads. It was an incredible individual effort that also happened to be his 500th career NHL point.

DECEMBER 4

LEAFS SCORE THREE SHORT-HANDED GOALS, 1966

L ate in the second period of a game against the Bruins on December 4, 1966, Tim Horton was in the penalty box for hooking. The 3–1 lead that Toronto had built up at the start of the frame had dwindled to a one-goal advantage, giving Boston the perfect opportunity to knot it up before the second intermission. But less than 30 seconds into Horton's penalty, Dave Keon potted a short-handed goal to restore Toronto's two-goal lead.

And just 13 seconds before Horton was due to exit the sin bin, Bob Pulford added a short-handed goal of his own to make it 5–2. After the Leafs added two more to start the final frame and really put the game out of reach, the team was killing off another infraction late in the period when John Brenneman scored to complete the hat trick of short-handed goals. Toronto's trio of shorties, as the kids say, matched an NHL record for the most in a game by one team. The mark held until Winnipeg put four past Vancouver on April 7, 1995.

DECEMBER 5

DAVE KEON SCORES 300TH GOAL, 1972

For a moment in the 1972 off-season, it looked as though Dave Keon's illustrious tenure with the Leafs may have been coming to an end. Following the 1971–72 campaign in which his production dropped to 48 points in 72 games, Keon, who was also not selected to be a part of Team Canada's entry for the Summit Series against the Soviet Union, looked to be contemplating a change. With the up-start World Hockey Association about to launch its inaugural season, he signed a letter of intent to play for the Ottawa Nationals in the rival league.

But as Leafs training camp approached, Keon denied that he was thinking about bolting. When the 1972–73 NHL season began, Leafs fans breathed a sigh of relief when he returned to the blue and white. While the ill-fated Nationals lasted just the year, Keon hit a couple of milestones with Toronto that season. A few weeks after becoming the franchise's all-time leading goal scorer, Keon recorded his 300th career goal on December 5, 1972, becoming the first-ever Leaf to reach the milestone.

DECEMBER 6

MITCH MARNER'S RECORD-SETTING POINT STREAK, 2022

itch Marner was in the midst of something magical. After recording a point in his 19th straight game, establishing a new Leafs franchise record for the longest point streak, it seemed as though it would never end. A few days later, on December 6, 2022, he had the chance to extend his benchmark when Toronto took on Dallas. Marner was also set to make NHL history by squaring off against the Stars' Jason Robertson (brother of Leafs rookie Nick Robertson), who was working on an 18-game point streak, marking the first time in which two players with active streaks of at least 18 consecutive games faced each other.

Although Marner took a penalty 30 seconds into the game, he redeemed himself a few minutes later by setting up John Tavares for the opening goal to push his streak to 20 games. But all good things must come to an end. Marner got as far as the 23-game mark, the fourth-longest point streak in the NHL in the last 30 years, an incredible testament to his dynamic skill.

DECEMBER 7

ED BELFOUR RECORDS 63RD
CAREER SHUTOUT, 2002

E d Belfour began his Leafs tenure with a shutout. In his first game for the blue and white, Belfour, who had signed as a free agent after spending the past five seasons in Dallas, stopped all 33 shots he faced to record his 59th career shutout. His strong play between the pipes continued as the season progressed. By the time November came to an end, Belfour had collected three more shutouts.

When the Leafs hosted New Jersey on December 7, 2002, Belfour's four flawless games were at the top of the league, tying him with former understudy Marty Turco and Jocelyn Thibault for the lead. That night, the Devils put Belfour's skills to the test. They outshot Toronto 38–14. While Belfour managed to turn aside every puck he faced to record his league-leading fifth shutout, he received offensive support from a rather unlikely source. Travis Green, who had been a healthy scratch the game before, returned to the lineup and scored the Leafs' lone goal just halfway through the first period.

DECEMBER 8

TORONTO PLAYS 5,000TH GAME, 1997

When the Leafs hosted the Stars on December 8, 1997, it was more than simply just another game in the schedule, it was an important milestone in franchise history: the 5,000th regular-season game played by Toronto since joining the NHL eight decades earlier. When Toronto joined the league in 1917, the club was known as the Arenas because they played out of the Arena Gardens on Mutual Street. Although the Arenas won the first Stanley Cup in the NHL era, the name didn't stick around for too long.

After 40 games as the Arenas, the club became known as the St. Patricks. For the next 217 regular-season games, they sported green, a nod to the team's Irish name. But midway through the 1926–27 season, the squad was purchased by an ownership group led by Conn Smythe and became forever known as the Maple Leafs. After ditching the green for blue, the Leafs went on to play 4,742 regular-season games before squaring off for that landmark game that night in December.

DECEMBER 9

LEAFS GET OFF TO A WAFFLE START, 2010

Who brings waffles to a hockey game? That was the question that befuddled Leafs forward Colby Armstrong following a game on December 9, 2010, in which a fan threw some waffles onto the ice in the final seconds of a 4–1 loss to the Flyers. Most of the breakfast treats landed near the Philadelphia bench, but one of them actually hit Toronto defenceman François Beauchemin as he skated by. While the team was left scratching their heads as to what the projectile was supposed to signify, another incident less than two weeks later provided a little more clarity.

Toward the end of a 6–3 loss to the Atlanta Thrashers, a fan named Joe Robb chucked a box of waffles onto the ice. Robb later explained to ESPN that if you drop the *W* in *waffle* it sounds like *awful*, which he felt summed up the season so far for the struggling Leafs. Although Robb was initially arrested for mischief, the charges were dropped in favour of community service, but he was banned from attending future games.

DECEMBER 10

LEAFS ACQUIRE JIM HARRISON, 1969

Darryl Sittler may have been the first player to score 10 points in an NHL game, but three years before that, Jim Harrison was the first to hit double-digit points in a professional hockey game. But before Harrison rewrote the hockey record books, he was actually teammates with Sittler. On December 10, 1969, the Leafs acquired Harrison from the Bruins in exchange for Wayne Carleton. After finishing the year with the Buds, he spent two more seasons in Toronto until he joined the Alberta Oilers of the World Hockey Association in 1972.

During his inaugural season with the Oilers, Harrison made history on January 30, 1973, when he recorded a hat trick and added seven assists in a 10–3 victory against the New York Raiders. Harrison finished the season with 39 goals and 86 points in 66 games, his most productive campaign since his junior hockey days with the Estevan Bruins, where he once scored a natural hat trick in 24 seconds, a Western Hockey League record that stands to this day.

DECEMBER 11

LEAFS BEAT FLYERS 6–4, 1999

eafs fans may have been rooting against the Flyers, but they were cheering for the team's head coach, Roger Neilson. No stranger to Toronto, Neilson made his NHL coaching debut for the blue and white more than two decades earlier, then made stops in Buffalo, Vancouver, Los Angles, Chicago, New York, Florida, and St. Louis before ending up behind the bench in Philadelphia in 1998. But prior to returning to Toronto for a game on December 11, 1999, Neilson announced that he was suffering from bone marrow cancer.

While Neilson, who was known as "Captain Video" for his pioneering video work, may have gotten some sympathy from the fans, he certainly didn't get any on the ice. Although the two teams were tied 2–2 heading into the second period, the Leafs scored three unanswered goals in the middle frame, including two from Garry Valk, to take a 5–2 lead. Although the Flyers mounted a comeback in the final session, coming within one, Jonas Höglund scored an empty-netter with 12 seconds remaining to put the game out of reach.

DECEMBER 12

ACE BAILEY INJURED, 1933

Eddie Shore was looking for payback. Halfway through the second period in a game against the Leafs on December 12, 1933, the Bruins defenceman was furious after he had been knocked down to the ice by a check. Thinking the perpetrator of the hit was Toronto's Ace Bailey, Shore went after him. He hit Bailey from behind, sending the Leafs winger to the ice, where he hit his head and was knocked unconscious. Bailey was rushed to hospital and underwent a series of operations to save his life.

When Bailey's father first heard the extent of his son's injuries over the radio, he went into a rage and vowed revenge. The story goes that he went to Boston looking to kill Shore, but when the Leafs' brass got wind of his plan, they were able to intervene and defuse the situation. While Bailey would make a full recovery, he would never play hockey again. A few months later, an all-star benefit game was held at Maple Leaf Gardens. In a touching moment, Bailey embraced Shore at centre ice.

DECEMBER 13

BRIAN SPENCER SCORES FIRST POINTS AFTER FAMILY TRAGEDY, 1970

B rian Spencer wanted to play for his dad. On the morning of December 13, 1970, the young Leafs winger learned that his father, Roy, had been killed the night before in Prince George, British Columbia. Although Spencer could have sat out Toronto's game later that day in Buffalo, he felt a duty to suit up. "He wanted me to play in the NHL more than anything, so I think I ought to play," Spencer tearfully told reporters.

That night, Spencer picked up two assists, his first big-league points, as the Leafs whitewashed the Sabres 4–0. It was only later that many learned the shocking circumstances of Roy Spencer's death. A few nights earlier, when Toronto took on Chicago for *Hockey Night in Canada*, Spencer was interviewed during the game. But since Roy was on the West Coast, he never saw the broadcast. Following the game, armed with a pistol, he stormed Prince George's only TV station to complain. After wounding a Mountie as he attempted to flee, Roy was shot and killed by police.

DECEMBER 14

LEAFS TRADE MIKE ALLISON TO L.A., 1987

J
ust a few games after making his NHL debut for the Rangers in 1980, Mike Allison scored his first career hat trick against none other than the Maple Leafs. He finished his rookie season with 26 goals and 64 points, but his three-goal performance against Toronto would prove to be his only hat trick in the big leagues. After five more seasons playing for the Rangers and their minor-league affiliates, Allison, who had been limited by knee injuries, was traded to the Leafs for Walt Poddubny.

In his first and only campaign with the Buds, Allison recorded 23 points in 71 games, the most he played in the NHL since his inaugural season in New York. But after getting into only half of Toronto's games to start the 1987–88 campaign, he was traded to Los Angeles on December 14, 1987, in exchange for Sean McKenna. Down the stretch with the Kings, Allison had one of his most productive stints since breaking into the league with the Rangers, recording 16 goals and 28 points in 37 games.

DECEMBER 15

TIE DOMI BECOMES ALL-TIME PIM LEADER, 2001

Dave "Tiger" Williams held the Leafs franchise record for the most career penalty minutes for more than two decades. Although he played only five full seasons in Toronto, he still managed to rack up an impressive 1,670 PIM. While Williams knew it was only a matter of time until the Leafs' feisty Tie Domi, who had surpassed his record for most PIMs in a single season a few years earlier, overtook him for the all-time mark, he was happy it would be him.

When Domi did finally pass him, Williams gave an endorsement that only he could give. "I'm glad it's him and not some other puke," he told the *Toronto Sun*. Domi also earned the record in a way that Williams, who earned 120 major penalties with the Buds, would have approved of. On December 15, 2001, Domi was sitting just three penalty minutes shy of matching Williams when he fought Reid Simpson in the third period, picking up a five-minute major to bring his career total with the Leafs to 1,672 penalty minutes.

PAT QUINN EARNS THE
BICKELL CUP, 2002

The Stanley Cup may be the best trophy in all of sports, but the Bickell Cup might be the most extravagant. Named after J.P. Bickell, who played an integral role in the early years of the Maple Leafs, including the construction of the Gardens, the trophy was commissioned by Conn Smythe in the early 1950s to honour Bickell's legacy with the club and recognize a member of the Maple Leafs for a singular feat, a season of superior play, or a distinguished period of service.

Made entirely of 14-karat gold, a nod to how Bickell struck it rich in the gold mining business in Timmins, Ontario, the cup sits atop a quartz base. Although the trophy was awarded rather regularly in the 1950s and 1960s, it has been bestowed only a handful of times in the decades that followed. A few years after Mats Sundin and Curtis Joseph shared the Bickell in 1999, head coach Pat Quinn, who was in his fifth season behind the bench in Toronto, received the honour on December 16, 2002.

DECEMBER 17

LEAFS ACQUIRE DAN DAOUST
AND GASTON GINGRAS, 1982

D an Daoust was hardly being used by the Canadiens, but it didn't make his departure any easier. Daoust, who managed to dress for only a handful of games in the 1982–83 season, was traded to the Leafs, along with defenceman Gaston Gingras, for future considerations on December 17, 1982. Although Daoust wasn't getting much ice time in Montreal, he thought he would stick with the team and told reporters he was close to tears when he got the news.

His teammate Gingras, who was also used sparingly, was a little more pragmatic. "Hell, I was No. 8 among the defencemen on this team," he said. "Where could I go? What could I do? I wasn't being used. They had to move me." Five days later, when they played their first game for Toronto, they each got on the scoresheet. Daoust scored a goal, his first in the NHL, and Gingras assisted on another in a 4–3 loss to Chicago. Daoust's immediate success continued, and he finished the season with 51 points in 48 games.

DECEMBER 18

JEAN MAROIS MAKES NHL DEBUT, 1943

With Turk Broda still serving in the Second World War, the Maple Leafs needed help in net. Coach Hap Day had convinced Benny Grant, who had previously played with the team a decade earlier, to come out of retirement and suit up again. Although the 35-year-old Grant, who hadn't played in a year, gave it his best shot, it was clear that the Leafs were going to need reinforcements. On December 18, 1943, they gave Grant the night off and put 19-year-old Jean Marois between the pipes.

Marois, who was unable to serve in the Armed Forces because of a heart condition, performed admirably in his first outing, turning aside 25 shots in an 8–4 victory against Chicago. It would, however, be his first and only game with Toronto. A week later, the Leafs got the help they were looking for when they signed former Canadiens goaltender Paul Bibeault after he was discharged from the army. Bibeault played 29 games down the stretch, picking up 13 victories in his only stint with the blue and white.

DECEMBER 19

TORONTO PLAYS FIRST NHL GAME, 1917

There was no shortage of goals in Toronto's first NHL game. The tallies started just one minute into their matchup against the Montreal Wanderers on December 19, 1917, and they didn't stop until just before the final buzzer. After the Arenas gave up the first tally, they traded goals with the Wanderers to close the first period trailing 5–3. The two teams nearly topped their eight goals in the first frame when they combined for seven in the second session, with the Wanderers leading 9–6 heading into the third.

While Toronto gave up its 10th goal just over four minutes into the final stanza, the Arenas then scored three straight to nearly pull off an incredible comeback in a game that was already one for the books. Although the Wanderers got the better of Toronto that night, it would prove to be their only NHL victory. A few weeks later, the arena they shared with the Canadiens burned down. While the Habs moved to the Jubilee Rink in Montreal's east end, the Wanderers ended up folding.

DECEMBER 20

NIK ANTROPOV SCORES
FIRST HAT TRICK, 1999

A few months before the Leafs drafted him 10th overall, Nik Antropov had the tournament of his life. Representing Kazakhstan in the lowest division of the European U18 Championship, Antropov racked up an improbable 23 goals and 31 assists in just five games. Kazakhstan, which had moved over from playing in the Asian junior tournament, ravaged its opponents, defeating Iceland 63–0 and hosts Luxembourg 39–0. Although Antropov's performance was one for the books, it was not why the Leafs had him rated so highly.

Standing at six-foot-six with plenty of offensive upside, Antropov was exactly the type of player any team would want down the middle. Although he scored just once in his first 22 NHL games, on December 20, 1999, he demonstrated his potent combination of skill and size. In a game against the Panthers, Antropov scored three goals, including the game-winner, to record his first career big-league hat trick. While Antropov would not exactly become known for scoring in bunches, he was a fixture in the Leafs lineup for nearly the next decade.

DAVID CLARKSON, WATER BOTTLE POLICE, 2013

There was no length David Clarkson wouldn't go to in looking out for his teammates. After earning an automatic 10-game suspension for leaving the bench in a pre-season game to protect Phil Kessel, a few months later, he was standing up for Jonathan Bernier. Well, for his water bottle at least. After Detroit's Todd Bertuzzi fired a puck at the Toronto goaltender's water bottle following a whistle during a game on December 21, 2013, Clarkson sprang into action.

While it was unclear what was going on during the broadcast of the game, HBO's *24/7 Red Wings/Maple Leafs: Road to the NHL Winter Classic* documentary, which had been following both teams for their New Year's Day outdoor game, later gave fans insight into what transpired. Following a series of profanities between him and Bertuzzi, Clarkson made it abundantly clear not to touch Bernier's bottle. Bertuzzi, clearly annoyed by the entire situation, reminded him it was just a water bottle, but Clarkson wouldn't back down. It finally ended when Bertuzzi asked him the question we were all thinking, "What are you, the bottle police?"

DECEMBER 22

BABE DYE SCORES FIVE, 1924

n just one night at the office, Babe Dye nearly doubled his goal output for the season. On December 22, 1924, in a game against the Boston Bruins, Dye scored five goals to bring his count up to 11. Not a bad day's work. It was just a few years earlier, when Dye made his debut for the St. Patricks, that he finished his inaugural season with 11 tallies. The following year, when the Quebec Bulldogs moved to Hamilton and were renamed the Tigers, Dye, a native of Steeltown, was loaned to the upstart franchise.

Following just one game with the Tigers, in which he scored two goals, Dye was returned to Toronto, where he went on to notch 33 more goals that season, the most in the NHL. Following another 30-goal campaign and a 27-goal effort the year after, he scored just 17 times in the 1923–24 season. But after his five-goal outing in December, Dye rebounded and finished the year with 38 to lead the league in goal-scoring for the fourth and final time.

DECEMBER 23

DOUG GILMOUR HITS 1,000 POINTS, 1995

After assisting on Mats Sundin's first goal of the night in a game against the Oilers on December 23, 1995, Doug Gilmour was on the verge of setting a career milestone. He was just one away from the 1,000-point mark. With less than six minutes remaining in the game, he appeared to accomplish the feat when he set up another goal to give the Leafs a 6–1 lead. His teammates came off the bench to congratulate him and the home crowd rose to its feet for a standing ovation, but the celebration was premature.

The goal was called back because the net had been knocked off its moorings before the puck crossed the line. But Gilmour wouldn't need to wait too long to reach the benchmark. Just over three minutes later, he set up Sundin's second of the evening to officially hit the 1,000-point mark, becoming just the third player in franchise history to accomplish the feat in a Leafs sweater. It was just as well for Gilmour, who ended up taking home two souvenir pucks.

DECEMBER 24

JOHNNY BOWER RECORDS CHRISTMAS EVE SHUTOUT, 1966

The only holiday performance that could top Johnny Bower's Christmas Eve shutout against Boston in 1966 was his rendition of "Honky the Christmas Goose." Two years before the 42-year-old netminder turned aside all 29 shots he faced from the Bruins, his best effort so far that season, Bower had been approached by Chip Young, a CBC producer who was looking to cut a Christmas record with some of Toronto's players.

Bower, who was known for dressing up as Santa Claus for the team's annual Christmas parties, didn't need much convincing, especially since all the proceeds would be going to charity. Trading in his pads for the recording booth, Bower, joined by his son John Jr. on backup vocals, sang a song about an overweight goose named Honky who could no longer fly but used his call to help Santa navigate the skies, thereby saving Christmas. It was an instant hit. In its first week of release, it sold 21,000 copies and through the holiday season became the bestselling Canadian record ever at the time.

DECEMBER 25

GERRY O'FLAHERTY GOES
HOME FOR CHRISTMAS, 1971

t was the best Christmas gift that Gerry O'Flaherty had
ever received. On the morning of December 24, 1971,
Flaherty, who was playing for the Tulsa Oilers, the Leafs'
affiliate in the Central Hockey League, received a telephone
call informing him that he would be suiting up for Toronto's
Christmas game at home against the Red Wings. Paul
Henderson was out with a knee injury, so O'Flaherty would
be taking his place in the lineup.

It couldn't have worked out better for O'Flaherty.
Originally from Toronto, it meant he and his wife, who was
also from the city, could return home for the holidays. And
even better was that O'Flaherty would be making his NHL
debut in front of family at Maple Leaf Gardens. Playing on a
line with Ron Ellis and Norm Ullman, O'Flaherty fulfilled
his dream of playing in the big leagues. Following a 5–3 victory against Detroit, in which the Leafs' Billy MacMillan recorded the last-ever Christmas hat trick, O'Flaherty was off to
Boston for a Boxing Day bout against the Bruins.

DECEMBER 26

BOXING DAY BLOWOUT, 1991

t was a Boxing Day blowout. On December 26, 1991, the Leafs were trounced 12–1 by the Penguins. Although the Penguins' Joe Mullen, who was coming off a four-goal performance on Long Island a few nights earlier, opened the scoring less than three minutes into the game, the Leafs tied the game just over a minute later. While Toronto gave up two more goals late in the frame, including another to Mullen, things didn't seem to be off the rails just yet.

Even when Jaromir Jagr scored 27 seconds into the second period, it was still a three-goal game and not entirely out of reach. But when Pittsburgh added two more to take a commanding 6–1 lead, it was safe to say the Leafs would need a holiday miracle to turn things around. It only got worse in the final stanza. The Penguins scored six more, including another two from Mullen to give him back-to-back four-goal efforts, capping off 11 unanswered goals to notch a 12–1 triumph, matching the franchise record for the largest margin of victory.

DECEMBER 27

MARIO LEMIEUX RETURNS AGAINST THE LEAFS, 2000

Even as a Leafs fan, it was impossible not to root for Mario Lemieux. One of the greatest players to ever lace them up, Lemieux retired early in 1997 after a successful battle with Hodgkin's lymphoma and chronic back problems had ravaged his body. But after being away from the rink for nearly four years, he was ready to return. Just a few months after becoming the owner of the Penguins, the team he rescued from bankruptcy and led to greatness, Lemieux announced he was making a comeback. His first game back was on December 27, 2000, when Pittsburgh hosted Toronto.

As he returned to the ice at Mellon Arena, which was fittingly known as "the House that Lemieux Built," he received a rousing ovation from the fans. It didn't take Lemieux long to find his game. Just 33 seconds in, he helped set up Jaromir Jagr for the opening tally, and in the second period, Lemieux lit the lamp. The Leafs lost 5–0, but it didn't matter. Lemieux was back and hockey was better for it.

DECEMBER 28

TOM PEDERSON SCORES
LAST NHL GOAL, 1996

Even before signing with the Leafs a few months into the 1996–97 season, Tom Pederson knew his NHL days were numbered. A defenceman from Bloomington, Minnesota, Pederson was selected by his hometown team, the North Stars, in 1989 but was taken by San Jose a couple of years later in the dispersal draft. During his time with the Sharks, he got acquainted with a fan who had invented a unique off-ice training puck. Pederson thought it was a neat idea and filed it away in his mind.

A few games into his tenure in Toronto, on December 28, 1996, Pederson scored what would be his final NHL goal. He would play a few more seasons in the minors and in Germany until a broken back forced him to hang up his skates. In searching for a life after hockey, Pederson remembered that puck from his days in San Jose. He ended up buying the patent for it and eventually launched a company called Green Biscuit, which I can attest to as being the ultimate road hockey puck.

DECEMBER 29

LEAFS HAVE THIRD-PERIOD SURGE
AGAINST NORDIQUES, 1988

t was a wild third period in Quebec City. Trailing 4–3 against the Nordiques in the final frame on December 29, 1988, Toronto, which had picked up only one victory in its past 14 contests, appeared destined for another loss. But Eddie Olczyk and Gary Leeman had other plans. After Olczyk scored just over five minutes into the session, Leeman potted another one 14 seconds later to give the Leafs a 5–4 lead. Less than five minutes after that, Olczyk and Leeman set up Paul Gagné for the insurance marker.

But 21 seconds after Gagné's tally, Quebec's Peter Šťastný found the back of the net to pull the Nordiques within one with plenty of time remaining. While the Leafs nearly managed to fend them off until the buzzer, Michel Goulet was awarded a penalty shot with just 12 seconds left after Börje Salming knocked the net off its moorings in a goalmouth scramble. Luckily, goaltender Allan Bester got a piece of Goulet's shot and the Leafs held on for the win, snapping a 10-game losing streak on the road.

DECEMBER 30

LEAFS STUN BRUINS WITH EPIC COMEBACK, 1989

D ecades before Leafs fans would get tired of hearing "It was 4–1," a reference to their epic Game 7 collapse against the Bruins, Toronto was on the other end of an improbable comeback against Boston. Granted, the stakes weren't as high, but with just over a minute remaining in the second period in a game against the Bruins, on December 30, 1989, the Leafs were trailing 6–1.

But before the frame came to a close, Vincent Damphousse scored to cut the deficit to four. Just before the five-minute mark in the final session, Gary Leeman notched a goal on the power play, and less than two minutes later, Luke Richardson made it 6–4. Suddenly the Leafs had life with plenty of time left on the clock. And then, in a span of just over three minutes, Eddie Olczyk scored a pair of goals to force overtime. A little over three minutes into the extra session, the club's beating heart, Wendel Clark, scored Toronto's sixth straight goal to complete an improbable comeback. It was 6–1.

DECEMBER 31

LEAFS PLAY FIRST GAME IN VEGAS, 2017

What happens in Vegas — well, you know the rest. That's certainly how the first period felt for the Leafs in Las Vegas on December 31, 2017. Just over four minutes into the New Year's Eve matchup, the Golden Knights scored two quick goals and would be up 3–0 when the period came to a close. Although the Leafs got on the board just over five minutes into the middle frame, a few minutes later, William Karlsson scored his second of the night to restore Vegas's three-goal lead.

But with less than a minute remaining in the second period, Auston Matthews found the back of the net to pull Toronto within two. Matthews scored again, 27 seconds into the final stanza, to earn his 100th career point and give Leafs fans on the East Coast a reason to continue watching instead of flipping to *Dick Clark's New Year's Rockin' Eve*. But after Vegas scored again, Karlsson notched his third of the night to record the first hat trick in Golden Knights history to seal a 6–3 victory.

ASSISTS (ACKNOWLEDGEMENTS)

This book wouldn't be possible without the Toronto Maple Leafs. They were the inspiration and the source material. Many years ago, in the acknowledgements section of my dissertation, I thanked the Leafs for not qualifying for the playoffs during much of my time in graduate school, allowing me to focus on my studies, but now I want to thank the team for giving me this book. I've been a lifelong Leafs fan, but I fell in love with the club all over again while researching and writing these stories.

Thanks to the team at Dundurn Press, chiefly Kwame Scott Fraser, Kathryn Lane, and Elena Radic, for allowing me to give my favourite team the Hockey 365 treatment.

Stick tap to Ron Beltrame for bagging a hat trick on this book. This is the third cover he's designed for me and, as always, it's fantastic.

Patricia MacDonald's copy-editing and proofreading business is Powerplay Editing and that's exactly what you get. A specialist on point who can help you cycle your words for an easy tap-in.

One time, when I wished Jeff Marek happy birthday on Twitter, he asked if that meant he got to be in the book. It was a great idea, so I threw him in. Thanks to Jeff for the suggestion and providing some of the details for the story he's featured in.

There are too many people to name, but I received a lot of feedback on social media about what stories to include. Many of them are in here because of your recommendations, so thank you. You know who you are.

You can always count on your mother to buy a copy of your book and *Leafs 365* is no exception. While my mom, Patti, always tries to be the first pre-order, she has also helped out with every book. She saw some of these stories in advance and offered some feedback to make sure I got my facts straight. So thanks to my mom and dad, Tony, for always supporting my work and buying it.

Special stick taps to my in-laws, Sue and Moe, for all the times you took the girls for a few hours on a Saturday, so I could sneak in a few pages.

People often ask me how I'm able to write these books on top of my full-time job, and my answer is — always, always, always — that I have a very patient and loving wife. Emphasis on patient. Writing is often a lonely pursuit, but you always give me the love and support I need. *Merci*, Chantal, for letting me chase my dreams. I love you.

As an author, there's nothing more exciting than unboxing your books for the first time, but it's even better when you get to do it with your kids. This will be the first time my beautiful girls, Zoe and Sophia, will both appreciate the significance of that moment, and I couldn't ask for two better teammates.

Finally, thanks to all the Leafs fans who share the passion and will read these pages. I hope in the not-too-distant future I'll need to write an addendum because the team's last Stanley Cup was won more recently than 1967.